I0447753

The ALBA

The ALBA

Inside Venezuela's Bolivarian Aliance

Joel D. Hirst

InterAmerican Institute for Democracy Publishing Fund
Miami, 2012

© Joel D. Hirst 2012
© This edition: Interamerican Institute for Democracy 2012
All rights reserved

Library of Congress Catalog Number: 2012939899

Design and Cover by: Alexandria Library, Miami

The Interamerican Institute for
Democracy is a non-governmental,
nonprofit organization created to
promote and support liberty, democracy
and institutionalism in Latin America.

InterAmerican Institute for Democracy
2600 Douglas Rd, Suite 906,
Miami, FL 33134, U.S.A.
www.intdemocratic.org
Email: IID@intdemocratic.org

Table of Contents

Introduction

Latin America finds itself today caught between to different systems of government. One is followed by countries who believe in a constitutional democracy; with respect to the checks and balances between a series of separate but equal institutions of government – such as the independence of the judiciary which protect our fundamental human rights and guarantee our right to free speech. The other model is followed by regimes, who, upon willing elections, totally abandon the trappings of democracy and have transformed their countries into authentic autocracies using occasional majorities. These governments follow a model called "Socialism of the 21st Century" and include Venezuela, Ecuador, Bolivia and Nicaragua (allied closely with totalitarian Cuba and an increasingly authoritarian Argentina). To be sure, these are a minority of countries, but their population of 100 million (mean 20% of Latin America) is forced to survive under this model.

Through the Bolivarian Alliance for the People's of Our America (ALBA), Hugo Chavez has used economic and other mechanisms to penetrate countries in the region as they seek support for their hegemonic project.

Perhaps the most significant risk that ALBA poses arises from ignorance. The majority of analysts and politicians in Latin America are unaware of the reality and implications of the project; as they are of its reach and the structure, which maintains it. This ignorance manifests itself, for example, in the lack of a response or even an interest in the topic; such as when an organization like FLACSO presents in academic discussions the ALBA as the only real project for the integration of Latin America.

The creation of the Bolivarian Alliance is a response both to ancient causes and current realities. Venezuela has always considered the Caribbean area as vital to its strategic and economic interests. Her diplomacy has also been oriented toward the non-Hispanic Caribbean. Within this paradigm, Venezuela has always used its oil resources to influence this region. Until the arrival of Chavez, these resources were used to counter the weight of Cuba in the Caribbean – a policy which reached its maximum expression during the second presidency of Carlos Andres Perez.

The use of oil nevertheless acquires a different significance under the regime of Hugo Chavez. It responds to a new, personal vision of Chavez.

To understand this, it is important to take note of his military background, which is dominated by a Cuban vision of geopolitics. For this reason, classical expressions of Venezuelan foreign policy (such as international cooperation, development and the advancement of integration based upon principles of free trade) experience a mutation towards a policy dominated by solidarity opposed to trade, confrontation instead of negotiation and the need to stand in opposition to other actors in the region – especially the United States – as is accurately described by Andres Serbin.

After 2004, and with President Chavez in full control of PDVSA and its almost unlimited oil resources, the Venezuelan president has at his disposal the perfect instrument for his Caribbean policy: the Bolivarian project called PetroCaribe. This is best seen as a bribe to purchase the Caribbean votes in the OAS. From there stems the initial silent respect to the ALBA – something similar to the rejection from the rest of the region.

It is only after the counter-summit in Mar del Plata – promoted by Chavez and Argentine President Nestor Kirchner- that the ALBA gains a more important role and begins to adopt its unique and belligerent expressions: the socialist agenda and the direct confrontation with the United States. It is also the time when ALBA begins to generate concern in the region; as these two pillars of ALBA generate significant discomfort within the rest of the countries of the region.

This reality has led the Inter-American Institute for Democracy to sponsor this book: and responds to the need of the international community to understand the political Project of Hugo Chavez and its geographic and economic reach. Despite the now-evident political, economic and cultural decline of Socialism of the 21st Century and its decreasing importance across the hemisphere – due in no small part to its failure both economically and the health challenges of Hugo Chavez – we believe that it remains important to disseminate the true nature of this Alliance.

Given that it should be the political community of the United States, which remains the most interested in averting the dangers of ALBA for the democratic integrity of the continent, this book is being published first in English.

In planning for this book, there was no doubt regarding the selection of the person to carry out the study. Joel D. Hirst has studied ALBA for many years, with a wide and deep experience in Latin America generally and Venezuela specifically. In any encounter where Socialism of the 21st Century or the ALBA are being discussed, Joel is an important voice. Be this at the Center for Hemispheric Policy or the Center for Latin American studies at the University of Miami; to American Enterprise Institute, Heritage Foundation, International Republican Institute, and the Council on Foreign Relations; or in his articles and television appearances on topics that affect hemispheric democracy and freedom: Hirst is an important voice in the discussion.

For this reason, it is with great satisfaction that the Institute presents "The ALBA: Inside Venezuela's Bolivarian Alliance."

Guillermo Lousteau
President
Interamerican Institute for Democracy

Acknowledgements

Very rarely is a person given the opportunity to step back and take a hard look at something that is going on in the world. For this reason, I thank the Council on Foreign Relations International Affairs Fellows program for allowing me the opportunity and platform to do just that, carrying out the research and study necessary for this book. I also am grateful to CFR for choosing this research project out of the thousands proposed – and for understanding the importance of better understanding the Bolivarian Alliance of the Americas. I would also like to thank the Inter-American Institute for Democracy, for enthusiastically supporting the publication of this research project.

For the book itself, I would like to thank Kate Pynoos who helped in the research of this project from her position as Research Assistant at CFR. I would also like to thank Dan Fisk, Vice-President for Policy and Strategic Planning at the International Republican Institute; and Ray Walser, Senior Policy Analyst for Latin America at the Douglas and Sarah Allison Center for Foreign Policy Studies at the Heritage Foundation for their vital help peer-reviewing the manuscript. I would also like to thank Arlene Robinson for her excellent work copy and line editing the manuscript, as well as Mindy Hirst for her support in content review and editing.

Finally, I would like to thank each person who took the time to read this book and interact with the ideas. Solutions to very real challenges comes from a better understanding of the issues at stake; for this reason I am grateful for those who look beyond the simple answers; and for bringing intellectual integrity to their fight to build a better world.

CHAPTER 1

The ALBA Rears its Head

A bright Central American sun was peeking over the deforested mountains of Tegucigalpa, Honduras' capital city, holding the promise of another sweltering Central American Sunday. Across the sprawling capital, poor and rich alike had awakened early in expectation. Today was June 28, 2009, the day chosen by the country's president for a crucial—if perhaps not entirely legal—election.

The much-anticipated nonbinding referendum was seeking authority to hold a vote on whether the country's executive could establish a Constituent Assembly. It was not to be. The morning of Sunday, Manuel "Mel" Zelaya, President of Honduras, was fast asleep in his bedroom within the presidential palace, located in an opulent area in the center of Tegucigalpa. At 6 AM sharp, Mel was jolted awake by the thunderous sounds that accompany the deployment of hundreds of heavily armed military. A pounding erupted from the gates of his official residence, and then the closed doors of the palace. Mel chanced a peek out the window only to see his official residence completely surrounded. The pajama-clad president wedged himself behind an air-conditioning unit while his presidential guard battled the military for a full twenty minutes before laying down their weapons in defeat. Mr. Zelaya, still dressed in his pajamas, was taken into custody and sped to a military base on the outskirts of the capital, where he was then ushered onto a military airplane and flown to San Jose, the capital city of Costa Rica.[1] The interim government, led by President of the Senate Roberto

---

1 Mary O'Grady, "Honduras Defends its Democracy," *Wall Street Journal*, June 29, 2009.

Micheletti, had decided that the only way to save lives during the instability was if President Zelaya was outside the country. This act was illegal, and while the removal of power did follow the rule of law and continuity of government was respected, this led to the immediate labeling of the kerfuffle as a "coup d'état."

In that short time, Mel found himself joining the ranks of other Latin-American presidents who, misjudging the national mood, now live their lives in exile across the length and breadth of our great hemisphere.

At least that's his story. Hondurans who were involved in the process of showing "Mel" the door insist that the Honduran President knew quite well his fate, that he was waiting for the military that morning and that he was dressed in his finest suit. According to their story, upon arrival in Costa Rica he rapidly changed back into his pajamas. Ever the actor, Mel knew he still had a role to play.[2]

It had not been an easy year for the polarizing president. His constitutionally mandated single five-year term was coming rapidly to a close—and with it the chance of making the deep and sweeping reforms being encouraged by his newly acquired mentor, President Hugo Chavez of Venezuela: most important of which was the extension of his mandate as precursor to other components of 21st Century Socialism. Seizing his last window of opportunity, on November 28, 2008, President Zelaya had issued a decree calling for a referendum on holding a Constituent Assembly to rewrite the country's constitution. Following a pattern of constituent assemblies in the other countries of Chavez's Bolivarian Alliance of the Americas (ALBA), Zelaya certainly thought he could use a victory to somehow stay in office indefinitely. Should the plebiscite, colloquially called the "fourth urn," succeed, the referendum would be held simultaneously with the Presidential, Congressional and regional elections in November 2009.

A lower court ruled that that the decree violated the Honduran Constitution, specifically Article 5, which states that only the Supreme Electoral Tribunal can call elections, plebiscites or referenda. Also in question were rticle 239,[3] which makes a president's attempt to extend his term

---

http://online.wsj.com/article/SB124623220955866301.html
2 Author interviews with confidential sources.
3 Honduras Constitution: Titulo VII: De la Reforma y la Inviolabilabidad de la Constitución, Capitulo I De la Reforma de la Constitución: Articulo 373.

limits an impeachable offense, and Articles 373 and 374,[4] which make the modification of term limits illegal: and high treason. The lower court ruling, nonetheless, was not based directly on these articles but on the aforementioned legality of the executive calling an election. The Supreme Court upheld the decision by the lower court, putting an end to the debate.

Not to be stymied by rule of law, President Zelaya then announced in March 2009 that he would hold a nonbinding referendum on June 28, 2009, to ask the people whether they wanted to have a referendum on holding a Constituent Assembly. The other, independent institutions of government continued to resist. On March 25, the Attorney General's office notified President Zelaya that he would face criminal charges should he proceed. On June 3, Congress passed a resolution warning Zelaya to correct his intended actions. On June 23, Congress passed another law forbidding holding plebiscites within 180 days of a general election. Zelaya rejected this law, stating that it was null and void due to the fact that it was passed after the plebiscite was scheduled. By this time the ballots (and boxes) for the polemic referendum had arrived, freshly printed, from his ally Hugo Chavez. To facilitate Zelaya's illegal vote and save the citizenry the trouble of turnout, the ballots were reportedly already filled out and deposited neatly in the urns.[5] These were seized by the customs office and held at an airbase outside Tegucigalpa.

On June 24, Zelaya, as commander in chief, ordered General Romeo Vasquez Velasquez to prepare to hold the referendum. President Zelaya and General Vasquez were old friends, and Zelaya was sure that the general would help him out of the jam. Much to Mel's surprise, the general refused, and was subsequently fired by an angry president. The following day the Supreme Court ruled 5 to 0 that the general was to be reinstated, stating that his firing was illegal since the order he refused to follow was itself unconstitutional. That afternoon Zelaya himself led a mob of followers and liberated the ballots from the airbase, holding them at the presidential palace until the 28th. Since no Honduran civil servant, military or civilian, was willing to risk their careers and possible jail time to support the political

---

4 Honduras Constitution: Titulo VII: Articulo 374. "Constitución De La República De Honduras, 1982" Part 2, Honduras.net; See also the Honduras Decreto (Decree) 169/1986.

5 Author interviews with confidential sources.

machinations of the insistent and increasingly desperate Zelaya, this same mob prepared to carry out the referendum and count the results in its aftermath. They worked late into the night, spending Mel's last night in the presidential mansion filling out ballots and stuffing the boxes to assure the overwhelming victory Mel needed for his coup.

The clarity brought by time has provided clarity as to then-president Zelaya's intentions. Following other Bolivarian Alliance (ALBA) countries in their pattern of "dictatorship of the majority," Zelaya planned to use an overwhelming "yes" vote on his nonbinding referendum to force the country into an immediate and sweeping Constituent Assembly. This would have allowed him to dissolve Congress and the Supreme Court and rule through an "interim" constituent period—and run again for office, having established a constitution more amenable to his Bolivarian political project.[6] The Bolivarian political project is what this book is about, and has as its most significant expression the Bolivarian Alliance of the Americas (ALBA – for its acronym in Spanish).

It is unclear how President Porfirio "Pepe" Lobo, the current president, who was already on the ballot for the upcoming elections and was ahead in the polls, would have responded. (Lobo's apparent willingness to change the Honduran constitution and make political deals with the exiled Zelaya, as well as his status as alumnus of a prestigious Moscow university where the then-Soviets trained political leaders from the world over, has brought his motives into question.) It is also unclear whether Zelaya himself could have won another election, given the low levels of domestic support at the time. According to a Gallup poll, his popularity was around thirty percent in February of that year.[7] One can only guess whether the constitutional instability was Mel's attempt to bolster domestic support to remain in the Honduran presidency, much like what happened with fellow revolutionaries Daniel Ortega, Evo Morales, Hugo Chavez and Rafael Correa. Perhaps he was seeking to create the very instability that ensued, but which he was then unable to control. Bolivarian Alliance countries are famous for their self-coups and other acts of self-generated instability, which they use to bolster popular support or hide illegal maneuvers. It seems likely that Zelaya was

6 Author interviews with confidential sources.
7 "Destituido Manuel Zelaya: Cronica de la Crisis," *Contacto Magazine*, Junio (June) 2009. http://www.contactomagazine.com/articulos/zelayadestituido0609.htm

simply trying to create a crisis he could exploit to increase his power and extend his time in office. A plan that, Zelaya now knows, was doomed to failure due to the democratic commitment of the Honduran institutions of government.

Yet there is a deeper question here. Where did Zelaya's revolutionary zeal come from? Zelaya himself is not known as a Marxist warrior or a left-wing ideologue. Even today in Honduras there exists debate as to his true socialist credentials: how far back they went and how real they were. Zelaya was born in 1952 to a wealthy ranching family in Juticalpa. After a privileged upbringing in the Honduran upper class, he received his degree in civil engineering from the Autonomous University of Honduras. In 1980 he joined the Liberal Party (the same party as Congress President Roberto Micheletti, who replaced him as interim head of government after his ouster) and in 1985 he joined the Congress, where he served until 1998. From 1998 until 2002 he worked in the administration of then-President Carlos Flores, in charge of the Honduran Investment Fund.[8] While known as a lawmaker who advanced pro-poor initiatives, he was far from the radical revolutionary that one saw in June of 2009. So, what caused the political shift from one moment to another? What was the motivating factor that brought Zelaya into conflict with the Honduran Supreme Court, Congress, Electoral Council, Military and even the Catholic Church? These fundamental questions are at the center of this book. Honduras itself is a case study in how Hugo Chavez's most important foreign policy initiative, the ALBA, works.

All analysis of events and conversations with people who closely follow Honduras seem to agree that Zelaya's embracing of extra-legal agendas, and the instability these brought to the country and the region, arose from the deepening relationship President Zelaya had with Hugo Chavez. For example, former US Ambassador to Honduras Cresencio Arcos has noted that Zelaya, from a wealthy family and whose own father was allegedly involved in rightwing death squads in the tumultuous seventies and eighties, had come into office as a center-right candidate.[9] Upon assum-

---

8 "Manuel Zelaya," Biografías y Vidas. http://www.biografiasyvidas.com/biografia/z/zelaya_manuel.htm
9 Heritage Foundation Forum, "Democracy at Risk: Central America Under Siege," November 18, 2010.

ing office, Zelaya had called Arcos, an old friend, asking, "What do you recommend I do?" "One thing," Arcos responded. "Stay away from Hugo Chavez." When outgoing Zelaya called Arcos several years later, and asked the question, "What did I do wrong?" Acros responded with the same answer, "I told you to stay away from Hugo Chavez." Nevertheless, to this day Zelaya is still deepening his links with the bombastic Venezuelan president.

Zelaya's post-presidency has been financed by Chavez, who appointed him as president of PetroCaribe, and continues to support Zelaya after his July 2011 return to Honduras.

The interaction of Latin-American presidents has always been based on camaraderie and antagonism, and the retreats they hold ad infinitum most often resemble a good old boys' club for rest and relaxation than the real diplomatic engagements they claim to be. Even such complicated relationships as Colombia's Alvaro Uribe with Hugo Chavez are often put aside, the show of backslapping and the flow of compliments more publicly important than personal disagreements and authentic bilateral challenges. President Chavez has managed these relationships well, and has built deeply enduring friendships with leaders across the region. He is also a patient man, someone willing to wait for the right moment to advance his hemispheric project. For Honduras, that time came on December 21, 2007 at the IV Summit of PetroCaribe, a Venezuelan-funded oil initiative. That day, Honduras, a nation with no energy resources of its own, was accepted into PetroCaribe, Venezuela's flagship energy treaty, as a full member, with all the corresponding benefits. This included provision of Venezuelan oil at preferential trade payments, which at a time when the global price of oil was reaching $100 a barrel was, for that impoverished nation, a welcome lifeline. It also meant access to the Fondo ALBA Caribe grants for development projects. On June 28, 2008, Honduras formally signed its admittance into the club.[10] This organization, discussed at length in Chapter 8, can best be understood as a gateway organization through which Chavez extends his tentacles into the hearts and economies of like-minded (or weak-minded) neighbors. It is also a mechanism to use official government debt to support partisan political activities of members.

---

10 "Zelaya anuncia ingreso de Honduras a PetroCaribe," Xinhua 28 de Enero, 2008. http://www.spanish.xinhuanet.com/spanish/2008-01/28/content_567861.htm

Through PetroCaribe membership, President Zelaya began a deeper personal and bilateral relationship with President Chavez and other members of the Venezuela sponsored Bolivarian Alliance for the Americas. Reveling in the power brought by a group of wealthy friends, he embarked upon a plan of initially timid social reforms, such as increasing the minimum wage and starting populist social projects in his country's poor areas. He also became more vocal in his condemnation of Honduras's wealthy and business class: a class to which he continued to belong. His foreign policy rhetoric began to align itself more closely with Venezuela and other ALBA countries and became increasingly hostile to the United States, which had been an important Honduran trading and foreign policy partner for decades and the global market infrastructure. Finally, as we know from statements of drug kingpins such as Venezuela's Walid Makled (addressed in Chapter 12), during Mel's presidency, drug trafficking into Honduras increased exponentially.

The real crisis moment seemed to come with President Zelaya's decision to bring Honduras into the Chavez-led ALBA. Up until this moment, President Zelaya had been increasing his squabbling with international donors, including the IMF, mostly over issues of transparency and governance. The IMF was seeking to pressure Honduras into devaluing its currency, the Lempira, to bring the national budget more into line with reality.[11] For Zelaya, membership in the ALBA represented an opportunity to receive support from a wealthy neighbor with no economic strings or calls for transparency, only political alignment. Upon his calculation, embracing Hugo Chavez' hemispheric anti-United States project must have seemed the lesser of two evils. The ALBA was overwhelmingly approved by the Honduran Congress amidst allegations that certain members had received up to $50,000 for voting in favor. It was even pushed by then-President of the Congress Roberto Micheletti, a fact that would cost him the nomination of his party for the presidency.

On August 28, 2008, the Liberal Party, in the presence of Hugo Chavez, Evo Morales and Daniel Ortega, held a massive rally to celebrate membership in the block, mobilizing a crowd of up to 30,000 by allegedly offering

---

11 "FMI aplaza labor económica de Zelaya," El Heraldo 12 de Enero, 2008. http://www.laprensa.hn/content/view/full/82502

21

payments from five to twenty-three dollars for attending.[12] During this rally, Hugo Chavez railed out against Zelaya's opponents, stating, "For me, any Honduran who opposes the adhesion of Honduras to the ALBA is a traitor or an ignoramus, one of the two."[13] To make matters worse, President Zelaya, hearing the insults directed from a foreign president at a sizable portion of his constituency—and on Honduran soil—followed up with, "There are those that call me center-left. If they are uncomfortable with this, take out the center piece." In the statement signed by President Zelaya, Honduras affirmed, "In Honduras the neoliberal model has meant the increase of poverty and a systematic process of social exclusion that keeps in danger the quality of life of the Hondurans, keeping them from reaching the equity necessary to live in peace, harmony and progress."[14]

This was too much for most patriotic Hondurans. "He came here, to our country, to insult us—and Zelaya stood by him," were one of the comments in regards to Hugo Chavez's declarations.[15] While his increasingly left-leaning agenda won Zelaya some supporters among the Honduran poor, it did not afford him the type of popularity among the lower classes that Hugo Chavez retains in Venezuela. It did, however, alienate the Honduran political establishment, the military, the Catholic Church and the business sector, eventually bringing about Zelaya's downfall.[16]

Immediately, the ALBA issued Honduras a line of credit for agricultural development of $30,000,000 as well as a $100,000,000 purchase of treasury notes to go toward the building of low-income housing. Other benefits were the inclusion of Honduras into Cuba's "Yes I Can" literacy program and technical assistance from the ALBA TV station TeleSUR to Honduras' Channel 8 television station, a station that would play a pivotal role during the crisis of June and July in 2009.

---

12 Thelma Mejia, "Joining ALBA, 'A Step Towards the Center Left' Says the President," August 26, 2008. http://ipsnews.net/news.asp?idnews=43681
13 Video "Chavez Insulta a Hondurenos," Daily Motion. http://www.dailymotion.com/video/x6jsim_chavez-insulta-a-hondurenos_news
14 "Declaracion de Adhesion de la Republica de Honduras a la Alternativa Bolivariana Para los Pueblos de Nuestra America (ALBA)," Agosto 25, 2008. http://www.alianzaboli-variana.org/modules.php?name=Content&pa=showpage&pid=1969
15 Author interviews with confidential sources.
16 Geoff Thale, "Behind the Honduran Coup," Foreign Policy in Focus, July 1, 2009. http://www.fpif.org/articles/behind_the_honduran_coup

Less than six months later Zelaya began his incessant pressure to change the constitution, leading to his ouster less than a year afterward.

After Zelaya was removed from office, and with the international community looking on, Hugo Chavez' ALBA mobilized the international response. The ALBA immediately called an emergency meeting on June 29, 2009 in Nicaragua attended by Presidents Chavez, Morales, Correa, and Ortega, and the recently unemployed Zelaya (with even the Mexican President Felipe Calderon participating as an observer). During that event President Chavez announced there would be "no return to the past" and placed the Venezuelan Armed Forces on high alert, threatening military action against the Honduran interim government led by Roberto Micheletti if Zelaya was not immediately returned to power.[17]

Pressure continued to mount on the tiny Central American nation. On July 5 ex-president Zelaya, aboard a Venezuelan airplane, crossed into Honduran airspace in a Hollywood-style attempt to land at the International Airport of Toncontin in Tegucigalpa. The aircraft was not given landing permission, and the Honduran military placed vehicles on the runway to impede landing. The airplane was instead diverted to El Salvador and finally made it back to Nicaragua. From there, the ex-president made his way to the northern Nicaragua city of Ocotal where, close to the border with Honduras, he set up a center of peaceful resistance. During this entire process, the ALBA turned on the funding stream to pro-Zelaya Social Movements, especially the National Front for Popular Resistance. Nobody knows the amount sent to the FNRP. The ALBA Social Movements (Chapter 8) are funded off budget and usually in cash. It was probably in the tens of millions of dollars.

In the middle of the crisis, the Organization of American States (OAS), originally established to deal with just these types of challenges to democratic governance, was co-opted by the collective weight of the ALBA countries. The OAS is a consensus-based organization. As such, it naturally gravitates to the centers of greatest power during regional crises. Answering a call from the ALBA countries, and probably with his own reelection in mind, the OAS Secretary General Jose Miguel Insulza orchestrated the immediate

---

17 "Chavez allies back ousted Zelaya," BBC News, June 29, 2009. http://news.bbc. co.uk/2/hi/8124100.stm

expulsion of Honduras from the organization: for the first time ever applying an Article 20 violation of the Inter-American Democratic Charter. The Obama Administration, committed to not repeating the perceived mistakes of the Bush Administration in the Venezuela coup of 2002, bequeathed full authority to manage the response to a debilitated and co-opted OAS.

Despite the OAS sanctions, the interim government of Honduras refused to capitulate to the demands of the international community to return Zelaya to power, and Insulza turned to Oscar Arias, the respected peace broker and president of Costa Rica who offered his services as mediator. Through deft negotiation, Arias received backing from all parties for the "Agreement of San José."[18] This agreement called for a truth commission, a government of national unity, amnesty for political crimes, and the commitment by all parties to leave aside any call for a national Constituent Assembly to rewrite the constitution. The agreement gave the final decision for the reinstatement of Zelaya to the presidency to the lower house of the Honduran Congress, which on December 2 voted overwhelmingly against this.

Inside Honduras, the situation had become very complicated for the interim government of Micheletti. Chavez immediately suspended oil shipments through PetroCaribe, handing the Micheletti government an energy crisis on top of their other challenges. Venezuela also called in the full amount of the $180,000,000 in loans they had provided to Honduras over the previous year. Martial law remained in place for several months, as the interim government attempted to control protests by angry Zelaya followers (with important internal support from Cuban, Nicaraguan and Venezuelan intelligence agents). Pro-Zelaya activists seized an important valley called Bajo Aguan, where they set up the center of the resistance movement. In Nicaragua, Venezuelan, Cuban and Nicaraguan intelligence agents reportedly began training a Honduran guerilla group.[19] Zelaya's followers had organized themselves into the National Front for Popular Resistance (FNRP), which would continue to receive more than a million

---

18 "Acuerdo de San José," 22 de Julio, 2009. http://www.elheraldo.hn/var/elheraldo_ site/storage/original/application/205307a26c541f7af1d173c22454bd5a.pdf

19 "La 'guerrilla zelayista' ya entrena en Nicaragua," El Heraldo, 1 de Enero, 2009. http://www.elheraldo.hn/Ediciones/2009/08/02/Noticias/La-guerrilla-zelayista-ya-entrena-en-Nicaragua

dollars a month from Caracas[20] and would eventually join the Forum of San Paulo and the Bolivarian Congress of the Nations, two organizations you will read about later in the book.

Meanwhile, the Supreme Court reverted Channel 8 to its previous owner, after the Zelaya government had orchestrated its illegal buyout and supported it with TeleSUR experts. The almost daily protests became more violent, and the teachers union seized upon the crisis as an opportunity to lobby for better pay. The antagonizing presence of the ex-president on the border made the country a tinderbox; add to that the almost constant calls of President Chavez for military action against Honduras, and the interim government was forced to deploy the military to guard the border crossing at Ocotal, from which Zelaya issued repeated threats to return to the country.

Only two months later, on September 21, Zelaya succeeded in returning to Honduras. Smuggled in the trunk of a car (and assisted by El Salvador's ruling party, the FMLN, and Venezuela's foreign minister Nicolas Maduro without President Funes' knowledge[21]), he reappeared at the Brazilian embassy, stating he had returned to reassume the presidency.[22] For four months he stayed as the guest of Brazil until, on January 27, 2010, he was given safe conduct out of the country to the Dominican Republic, where he remained until July 2011.

In his final act as interim president, before handing over power to the newly elected Porfirio Lobo, President Micheletti pushed through Congress the withdrawal of Honduras from the ALBA.

Throughout the entire process, the ALBA countries, led by Chavez, continued to manage the OAS's response and dictate the measures to be taken against Honduras. On various occasions, President Chavez threatened the country with invasion. For an extended period of time, ALBA countries continued to maintain their economic and political blockade of the government of Honduras despite growing desire by the international community, led by the United States and the European Union, to usher Honduras back into the Inter-American community.

---

20 Author interviews with confidential sources.

21 "FMLN y Chavez regresaron a Zelaya," La Prensa, 8 de Diciembre 2010. http://www.laprensa.com.ni/2010/12/08/nacionales/45854

22 Zelaya consigue entrar en Honduras," La Verdad, 22 de Septiembre, 2009. http://www.laverdad.es/murcia/20090922/mundo/zelaya-consigue-entrar-honduras-20090922.html

In July of 2011, President Zelaya returned to Honduras to lead his political party, the National Front for Popular Resistance. Upon recommendation from the truth commission of the Organization of American States (OAS), President Lobo began to discuss the possibility of a popular consultation to change the constitution. The ALBA countries (except Ecuador) reestablished diplomatic relations with Honduras after a new agreement, the Cartegena Accords (mediated by Colombian President Juan Manuel Santos), paved a way for the return of President Zelaya without the unacceptable components of the San Jose Accords (namely, the assurance that no party will discuss constitutional reforms).

The new government of Honduras has suspended investigations into the destination of $98,000,000, part of a lot of $100,000,000 transferred to the Honduran Ministry of Finance and passed over to the presidential palace months before Zelaya's ouster.[23] The money has vanished. Zelaya, responding to the accusations of corruption, assured that his successor, interim president Micheletti, in fact took it, which Micheletti denies. The FNRP, an ALBA Social Movement (which I will discuss later) has collected over 1,300,000 signatures (of a voting block of 3.9 million) demanding a Constituent Assembly. This is a strange story, a real Latin-American story, and one without a happy ending. Honduras continues to face international pressure by governments controlled by ALBA, and it continues to suffer from the internal polarization due to Zelayistas who strive for the return of their president to power and the writing of a new constitution. The story is by no means over. The future of Honduras continues to be written by the social actors at the grass roots, and by the way President "Pepe" Lobo is able to manage the ongoing crisis and create a broader base of well-being for the nation's citizens, while resisting Chavez's attractive trap of authoritarianism and easy money. Just as important, drug trafficking, which increased exponentially during the Zelaya Administration, is threatening to corrupt Honduras' weak institutions and plunge an already internally violent Honduras into chaos.

For ex-president Zelaya, I continue to be intrigued by the behavior that brought about the crisis. The decisions made seem to be counterintuitive, especially for a politician with as much experience as he had. It is unclear

---

23 obal/detalle.aspx?idart=3281318&idcat=56658&tipo=2

what he hoped to achieve from the chaotic vote that Sunday morning except, perhaps, forcing a political crisis. From his ouster through the present, he seems to be basing decisions on the assumption that a broad-based popular revolt is in the making—a revolt that did not happen when he was removed from office, did not happen when he attempted to land his airplane and clash with the military, and did not happen even when he returned to the Brazilian embassy. The FNRP has an approval rating of less than ten percent.[24] Yet the instability created by Zelaya's insistence upon illegal changes has done nothing but harm the Honduras he says he is attempting to deliver out of poverty. The suspension of the IMF funding, the European Union and United States' support, as well as the sanctions that accompanied the expulsion from the OAS, left Honduras in a deep fiscal hole, all this happening when the world economy itself was struggling with its most significant recession in a lifetime. The only reasonable explanation for his bizarre behavior is that of a zealot advancing a personal political project, a person who projects a grandiose revolutionary vision to be sold using inflammatory language disguised as retribution, redistribution and revolution—while subverting the very pillars designed to protect against tyranny.

But why advance a vision that in fact has only brought instability, ostracism and pain to the people of his country, people he was elected to represent, by violating a constitution that he swore his oath to defend? I think the answer is to be found in Zelaya's relationship with Hugo Chavez and the ALBA countries as a whole, who have bound themselves together in a revolutionary alliance that seeks to advance a political project, at the margins of legality even in their own countries, and expand its influence in the region and beyond.

This is a book about that project.

---

24 Author interviews with confidential sources.

CHAPTER 2

The ALBA in History

In the winter of 1830, Simon Jose Antonio de la Santisima Trinidad Bolivar y Palacios, liberator of a continent, revolutionary, thinker and philosopher, military leader, president and dictator, lay dying in the *quinta* (colonial farmhouse) of San Pedro Alejandrino in Santa Marta, Colombia. The liberator had taken ill with a fatal case of tuberculosis. As he gasped his last breaths, exiled from his country of birth—a country that only a few precious years before, he had helped to free from Spanish dominion—he must have been pondering his fate, and his failure. Only forty-seven years old,[25] he had led one of the most spectacular lives imaginable and had carved his place into the annals of world history by the might of his sword and the strength of his unassailable vision. He would be remembered: from the Hall of Bolivar in the Organization of American States in Washington DC; to the statue of The Liberator astride his horse in an opulent neighborhood of Tehran; to the thousands of plazas named after him in town after town across Latin America. For two centuries, people across a wide continent have sung the praises of this powerful man.

Yet despite the fame, the glory, and the undeniable victories, he died an outcast, a man on the run from former friends-turned-enemies as he looked over his shoulder, fearful of assassins' bullets or unseen betrayal. It must have been a heartbreaking end for a man with such a grandiose vision, to see everything he built collapse around him. It must have been

25 Ignacio Arismendi Posada; *Gobernantes Colombianos*, trans. Colombian Presidents; Interprint Editors Ltd.; Italgraf; Segunda Edición: 19; Bogotá, Colombia; 1983.

29

humiliating to have to die depending upon the simple charity of a friend. But more than anything else, to know, as he must have in his heart, that the great, powerful nation he envisioned in his mind's eye and worked so hard to achieve was instead destined to suffer for the next two hundred years in an endless line of misery, despotism and poverty.

The idea, Bolivar's grand idea, had been first proposed by Francisco de Miranda, a great thinker in his own right and one of the founding fathers of Venezuela—and young Simon Bolivar's mentor. He had written about the idea of Hispano-American unity from 1790. In 1797, together with two other thinkers, Jose del Pozo y Sucre and Manuel Jose de Salas, he signed the Act of Paris, which called for the creation of a continental representative body. This idea, adopted so enthusiastically by Bolivar, would meet its final inglorious end with Bolivar's premature death.[26]

To understand what the Bolivarian Alliance of the Americas (ALBA) is, one must go to the very dawning of Latin-American independence. It is there, in the grandiose vision and the incredible struggles of those few founding fathers of an independent Latin-America, that one finds the seed of the ALBA, a seed that sprouted into only a sapling before it was to die upon the parched and withered earth of Simon Bolivar's unquenchable ambition. It was an audacious scheme: a vision of a powerful Latin-American continent under one ruler, subordinate to the cause of one empire and steadfast in its opposition to the United States and the imperial advances of Europe—"La Republica de Colombia," what we today refer to in popular jargon as the "Gran Colombia." That was Bolivar's vision, and the only way he saw Latin America being able to stand up to what he believed were the predatory instincts of the giant to the north. This failed vision, which plunged South America into war against itself less than two decades after independence, is the vision being revisited upon the countries of the former Gran Colombia by another authoritarian leader, Hugo Chavez.

Simon Bolivar was born in Caracas, Venezuela on July 24, 1783, into a wealthy family that had interests in copper and agriculture, and was an important member of the colony's aristocracy. Bolivar's house, a beautiful three-century-old colonial masterpiece, has been turned into a museum in central Caracas. The house still contains The Liberator's uniforms, the bed

---

26 Cuadernos de Emancipacion, No. 35, ISSN 0328-0179 April 2009.

in which he was born and the accoutrements of daily colonial life—at least for the wealthy. As one walks through this spectacular mansion you can still feel the reverberation of that Spanish colonial life, and sense the strength of this man's personality and the power of the word that still resonates through the country: revolution.

The young Simon was raised in his early years by the Bolivar family's slave, referred to in history books as *la negra Hipolita* (Hipolita the black woman), until he was old enough to begin his schooling under the careful tutelage of Andres Bello and Simon Rodriguez (both important and oft-repeated names in Venezuela). At the age of fourteen, like all good colonial aristocrats, he began his military training, which eventually led him to Paris, France where he gained his first experience in revolution.

Returning to Venezuela in 1807, Bolivar began to conspire with those in the colony who were advocating independence from Spain. As in the United States only three decades earlier, the colonials were chafing under the weight of an empire run from three thousand miles away. He raised arms against the Spanish colonialists in 1811, and by 1813 he took his first revolutionary military command in New Granada (now Colombia) and marched on Venezuela, entering the capital city of Caracas on August 6, 1813, where he was glorified as "El Libertador." A revolution in the ranks forced him to flee back to Colombia to seek support, which he finally obtained from Haiti's dictator Petion.[27] Accompanied by Haitian soldiers, he decided to focus his attack on the Viceroyalty of New Granada, believing that if he could chase the Spaniards out of that important stronghold, he could then free the less important and less fortified captaincies of Caracas and Quito. On February 15, 1819, Bolivar called together the nobles and aristocrats in open rebellion against the Spaniards in the Congress of Angostura. At this Constituent Congress, the Gran Colombia was officially formed—and the battle to expel the Spaniards from the newborn nation began in earnest.

From the congress, Bolivar moved to challenge the Spaniards in the capital of the viceroyalty in present-day Bogota, Colombia. He believed that should he be able to beat the Spaniards where they were strongest, he could then quickly piece together the other components of the great

---

27 David Bushnell, *The Liberator, Simón Bolívar*. New York: Alfred A. Knopf, 1970. Print.

nation. On August 6, 1819, the thirty-six-year-old Bolivar faced off against the Spanish in the Battle of Boyaca. Bolivar's revolutionary armies won.[28]

From there, Bolivar launched attacks into both Ecuador and Venezuela, routing the Spanish in battle after battle until in the Battle of Carabobo in Venezuela in 1821 and the Battle of Pichincha in Ecuador in 1822 put an end to the Spanish occupation of the region. On August 30, 1821, the revolutionary Congress of Cucuta met, a re-assembly of the members of the 1819 Congress of Angostura. There The Liberator delivered his famous speech declaring the formal independence of the region from Spanish control.[29] This reassembled congress was comprised of twenty-six elected leaders from the various parts of Gran Colombia that were in open revolt against Spain. There, they quickly wrote and approved the Constitution of Cucuta, which replaced the one of Angostura, an interim document meant to facilitate revolution.

On September 7, 1821, newly elected President Simon Bolivar, with Vice-President Francisco de Paula Santander at his side—announced the creation of "La Republica de Colombia," "the Gran Colombia."[30] This new construct did away with the regional vice-presidencies of Francisco Antonio Zea and Juan German Roscio, set in place at the Congress of Angostura, and organized a more formal, centralized government based in Bogota.[31] This new independent republic encompassed most of the territory of the Spanish Viceroyalty of Nueva Granada, and included the present day countries of Venezuela, Colombia, Ecuador and Panama, parts of the Caribbean coast of Costa Rica, parts of the Peruvian and Brazilian Amazon, and a large slice of Western Guyana (still under contention by Venezuela to this day). Bolivar also assisted Bolivia, named after him, in their fight for independence—and was briefly president of that country before appointing his friend and fellow general Antonio Jose de Sucre to the role. Bolivia had been part of the Viceroyalty of Peru, known as Upper

---

28 "La Batalla de Boyaca," Efemerides Venezolanas. http://www.efemeridesvenezolanas. com/html/boyaca.htm

29 "Simón Bolívar, An Address of Bolivar at the Congress of Angostura" (February 15, 1819), Reprint Ed., (Washington, D.C.: Press of B. S. Adams, 1919), passim.

30 David Bushnell, *The Santander Regime*, 12. (Bushnell uses both "Colombia" and "Gran Colombia.")

31 "Gran Colombia," Encyclopedia Britannica online. http://www.britannica.com/ EBchecked/topic/241012/Gran-Colombia

Peru, and its political independence, mixed with the expansionist vision of Simon Bolivar, brought considerable consternation to the newly independent government of Peru in Lima. However, either due to geography or a backroom deal with fellow liberator San Martin of Argentina and Peruvian president Jose de la Mar—and perhaps understanding that any move on Bolivia could lead to war, a fact confirmed only a few years later—Bolivia was never brought into the nation-state of Gran Colombia.

Immediately upon centralization of government in Bogota, frictions began to occur between the Federalists and the centralists. Santander, Bolivar's vice president, held Federalist views, while Bolivar wished to maintain a highly centralized state with power vested in a strong executive.[32] At the same time as these rifts began to occur, war broke out in Peru, which kept Bolivar's attention focused on the military conflict, his forte, but requiring him to tighten his grip upon the Department of Ecuador. Resentment in Ecuador began to spill over as its economy was hurt by supplies of cheaper textiles from the other Departments. The quasi-dictatorial rule of Simon Bolivar—who was still governing under special wartime authorities—exacerbated the discontent. Even many low-level civil servants in Ecuador were being brought from the Departments of Venezuela or Cundinamarca (now Colombia).

By the middle of the 1820s, the military alliance that had held the unwieldy nation together, for the purpose of fighting the Spaniards, started to shred. Federalist forces within the government, led by General Jose Antonio Paez in Venezuela, began to gain ground against the centrist Bolivar. In 1826, the congress began impeachment proceedings against Paez, who ignored the proceedings, continued on his push for Federalism, and refused to leave his post. Soon he was joined by disgruntled voices from Guayaquil and Quito, who were also chafing under the heavy hand of Bolivar's government in Bogota.[33] During this time, Simon Bolivar had been busy with the organization of the newly independent Republic of Bolivia. Bolivia had been freed from Spanish (and Peruvian) rule, and in 1825 General Sucre had organized a Constituent Assembly. However, Bolivar was un-

---

32 David Bushnell (1970), *The Santander Regime in Gran Colombia.* Westport, CT: Greenwood Press. ISBN 0837129818. OCLC 258393.
33 John Lynch (2006), *Simón Bolívar: A Life.* New Haven and London: Yale University Press. ISBN 0-300-11062-6.

happy with the constituent process and drafted his own constitution for the Bolivian state emphasizing sovereignty and establishing, among other things, a presidency for life.[34]

In response to the Paez revolt of 1826, Simon Bolivar began proposing use of the model of the Bolivian constitution as a possible solution to the crisis. In his mind, perhaps he was thinking that the acceptance of a centralist constitution would finally end the squabbling of regions becoming disenchanted with rule from Bogota. Whatever his reasoning, his attempts to use the Bolivian constitution as a model for Gran Colombia were met with outright hostility by political actors already wary of what they saw as Bolivar's creeping authoritarianism. Vice-president Santander himself, a longtime advocate of Federalism, was dismayed by the new constitution. The situation continued to deteriorate, with various assemblies in Caracas discussing (but never agreeing upon) succession, and outright violence breaking out between pro-Paez and pro-Bolivar factions of the military. Late that year, with no other option left to hold together the shattering country, Bolivar marched an army to Maracaibo, in western Venezuela, intent upon invading the wayward department. The attack never materialized, however, and Bolivar offered as a solution the instatement of the Constituent Assembly promised in the last Congress of Cucuta for the creation of the new constitution.

Tension continued to simmer for the following year until, in January of 1828, the Constituent Assembly met. Bolivar again took the opportunity to push his Bolivian constitution with its president-for-life clause. Bolivar's proposal again met with resistance, and the final constitution that emerged from the assembly was of a Federalist bent. Pro-Bolivar hardliners walked out of the assembly, marking an end to the process. With no options remaining to hold together the great nation, on August 27, 1828, Bolivar declared himself dictator.[35]

---

34 "Constitucion Politica de Bolivia de 1826," http://www.dircost.unito.it/cs/docs/Bolivia%201826.htm

35 Juan Jose Canavessi, "Simon Bolivar: Sintesis Biografica de Bolivar," Reportario de Ensayistas y Filosofos. http://www.ensayistas.org/filosofos/venezuela/bolivar/semblanza.htm

During this time, war was brewing in the south between the newly independent Republic of Peru, which Bolivar himself helped to gain its independence (and had even served for a short time as president), and the Gran Colombia. Upon liberating Peru (alongside San Martin, who came from the south in 1821), Bolivar assumed the presidency and attempted to bring the newly independent country into his Pan-Latin-Americanist vision. By 1827 it was clear he would be unsuccessful, and he resigned as president of that nation, to be replaced by a succession of presidents ending with President Jose de la Mar, who was himself later overthrown.

Ostensibly, Bolivar failed because of the quite different dynamics between the Gran Colombia countries and those of the Spanish Viceroyalty of Peru. However, during this time Bolivar had also been appointed (and had accepted) the presidency of Bolivia by the newly independent assembly. Up until independence, Bolivia had been a province of the Viceroyalty of Peru known as Upper Peru. In 1826, while assisting Bolivia with its new constitution, Bolivar stepped aside as president to return to Bogota and focus on the administration of the Gran Colombia, leaving his general and friend Jose Antonio de Sucre (who had also served a short time as President of Peru) as the new President of Bolivia.

The year 1826 was a crucial year for Bolivarianism. The wars of independence were over and the newly independent countries were exploring mechanisms of self-governance: through constitutions, assemblies and multilateral agreements. Bolivar seized the opportunity to again pursue his idea of a Latin-American Confederation, an idea that had been with him from the beginning. In his 1815 Letter from Jamaica, he wrote about this ambitious project:

It is a grandiose[sic] idea to attempt to form from all the new world a single nation, with one sole link which connects its parts among each other and to everything else. Since it already has an origin, a language, customs and a religion, it should also have one sole government which confederates the different states that are forming … how beautiful it would be that the Isthmus of Panama were to become for all of us what Corinth was for the Greeks. Hopefully someday we have the fortune to install there an august congress of the representatives of the republics, kingdoms and empires and attempt to discuss the high interests of peace and war, with the nations of other parts of the world. This type of cooperation could have a place in some lucky moment of our regeneration.…

Beginning on June 22, 1826 and for a period of three weeks, representatives from Gran Colombia, Peru, Bolivia, Mexico, and the United Provinces of Central America held the first (and only) session of the Congress of Panama. The tone of this congress was the open opposition to England and the United States (and of course Spain), which Bolivar saw as the greatest threats to the creation of his Gran Colombia.[36] Simon Bolivar said of the conference, "The object of this perpetual pact will be to sustain in common, defensively or offensively if it becomes necessary, the sovereignty and independence of all and each one of the confederated powers of America against all foreign domination." The undercurrent of the meeting was the attempt to also seek the liberation of Cuba and Puerto Rico, which were still under Spanish domination, and to bring them into the Latin-American confederation. There, the ambassadors present made sweeping agreements for unity and proposed ambitious joint projects. However, when the lofty rhetoric fell silent, the confederation's final agreement was signed only by the Gran Colombia. When Bolivar heard the news of the conference's failure, he said, "The Congress of Panama will only ever be a shade."[37]

Witnessing Bolivar's weakness in Gran Colombia and the failure of the Congress of Panama, Peru perceived an opportunity to retake the wayward province of Upper Peru (now Bolivia). This angered the soon-to-be dictator Simon Bolivar, who saw the new Bolivian country and its constitution as a mechanism to expand his Gran Colombia into a hemispheric project. He appointed Sucre as the general for the Colombian armies tasked with retaking Bolivia. On June 3, 1828, Bolivar declared war on the Republic of Peru.[38] That same day the Peruvians under President Jose de la Mar responded in kind, ordering the mobilization of ground and sea forces. On November 22, 1828, the Peruvian army attacked Guayaquil, Ecuador, in an attempt to take control of that important city. The Peruvian victories were short-lived, however, and General Sucre began to turn the tide. The

---

36 Cuadernos de Emancipacion, Edicion #35, ISSN 0328-0179, April 2009.
37 *Germán A. de la Reza, El Congreso de Panamá de 1826 y otros ensayos de integración en el siglo XIX. Estudio y fuentes documentales anotadas*, UAM-Eon, México, 2006. ISBN 970-31-0656-0.
38 "Guerra de Gran Colombia – Peru," http://www.worldlingo.com/ma/enwiki/es/Gran_Colombia-Peru_War

Peruvians held Guayaquil until July 10, 1829 when, in an armistice, the Peruvians agreed to cede control of the city to Gran Colombia. A formal peace agreement was signed on September 22, 1829.

While this conflict played out to the south, Bolivar was leaving the problems of his own disintegrating country unattended. From November 23, 1829, two separate congresses were held in Valencia and Caracas, Venezuela. They unanimously agreed to dissolve all ties with Bogota. On March 20, 1830, the last Congress of Gran Colombia met with the purpose of discussing strategies with the Venezuelan delegation, an attempt to keep the union together: a last-ditch effort that proved futile. At this congress the troubled union, which had lasted from the 1819 Congress of Angostura to 1830, was finally and permanently dissolved. Saying, "All who served the revolution have plowed the sea," Simon Bolivar resigned the presidency on April 27, 1830.[39] Feeling defeated and ill from what we now know was advancing tuberculosis, he left the administration of the country to Rafael Jose Urdaneta y Faria, another Venezuelan general and faithful Bolivarian. On December 17, 1830, Simon Bolivar died.

The collapse of Bolivar's emblematic project, Gran Colombia, has had reverberations through Latin-American history. Since that time, and using countless bilateral and multilateral treaties, these nations—brothers in culture, religion, language and ethnicity—have attempted to create mechanisms for unity that Bolivar had initially sought. These mechanisms have always been short-lived, and the incessant conflicts between Latin-American countries, beginning with Bolivar's war with Peru, have planted seeds of a bitterness that has never been entirely overcome. This, nevertheless, is the political project of Hugo Chavez's ALBA. What Bolivar called the Congress of Panama is today the Bolivarian project called the "Patria Grande (Great Homeland)." This is what President Chavez is seeking to build through his Bolivarian Alliance, using mechanisms, which are laid out in this book, to link the countries of Latin America together under his indomitable rule: as the reincarnation of, if not literal, at least figurative Gran Colombia: the second coming of Simon Bolivar.

---

39 German de la Reza, "La invención de la paz. De la república cristiana del duque de Sully a la sociedad de naciones de Simón Bolívar," México, Siglo XXI Editores, 2009. ISBN 978-607-03-0054-7.

CHAPTER 3

Socialism of the 21st Century

In Bolivia there is a democratic, decolonizing revolution. A progressive annihilation of the mechanisms of economic and cultural exclusion, that have marginalized indigenous sectors, leaving them culturally oppressed and economically exploited. And, along with that, there is in progress a process of amplification of rights, democratization of functions and strengthening of communitarian nuclei, which merit a medium or long-term post-capitalist horizon, but which today are internal, in the fight against capitalism itself. My idea of Socialism of the 21st Century is the one that Marx had in the 19th century: a corpuscular overcoming of the existing capitalist order.

— Alvaro Garcia Linera, Vice-President of Bolivia

Any discussion of the Bolivarian Alliance for the Americas would be incomplete without an analysis, however brief, of the economic and political project that this regional block is enthusiastically promoting. This chapter is a summary of the precepts of the new socialism.

The political and economic project has definite Marxist overtones. Cuban influence upon Chavez's ALBA has been immense, and the Chavez government itself is full of adherents to Marxism, Leninism and Trotskyism. Nevertheless, for Chavez, "socialism" is a means to an end.

It is a common mistake to disavow the important political changes in Latin America, or to confer upon Hugo Chavez the title of "clown" or "buffoon," or to assume that the political process dubbed "21st Century

Socialism" is merely at best an exercise of populism by the bombastic Venezuelan leader, or at least an idiot's ridiculous ramblings. Sometimes in the United States, analysts looking at Latin America attempt to compare their political paradigms with our US realities, and this too often makes us miss some important nuances of Latin-American politics. They seem unwilling to confer upon Latin America's colorful and colloquial political movements the respect of their quite real political project. The success of this project is still in doubt. As FLACSO's Josette Altmann has said, "This project is doomed to failure, because it denies the irreversible forces of globalization in this new century." Even Chavez has said, "Globalization is real, whether we like it or not." However, doomed to failure or not, Bolivarians are embarking energetically upon their bold project: "We must save (the world) from the claws of imperialism and the threats of capitalism, the destroyer of peoples, of rivers, of oceans and of mountains," as said President Hugo Chavez.

The project is itself colorful and messy. Students of Gabriel Garcia Marquez or Alvaro Vargas Llosa will revel in its magical realism. Nevertheless, behind the project are a group of serious philosophers and intellectuals and an army of hundreds of thousands, or millions, of activists. These activists have come from all the world over to participate in Chavez's political revolution; from the now famous Foro de San Paulo, the anarchists, the communists, the environmentalists, the anticapitalists, and others have arrived, then assembled under the mantle of the ALBA Revolution to advance their joint project.

The story of how Hugo Chavez has assembled the ALBA's economic and political philosophy is circumfluous. Many thinkers have influenced his ongoing learning. Chavez is a famously avid reader with an active intellectual curiosity. Repeatedly, the Venezuelan opposition and the United States underestimate him, assuming his bombastic style makes him a clown instead of a political master who understands his constituents well.

In 1983, Chavez gathered with thirteen other clandestinely rebellious soldiers under a tree in the city of Maracay called the "Saman de Guere." This was the tree where The Liberator Simon Bolivar was said to have rested. There, they formed a secret organization called the MBR200—named for the 200th anniversary of the Liberator's birthday—and swore their oath to refound their republic. This led to the eventual creation of what has become known as the Fifth Republic. Since his days leading the MBR-200, Chavez has had important influences. His brother, Adan Chavez, instilled him with communist ideas. Contact with FARC and terrorist organizations as they planned their insurrections gave him a sense of the struggle and relationships in that shadowy world. The Cuban influence, especially that of Fidel Castro, is undisputed. Other important mentors have received less attention. Jose Vicente Rangel and Luis Michilena, his former vice presidents, held important roles as institutional leftists to convince Chavez of the need to work within the system. Luis Michilena, in whose house he lived after he was released from jail, taught him about politics, party building and campaigning, Jose Vicente Rangel about negotiations and building coalitions for power. An important thinker who started the nouveau discussion of dictatorship in Latin America was the former president of the Dominican Republic, Juan Bosch. In his famous book, *Dictatorship with Popular Support*, Bosch laid out a long and tedious list of grievances against the United States abroad and the "oligarchs" within. This laundry list of complaints has been heard repeatedly in countries where the executive seeks to perpetuate himself in power. According to Bosch,[40] the new, popular dictators will be able to carry out the following:

1. Guarantee work, health care and education to those who currently are excluded.
2. Serve as the absolute guarantor of all the fundamental freedoms of humanity, eliminating hunger, exploitation, and "governmental terrorism."
3. Guarantee the equality of citizens, not only following the written laws of the land but those that are not written, yet keep citizens divided by reason of sex, culture, social status, and those who launched a struggle, one against the other, to seize, and not allow to be seized, their food, position and rights.

As can be demonstrated, this authoritarian trend, said to be necessary to guarantee the basic rights of the majority, has been discussed for decades. The argument is not new, and has not gotten any more palatable or viable over the last forty years. Nevertheless, there have been others more

---

40 Juan Bosch, , (1969): P116.

recently who have added to this argument and enriched the discussion. And there are several who stand out by the force of their ideas. 21st Century Socialism is a political, economic and military project; each of these components has had its main influence, built rationally in true Latin fashion.

The political project was best summed up by long-time Chavez friend and mentor Norberto Ceresole. Norberto Ceresole, one of Hugo Chavez' most important mentors, himself stated, "Lastly, it is in my personal interest that my thoughts remain unaligned, with the utmost clarity possible, to both the infantile leftist pro-Cubanism as well as whatever form of social democratic modernism neo or post capitalist." The political project, in Ceresole's mind, was about power and the re-positioning of Latin America. It was not ideological.

In his book *Strongman, Army and the People: The Venezuela of President Chavez*, Ceresole lays out his vision of the future of Hugo Chavez, resident of Venezuela and re-unifier of the Grand Colombia. According to Ceresole, it was essential to speedily reinstate Venezuela in a different way in the international order. To do this, a physical person, not an abstract idea, was delegated by the Venezuelan people to carry this out. The emerging Venezuelan political model is not a theoretical construction, but an "emergency of reality." This emergency created a revolution that didn't focus on ideological ideas, but hinged upon a basic relationship between a national caudillo and the popular masses who, in their absolute (and permanent) majority, designated Chavez as their representative. This resembles more a feudal model of government represented by the shire charters of 16th-century England than modern constitutional-based governance. As will be discussed in the future, the Bolivarian model of "communes" is of locally governed units that pay homage to the center for support and protection. Here again, this time with Ceresole, we see the idea of a permanent majority, a concept that has become essential to the ALBA. According to Ceresole, the ALBA political model has four unique and discrete differences from anything ever seen before:

1. Ceresole advocates for a "post-democratic" model different from the democratic model in that it emphasizes that power must be centralized. Neither institutions nor ideas have any place in the creation of the new ALBA political model.

2. He also stresses the divergence from traditional 20th Century Socialism (communism) in that neither ideology nor party should play a role in leadership. Chavez has always stressed this himself, concerned less with the creation of a "unitary party" and more with the "patriotic pole," which brings together different electoral machines under his leadership. His primary party, the Fifth Republic Movement, was less a party than an electoral movement and platform for winning elections. With the advent of the United Socialist Party (PSUV), Chavez ventured into the realm of more institutional communism. He has quickly backtracked as he has seen the party fail to produce the same level of electoral victories as his "patriotic pole." This has been an ongoing problem with the Venezuelan, Bolivian and Ecuadoran "revolutions"; they have fallen back upon more institutional ideological communism, which has heralded the demise of their project (as Heinz Dieterich, the father of 21st Century Socialism, has said on multiple occasions).

3. The ALBA political model differs from traditional caudillo models of government in that it was expressed as a democratic choice of the "permanent majorities," but also, power was conveyed to Chavez for a specific purpose. This purpose is the national independence (from the "empire," the United States) and radical transformation of the society. Old feudal models were simply about the perpetuation of the lords. This model is the power of a feudal lord not for his own personal project, but for a grandiose scheme to create a "new world order" in Latin America.

4. The model is also different from the European nationalists (such as Germany, Spain or Italy) in that it is not ideologically focused, and for the reasons stated above.

Ceresole, who passed away in 2003, was an enigmatic character who embodied his vision. He considered himself a post-ideological figure. He had been part of the Argentine Montonero group of leftist revolutionaries.[41] He joined the Peruvian dictator Juan Velazco Alvarado in the early seventies as an advisor. Velazco Alvarado was a leftist dictator whose political project closely resembled Hugo Chavez' Bolivarian Revolution. Exiled to Spain because of unsavory relationships, Ceresole became the spokes-

---

41 "Ha Muerto el Camarada," Altermedia Castellano 7 de Mayo, 2003. http://es.altermedia.info/general/ha-muerto-el-camarada_419.html

person for Hezbollah in that country and joined the *carapintadas*—a radical right-wing Argentine revolutionary group. Following the coup attempt in 1988 by Aldo Rico, Argentina's most famous carapintada, Ceresole returned home as an advisor to Rico. He became known as a rabid anti-Semite, denying the Holocaust and famously writing books blaming Mossad for the bombings of the Jewish center in Buenos Aires.

Hugo Chavez met Norberto Ceresole in 1994 in Buenos Aires.[42] Chavez, recently pardoned by Rafael Caldera for his failed coup attempt of 1992, was in Argentina ostensibly meeting with Aldo Rico and his carapintadas, and it was through them he was introduced to Ceresole. "When I met Chavez," Ceresole said later in an interview, "I felt a revelation, that is, I saw a character that somehow I had imagined.... I had imagined (him) as a possibility. I had a negative experience with some Argentine military and when I saw Chavez it was, frankly, like a breath of fresh air. However, I immediately understood his left-wing line, which I didn't like, and therein emerged the fraternal struggle between Chavez and Ceresole."[43] Ceresole traveled back to Venezuela with Chavez, intent on converting Chavez to his vision. Together, in Ceresole's own words, they drove around the country three times and discussed Ceresole's ideas and the role that Chavez would have in the remaking of Venezuela and the Patria Grande.

These were the days that Chavez, in his red Volkswagen Beetle, was connecting with the Venezuela population and building his constituency. He would stop in a village, climb up onto his car and start delivering the fiery speeches about remaking Venezuela for which he has become famous.[44] But back then, he was an unknown. A pardoned coup-monger, an irrelevant politician, the wrong color and with the wrong trajectory to ever lead Venezuela. Yet Ceresole saw something different, and spent years with Chavez, training him on the ideas for which Ceresole has become reviled.

Ceresole was expelled from Venezuela after the Venezuela political police (DISIP for the letters in Spanish) found him in possession of a book[45]

---

42 Maria Victoria Cristancho, "El Incomodo Amigo de Hugo Chavez," El Tiempo, 20 de Mayo 1999. http://www.eltiempo.com/archivo/documento/MAM-872606

43 Ilan Stavans, "Hugo Chavez's Advisor: The Anti-Semitic path of Norberto Ceresole." http://zeek.forward.com/articles/116835/

44 Cristina Marcano, "Hugo Chavez sin Uniforme," Debate Publishers, November 30, 2005, ISBN 9871117183.

45 Maria Victoria Cristancho, "El Incomodo Amigo de Hugo Chavez," El Tiempo, 20 de

called, *"Proclamation to the Venezuelan Nation of the National Bolivarian Front,"* which defended Chavez' 1992 coup and outlined the new Venezuelan political order which would be led by Hugo Chavez.

Upon Chavez' victory in 1998, Ceresole re-appeared in Venezuela and authored the book, *Strongman, Army and the People: The Venezuela of President Chavez.* After an outcry by the Venezuelan Jewish community, who were concerned about the influence of this vocal anti-Semite upon their new and volatile president, Ceresole was expelled yet again, this time by then-vice president Luis Michilena. Michilena, an institutionalist, saw the dangers in the political project sold to Chavez by Ceresole. Michilena would attempt to moderate President Chavez's growing authoritarianism, and would find himself as one of the first casualties of the Chavez Bolivarian project. Chavez, an increasingly polished politician, undoubtedly understood the uncomfortable nature of the relationship with Ceresole, and allowed the expulsion. Nevertheless, the relationship remained strong. After learning of his death, Chavez described Ceresole as a "great friend" and an "intellectual deserving great respect." [46] He reminisced about a conversation they had on the banks of the Orinoco River, where they discussed the importance of Venezuela geopolitically and the importance of looking south instead of north—conversations quite similar to the third tenet of Bolivarianism by Fernando Bossi outlined in the previous chapter. In his 1998 book, *The Commander Speaks*, Chavez reflected he was "reconsidering the ideas of Norberto Ceresole, in his works and studies, where he planned a project of physical integration in Latin America … this will be a project which will integrate the Continent along Venezuela, Brazil and Argentina and their ramifications (a vision of what would become the 'Buenos Aires Consensus' envisioned under Nestor Kirchner and Chavez)." The idea for the ALBA was born.

Before continuing, a caveat. There are those who see a great conspiracy behind the relationship between Chavez and Ceresole, a clandestine scheme to control the levers of power of a continent. It is more complicated than this. President Chavez's ALBA Project has had many influences, and there exists a creative intellectual tension within the political and economic project

---

Mayo 1999.
46 http://www.eltiempo.com/archivo/documento/MAM-872606

espoused by the Bolivarians. Ceresole himself stated he was less than comfortable with Hugo Chavez's leftist bent. In his mind, he was concerned about "letting the process disintegrate into, for example, the delirious left, decrepit and without plans. That would be a catastrophe. That would be the end of the country. I observe with consternation some of the comments of Hugo Chavez about Cuba, with great concern. And I want it to be clear, I have nothing to do with that."[47] As with any political construct, there are many influences both ancient and new—Victor Hugo to Lao Tsu to Norberto Ceresole. This is part of the battle for the political project of not only Venezuela but also the Bolivarian Alliance countries. However, the main tenet of Ceresole's vision struck a chord in an authoritarian Chavez looking for justification for the centralization of power. In this, Ceresole's political project weighed heavily in the construction of the ALBA.

According to Ceresole, to consolidate this political project requires the perfect harmony of his holy trinity: caudillo, army and the people. This mechanism is the only way to stand up to the attacks from the right and the left. The right will demand the distribution of power and the creation of supra-human institutions. The left will demand citizen participation, a powerful party, and eventually a bureaucratized socialism that will replace the very real, physical leader with the abstract idea of the people. Neither will allow the Venezuelan ALBA Project to succeed.

The caudillo in this political project, naturally, is Hugo Chavez. Ceresole was convinced of the historic nature of Chavez' leadership when he, in his own words, "journeyed together, several times, almost all the Venezuelan country, in a long voyage that began in faraway Buenos Aires and then, afterwards, continued in Santa Marta, Colombia. I could see, in practice, how 'charisma', which I had studied in books but never seen in reality, works. I could watch, definitively and in a moment of 'significant risk,' as an exceptional politician fought against the great adversities of history and the small miseries of daily life."[48] In his "post-democratic" model, the figure of Hugo Chavez stood astride the world stage "anti-institutionally" and met the needs of his people through a direct connection with them.

47 "Ceresole Visto por El Mismo," Analitica.com, 21 de Junio, 2000. http://www.analitica.com/va/entrevistas/1867848.asp
48 "Caudillo, Ejercito y Pueblo: La Venezuela de Presidente Chavez" Norberto Ceresole, (1999): P15.

Naturally, any powerful leader needs mechanisms to make his politics felt. There are simply too many issues for one person to deal with, and too many people to address their concerns individually. It's not that Chavez didn't try. At the beginning of his presidency, he would use his *Alo Presidente* program to hear and resolve individual concerns. He would take his cabinet meetings around the country. But this became untenable. In democracy, we believe in powerful institutions that are managed at the local level by decentralized representative government, and who are best responsible to address citizens' concerns. In Ceresole's (and Chavez') vision, there must be a mechanism to sustain the leader-people link while providing disciplined efficiency. This mechanism is, according to Ceresole, "the permanent participation of a dignified people and a strong, industrialized military."

For Hugo Chavez, this became the "civic-military alliance" he believed could govern the country. Chavez, even today, constantly refers to the "civic-military alliance" that upholds his revolution. This alliance is the marriage of a military that defends only the revolution and the president, with a people who see themselves as the vassals of the caudillo. In Venezuela, the government organized the Bolivarian Militia, and renamed the army the Bolivarian Armed Forces, changing their mandate to defend the revolution. They carry out important social activities such as Plan Bolivar 2000, Chavez's first social project involving the military. (Many more would follow.) In an October 2002 interview, Chavez stated:

My order was: "Go house to house combing the terrain. The enemy. Who is the enemy? Hunger." And we started it on February 27, 1999, ten years after the Caracazo[49] as a way of vindicating the military. I even used the contrast and I said: "Ten years ago we came out to massacre the people, now we are going to fill them with love. Go and comb the terrain, look for misery. The enemy is death. We are going to fill them with bursts of life instead of gunshots of death." And, in truth, the answer was really beautiful. While we, the politicians, were engaged in the political struggle, forty thousand soldiers were on a campaign to attend to the health of the people; opening roads with military engineering equipment; flying passengers in military planes to the most poor areas, charging them at cost.

49 A popular uprising in February 1989 in response to an increase in gasoline prices, which was brutally put down by the National Guard upon orders from then President Carlos Andres Perez.

They also safeguarded elections, carried out humanitarian work, and were involved in social work at every level of the "revolution."

In Bolivia, the army also has begun to proclaim, "Socialism, Fatherland or Death" and declare their undying loyalty to their regional caudillo, Evo Morales. In Nicaragua, the document "Revolutionary Brotherhood" talks about the need to co-opt the army in service of the revolution, and the trinity of national security laws passed by President Daniel Ortega in December of 2010 set the stage for doing just this. Rafael Correa has put the military in charge of local police services after the police dustup of 2010. The progression of the military involved in daily life continues.

For the civic component of the civic-military alliance, it is important to create the caudillo-people link. This is done through giving local people the opportunity to participate, in a centralized manner as authorized and ordered by the center. Venezuela has experimented with this extensively over the twelve years of Chavez's presidency: through the missions (social projects reporting directly to the executive), then through the Local Councils of Public Planning, through the communal councils, through the Bolivarian Circles, and through the party. Finally, in December of 2010, in the waning days of Chavez's absolute majority in the National Assembly, they passed a set of laws called the "Popular Power" laws. These set in place partisan communes at the local level, to wrest control from the municipalities and give them the authority for local governance. These are "revolutionary" councils, and leaders are elected from out of the government's supporters. These laws are: Popular Power, Popular and Public Planning, Communes, Communal Economic System, and Social Control. To support these laws they passed the Law to Transfer the Competencies of the Municipalities to the Popular Power.

To promote this caudillo-people linkage in Nicaragua, citizen participation is organized through the Committees of Citizen Participation that are organized in each community and report directly to Rosario Murillo, Daniel Ortega's wife and the coordinator of the ALBA in Nicaragua. These committees are in effect a parallel institution of government, and have authority similar to local mayors. Evo Morales has relied more on the grassroots indigenous structure, empowering them and providing mechanisms and opportunities for them to become involved without challenging the leadership at the center. In Ecuador, the country's new constitution in Article 95 states that, "citizens will individually and collectively participate in a protagonist manner in decision making, planning and management of public issues."[50] Naturally, most of the experience for these citizen participation mechanisms at the grass roots comes from Cuba's Committees for the Defense of the Revolution. There are literally thousands of Cuban advisors in Venezuela and across the ALBA assisting in writing the legislation and the setup of these organizations.

An important point to note is that these are all mechanisms to participate *within* the revolution. Ceresole states emphatically that it is important to completely eliminate—pulverize—the old and corrupt system and all the institutions that defend it, including the old economic "oligarchs who are constantly conspiring." Translation: the opposition must be destroyed. Following his advice, Chavez, Morales, Correa and Ortega have attempted to destroy the opposition. In Venezuela, Chavez has nationalized over eight hundred businesses and driven more than one million Venezuelans from the country. In Ecuador, Correa has gone after first the private media and then the banks. In Nicaragua, Ortega has instead (and perhaps more intelligently) threatened the businesses with destruction if they do not fully support his political project—and offered them economic rewards for their subservience, a plan that has paid dividends within Nicaragua. Dissent is not permitted, with only the civic alliances managing themselves communally and in constant homage to the center. "The Venezuelan process establishes a *necessary* and *just* exclusion of a new type: the exclusion of the oligarch minorities," says Ceresole.[51]

The next component of protection of the new ALBA order is the creation of a network of solidarity with the ALBA revolutionary process: from public personalities, political parties, cultural and business organizations, and others the world over destined to defend the legitimacy of the Bolivarian revolutionary processes. This, the ALBA has done par

---

50 "Constitucion de Ecuador." http://www.asambleanacional.gov.ec/documentos/constitucion_de_bolsillo.pdf

51 An interesting point is that Heinz Dieterich, the father of 21st Century Socialism makes the same assertions. According to Dieterich, Chavez' inability to completely "pulverize" the opposition in the run-up to 2012 presidential elections marks the death knell of the Bolivarian project.

excellence through the ALBA Social Movements—who even participate through a council in the ALBA's organization. These Social Movements come from different arenas. Politically, they emerge from the Foro San Paulo, a network of left-leaning Latin-American political parties organized by Fidel and Lula in the early nineties. They also include personalities such as Danny Glover, Sean Penn, and so many others who constantly come to the defense of Chavez, Correa, Morales and their political projects. They include politicians such as Joe Kennedy, Congresswoman Sheila Jackson Lee and Senator Chris Dodd. And they are well defended by American and European intellectuals such as Noam Chomsky, and even a wide array of nongovernmental organizations. The FARC, according to emails emanating from the computer of Raul Reyes, the FARC commander killed in the Colombian military bombing raid on his camp in Ecuador in 2010, has established a network of more than seven hundred organizations that defend them and the ALBA. Many of these groups (and the FARC itself) participate in the Foro de Sao Paulo. These organizations defend the Bolivarian Revolution abroad while Chavez and his mini-caudillos consolidate political power at home.

In 1999, Ceresole foretold that the consolidation of the civic-military alliance at home would allow the internationalization of the leadership of Hugo Chavez. This has already happened. The Bolivarian Alliance is the maximum expression of Chavez' response to Ceresole's assertion that, "Today exist all the elements which will make Hugo Chavez the leader of all Hispanic-America (...) This projection will be the result only of a laborious political-strategic building process within almost all of the popular movements of the region. In terms of power, the regional-international projection of the leadership of Hugo Chavez will give to the Venezuelan (Bolivian, Ecuadorian, Nicaraguan, and Cuban—*author additions*) internal process a degree of protection against conspiracies which it (they—*author addition*) lacks today." Thus arises the Bolivarian Alliance. According to Ceresole, the next steps are: (1) use intelligence to diffuse internal conflicts; (2) pulverize at long last the opposition; and (3) develop an international campaign to defend the revolution. He further said:

Venezuela has become, perhaps for the first time in its independent history, a strategic center of interests within the political world. That geopolitical reality is the product of the emergence of an original and genuine leader: Hugo Chavez. Chavez has the capacity not only to direct Venezuela: he could be, as well, the reference point for the disinherited masses and the humiliated national armies of Hispano-America (...) it's for that reason that being in Venezuela, today, is being with something that is greater than Venezuela: it is being in the possible origin of the Patria Grande, the old hope of all of us[52].

These words whispered sweetly in Chavez's ears over a period of years when he and Ceresole toured around the countryside—alone—must have been a powerful aphrodisiac. As Chavez, ever the romantic, stated, "Sitting on the banks of the Orinoco talking about the *Patria Grande*" must have been a powerfully formative experience for a burgeoning narcissist. Ceresole justified within Chavez his desire to establish himself as the "caudillo." But more importantly, Ceresole set the seeds within a young Chavez of an international role for himself, a role that came to fruition with his creation of the ALBA.

Despite the clear vision of a society organized around "strongman, army and the people," there existed the clear challenge on how to go about doing this at the grass roots. Simultaneously, there existed the important influence of another of Chavez's mentors, Fidel Castro, who was pushing for the creation of a Castro-Communist satellite state in Venezuela. Unwilling to play a secondary role to anybody, yet understanding the importance of establishing a relationship with the western hemisphere's most long-serving despot, Chavez went to work on his model of political participation. Chavez initially shied away from the USSR's Leninist model of state control, state capitalism and a preeminent party. As Ceresole undoubtedly convinced him, subservience to an almighty party was just another limitation on the power he believed he needed as maximum leader to build his regional political project. Nevertheless, as I'm sure Castro told him, communism has been the best mechanism for social control that ever existed in the history of the world. This fact was not overlooked by Chavez. He even admitted during a program of *Alo Presidente* to studying dictatorship with the help of Lukushenko (the president of Belarus, sometimes called

---

52 "Caudillo, Ejercito y Pueblo: La Venezuela de Presidente Chavez" Norberto Ceresole, (1999)

Europe's last dictator), Ortega, Fidel and Gaddafi. He found in communism the perfect platform around which to organize the leader-people link (as outlined above), co-opt the military and tap into the massive groundswell of social actors willing to be used by anybody as long as it was within the bounds of a fight against the United States.

His problem emerged in how to do this while not allowing the institutionalization of a party that would challenge him for control and the leadership of Venezuela, and would not place limits on his own authorities or powers. This creative tension still exists within the heart of Chavismo. Hugo Chavez is increasingly reliant upon the Cuban government for technical support. Within his own government has existed a powerful confrontation between the militarists, the institutional communists and the pragmatists. Chavez has not managed these conflicts well, and has allowed the Cubans to assume important control over groups such as the armed forces. This has weakened his "caudillo-army" link as nationalist Venezuelans see Chavez's capitulation to the Castros as nouveau domination by yet another foreign power. This conflict is still there today, and is a very real threat to Chavez's control of the military.

As he studied the economic model to follow in a world without a Soviet Union, where the markets are the undeniable, unchallengeable global force for commerce, the answer to his fundamental challenge of grassroots organization was found in another important relationship—that of Heinz Dieterich, a German sociologist and post-USSR reformist Marxist. Dieterich, a professor of sociology at the Autonomous University of Mexico who has authored more than thirty books, is the inventor of, and the man who quite literally wrote the book on the aforementioned "Socialism of the 21st Century." The economic and social project of 21st Century Socialism itself, to nobody's surprise, has a heavy Marxist component to it.[53] It is interesting, however, that there are some differences or, as they would say, improvements (or criticisms of) the Soviet model. They adopt a reformist model of socialism using cybernetics and quantum mechanics to reinvent the old Soviet Value of Labor idea. While many of the two-hundred-year-old precepts are the same, the Bolivarians have invented new language to use as they sell their communism abroad. But Socialism of

---

53 Marta Harnecker, "Hacia Donde Avanzar—El Socialismo del Siglo XXI," (2010): P33.

the 21st Century is more a political and social construct than an economic model. These ideas are based upon so-called "Participatory and Protagonist Democracy" that feeds and nourishes their political and economic model. As in traditional communism, politics and economics are inseparable.

Apart from Heinz Dieterich, other important thinkers and economists of this nouveau socialist model are Marta Harnecker, a Chilean communist who cut her teeth on Salvador Allende's revolution; Fernando Bossi, an Argentine thinker, managing editor of *Emancipation* magazine, and former head of the Bolivarian People's Congress; and finally Michel Lebowitz, author of *Beyond Capital* and winner of the Isaac Deutscher Prize in 2004. Chavez' current economic advisor is Alan Woods (from the United Kingdom) who is also a Trotskyite—as is to an extent Dieterich—but whose ability to influence Chavez is limited at this point in the revolution's economic entropy (and due to Dietrich's very public rift with Chavez). Heinz Dieterich has disavowed Bolivarian economics and President Chavez's version of "21st Century Socialism" as having turned its back on his initial vision.

There is one fundamental tenet of the new socialism that is unquestionable and, in their minds, unarguable. It is also, in their political project, something they must retain at all costs. This principal idea is fed through the system, is present in the speeches of the leaders, and is the back upon which rests the legitimacy (and the success) of the entire model. This "New Historical Project" is, in their words, the project of the "permanent majorities."[54] Being the political voice of the permanent majorities (as Ceresole said, the absolute, permanent majority) has allowed them to redesign and remake the legal topography of their nations, rewriting their constitutions, reforming their laws and reinventing their economies. They do this, they repeat as they point to the elections foisted on the people ad infinitum in each of their countries, to respond to the desires and needs of the majorities kept in constant subjugation by the capitalist system. They also do this, following the plan of Dieterich and Ceresole, to destroy the opposition—election by election. For this reason they must, at all costs, demonstrate to themselves and the world that they retain the majorities. This is their veneer of legitimacy, their calling card to revolution, and their final safeguard. They protect these majorities ruthlessly, with brutal

---

54 Heinz Dieterich, "El Socialismo del Siglo XXI," (2005): P3.

propaganda, electioneering, intimidation and populism, for if they lose them, they are lost.

Basing their plan on this undeniable fact, what type of world are the ALBA countries attempting to create? Mr. Chavez himself is not a philosopher, an economist, or a political historian. He is, as he will remind you, a military man. He sees the world very much in military terms. He has, however, with his publicly embracing (but rarely defining) of 21st Century Socialism, opened the door for debate, for proposals and counterproposals, for ideas and for inventing. As long as the direction is toward a hazy Marxist model—that would wrest power from capitalism, from the "oligarchs" and the United States—and he is at the top in true caudillo fashion with no limits placed on his own power, he is comfortable letting the discussion continue. Marta Harnecker, in the spirit of the ongoing learning titled one of her books, *Latin America and 21st Century Socialism: Inventing to Avoid Mistakes*.

The problem, for the Bolivarians, is couched very much in similar terms as it was centuries ago by the Marxists, but with a few added twists learned from the failure of the Soviet Communist model. According to them:

During various years after the disappearance of Soviet socialism there was more talk about what socialism shouldn't be than about the model that they wanted to build. Among the aspects rejected—and with good reason—were the following: statism, state capitalism, totalitarianism, bureaucratic central planning, collectivism which pretended to homogenize without respecting differences, production which emphasized the advance of productivity without taking into consideration the need to preserve the environment, dogmatism, atheism and the need for a one-party state to guide the transition process.[55]

All these items that came to define Soviet Communism have been rejected, in the minds of Bolivarians, as having led directly to the failure of that model and the abridgement of their socialist project. However, again according to the Bolivarians, the emphasis that President Chavez has placed on the socialist debate has added or returned value to the principle of socialism. The global economic crisis of 2008 and 2009 has played directly into the Bolivarians' hand as they capitalize upon global disenchantment with market-based capitalism and drum up support by loudly denouncing its failure and

---

55 Marta Harnecker, "Hacia Donde Avanzar—El Socialismo del Siglo XXI," (2010): P25.

imminent collapse. However, the proclaimed failure of global capitalism has for the Bolivarians a more significant, more meaningful positive aspect. Since the fall of the Soviet Union, countries such as in Western Europe, and especially the Mediterranean states, have been emphasizing the emergence of a "New Socialist Model" which rests more firmly upon the back of Social Democracy than upon Marxist communism. In essence, they took the wind out of the sails of the communists, heretofore undefeated in spirit despite the collapse of their great hope, by demonstrating that the way toward social evolution is through a marriage of government regulation and entitlements for the promotion of national social justice embedded within the dominant, unchallenged system of market-based capitalism and representative democracy.

For the Bolivarians, this could not be the case. They were discontented with their own continental history of Social Democracy, which ranged between Christian democratic and Social democratic parties mentored by the German Adenauer Schiftung (Adenauer and Ebert) foundations and other European parties. The Bolivarians were therefore looking for an opportunity to alter the model completely, clarifying that bourgeois social democracy and socialist democracies are antagonistic projects, not rungs on a ladder leading to the same point.[56]

The regulation of the markets, the widening of public space and municipal action are controversial themes in participatory democracy. In the absence of socialist perspectives, the democratizing initiatives in these fields *do not modify the existing order*. The participatory example of budgeting process in Porto Alegre gives an example of these limitations, but in Venezuela exists the search for another way, as they continue the radicalization of the Bolivarian process.[57] (emphasis added by author)

So, rejecting the Soviet communist model and seizing upon the window of opportunity given them by the political power of President Chavez, the exploding prices of natural resources (especially oil) and the failure – at least in their collective mind – of the capitalist model, they have embarked upon the creation of their new socialist economies. For the Bolivarians, "21st Century Socialism" is *not*:[58]

---

56 Claudio Katz, "La Democracia Socialista del Silgo XXI," P4.
57 Claudio Katz, "La Democracia Socialista del Silgo XXI," P1.
58 Michel A. Lebowitz, "Que es el Socialismo," Cuadernos para la Empancipacion, #28, ISSN 0328-0179, P4.

1. A society where people sell their labor and are directed from above by others whose only goals are profit, where the owners of the means of production are the only beneficiaries of the products created.
2. A statist society, where decisions are imposed upon the decisions of government bureaucrats. Precisely because it is socialism, it focuses on the development of the individual and depends on participatory democracy. This model rejects the Soviet, statist approach.
3. A populist model. A state that provides resources and solutions to all the problems of the citizenry is not a state that works toward the development of the individuals.
4. Totalitarianism. Precisely because human beings are different and have different needs and ideas, their development by definition demands that recognition of those differences. Government pressure to homogenize productive activities, alternatives for consumption or styles of life cannot be the base for unity based upon the recognition of differences.
5. A system with specific characteristics, laws and limits. Socialism is instead a process.

According to Heinz Dieterich, the new social model cannot have any of the four components that have led to the dictatorship of the bourgeoisie: national market-based economy, formal plutocratic democracy, classist society, and the liberal individual.[59] [60]

What the thinkers behind 21st Century Socialism are trying to do is to rewrite the dialogue behind the ideas of socialism and communism, especially in contrast to democracy and capitalism. They see democracy and capitalism as inextricably joined in freedom—wherein socialist countries are seen as less free (economically and politically) than democracies. The Bolivarian thinkers reject this idea in whole, just as they reject the notion that communism is unfree and that social democracy is the same as socialism.[61]

Dieterich comments that the system of liberal democracy is able to be transformed in form and function to the following: a non-mercantilist

---

59 Heniz Dieterich, "El Socialismo del Siglo XXI," (2005): P9.

60 The reality of what ALBA's political model has become is quite different from the design. The communists continue to support it because, frankly, they have no other option. Arguably, they also believe they will still be able to fix the process; as Harnecker has stated on multiple occasions, the process allows them to continue to learn.

61 Rosa Luxemburg, "Reforma o revolucion, Obras escogidas tomo 1 Ed Pluma, Buenos Aires, (1976).

economy based on the value of use, real participatory democracy, a democratic state and an individual rationally/ethically exercising self-determination.

At this point, one should understand how Bolivarians see the differences between 21st Century Socialism and Soviet communism. The best guide to this difference is Heinz Dieterich, the person who coined the phrase 21st Century Socialism in 1996 and developed the new model.[62] This new model for a socialist world economy has four elements.

Economy of Equivalencies

Dieterich rejects the idea of market-based capitalism for one basic reason. He argues in his book that the market is an inappropriate mechanism to set the prices for goods and services.[63] First, the system is fundamentally unstable. It is completely unsupervised, subject to fluctuations and abuses, and therefore cannot be relied upon. Second, the system is fundamentally asymmetric. The chrematistic (literally, the art of getting rich) nature of capitalism leads to an inevitable concentration and centralization of capital in the hands of a few. Thirdly, the mercantilist/nationalist nature of transnational companies in our globalized world leads the governments of the most powerful states (where the transnational companies are based) to use political and military protection, which brings about neo-colonization. Fourth, transnational companies are exclusive and don't give people, especially the people affected by their activity, a voice over that same activity or the company's governance. This fits neatly into the ALBA's rejection of the FTAA.

Dieterich uses this argument to explain why the productive capacity of the world is not geared toward meeting the needs of the most vulnerable, but is organized to meet the wants of a select rich few. Finally (and most importantly), the universalization of this model is environmentally unsustainable. In short, for the entire world to have the same lifestyle as the citizens of the United States would require four planets.

For this reason, argues Dieterich, the market-based capitalist model cannot work. It must evolve into a new way of interacting. This is where he comes up with the idea of what he calls a democratically planned economy.

---

62 Cristina Marcano, "Entrevista a Heinz Dieterich," Aporrea.com, 3 de Enero, 2007. http://www.kaosenlared.net/noticia.php?id_noticia=28818
63 Heinz Dieterich, "El Socialismo del Siglo XXI," P39.

According to Dieterich, three characteristics must be resolved for an economy to work for the "Historical Project of the Majorities." The first is that it must eliminate the model of exploitation (that is to say, the rich becoming wealthy upon the backs of the workers). The second important characteristic is that of domination, seen as a lack of individual freedom. The third is the idea of distraction. That is to say, the economic system is distracted from its true purpose of assuring that "majorities have the greatest degree of control historically possible over the economic, political, cultural and military institutions that guide their lives."[64] In Dieterich's model, the three systems that have been tried in recent history have been that of free-market capitalism, traditional bourgeois socialism (represented by the Sovietstyle communism), and what he calls real democracy. The current capitalist model is rife with exploitation, domination and distraction. It is not a true democracy, because it is set up to maximize the profit of a certain small group of bankers and businesspersons who have full control over the mechanisms of production. This is the only explanation for the reason that in a world where we have a surplus production of food, we also have a billion people going hungry. Also, in a world where millions die of malaria, the medical research is being done to improve plastic surgery methods for the elites. That is to say, the market-based capitalist approach doesn't work because it does not assure the fundamental needs of the majority are met.

Dieterich argues that while this remains true, the communist model did not work either. The reason given is that while it did lower the levels of exploitation, there continued to be significant degrees of domination (that is to say, lack of freedom) and a distraction of the system in focusing on the provision of the basic needs. The rich bankers were, in effect, replaced by an undemocratic party committee that actually increased domination in their attempt to undemocratically decrease exploitation. This led to lack of context and contact with the majorities, which resulted in arms races and other distractions due to the need to compete through productivity with the capitalist model. Again, this is to say the Soviet Union did not replace the capitalist model, they simply exchanged free-market capitalism with state capitalism. This brought the corresponding environmental damage and

---

64 Cristina Marcano, "Entrevista a Heinz Dieterich," Aporrea.com, 3 de Enero, 2007. http://www.kaosenlared.net/noticia.php?id_noticia=28818

conflict for power with other states. Real democracy will reduce exploitation, domination and distraction.[65]

According to Dieterich, "this type of economy, coordinated in an unstable, antidemocratic and predatory fashion by the markets," will be substituted with a democratically planned economy. But what does this mean and how would it work? The main problem Dieterich finds in the market-based economy resides on the *price* of the item in question being decided by the *market*. This means that the price becomes what people are willing to pay for something, or what the bankers and owners of industry decide it should be. This includes, naturally, the aspect of profit, which is what makes the price so unaccountable and lends itself to undemocratic and unsustainable process, because economic activity becomes about chrematistic skill and not about the true worth of the item in question. Therefore, the solution to this problem requires replacing unstable market forces deciding the prices, with prices being decided solely by the *value of the time* (a play on the old Value of Labor arguments of 20th century communism) that went into creating the item. And all people's time has the same value; there is no one's time more valuable than someone else's simply because of skin color, age, sex, or education. All time is of the same value.

This, Dieterich calls an economy of equivalencies.

An example of this would be setting the value of, say a loaf of bread compared to a cellular telephone. To obtain the value of the bread, you would have to sum up all the time worked by all the people who contributed to its creation. . Therefore, you would have to add the time of the people who tilled the land, who grew and harvested the wheat; the time, including research and production, to produce the pesticides; the time worked sending the wheat to market; the value of the time of use of the truck and gasoline needed to get the item to the market; the time it took in storage; and on and on until all the infinitesimally small units of time were added and led to the ultimate value of the item. The same would be done for a cellular telephone, including research and development; marketing; mining of the coltan used in its circuitry; creation of the plastic; transportation; hours worked, and the list would go on. At the end, this would produce a price for an item that is *solely related* to the value of the time used to design it

---

65 Heinz Dieterich, "El Socialismo del Siglo XXI," P9.

and bring it to market. There is no speculation, no profit, no hoarding, and no undemocratic economic machinations.

The specific calculations follow the analysis of Arno Peters, a German thinker who developed the visual representation of this model – called Peters' Rose. The model would eliminate profit, speculation, and everything else that, 21st century socialists believe makes the market-capitalist model unsustainable.

The natural response to this is that the calculations necessary to make an economy of equivalencies work, all in real time, make the model unrealistic—as it was in the past. However, Dietrich argues[66] that the element that makes the practice of an economy of equivalencies possible in the 21st century is the rapid advance of information technology. It is, in fact, the information revolution that allows the immediate calculation of the billions upon billions of transactions each purchase or sale would require. In his mind, the price then would be pure and he would have solved the problem which led "Value of Labor" to fail.

Then, when the economic interests of the accumulation of profit are taken out of the equation, the industrial-military complex that protects that capital would also naturally fall by the wayside, as would the inequalities spawned by the entropy inherent in the current developmentalist model (see later in this chapter) between industrialized and nonindustrialized countries. This developmentalist entropy causes technologically advanced, industrialized countries to increase their wealth and power at the expense of the developing world nations where the raw materials are found—again, all according to Dieterich.

Participative and Protagonist Democracy

The second, and perhaps most unique, component of 21st Century Socialism is the idea of participative and protagonist democracy. This is the piece of the project Chavez and the ALBA have most advanced. In this local participatory democracy, they have found their locus of defense of their model as well as their mechanism for internal control. For the Bolivarian thinkers, western countries with representative democracies are not true, full democracies because the majorities of their populations are

---

66 Heinz Dieterich, "El Socialismo del Siglo XXI," P41.

never allowed to truly participate in the construction of their democracies. The occasional vote afforded by the representative model, in their minds, is insufficient to assure popular control over the national democracies.[67] In their arguments, the same people who control the worldwide capitalist economy, which has proven unable to provide for the basic goods and services needed by the majorities, are the same *class* of people who usurped the reigns of representative democracy and control all the seats in the assemblies of the west. The assemblymen and women, elected to represent the people who voted for them, in point of fact ultimately represent the interests of capital and of themselves. This system cannot lead to a greater good but instead has led to the crisis of confidence in the world's peoples toward their parliaments in most western countries. According to the Bolivarians, the structure of the representative system has made the option of real citizen participation impossible.

So, what are the components of representative democracy Bolivarians believe has reached its point of collapse? They are the following: the division of power, constitutions with clear definition of formal democratic mechanisms, a formal system of electing representatives, the parliament as the responsible office in which rests the sovereignty of the people, a federal structure of government, the existence of media houses that are not the property of the state, free use and protection of private property, rule of law—including protection of minorities, and the dichotomy between public and private life. All these areas have become controlled, according to Dieterich, by the bourgeois elites, meaning that for a post-bourgeois society they need to be broken and reformed to reflect the desires and needs of the permanent majorities. This system will be replaced by a democracy that is the property of the society and can be conceived in three forms: (1) the social, understood as the quality of material life (of the majorities); (2) the formal, which becomes less a structure and more a system of basic rights, powers and obligations under which participatory democracy functions (similar to the old caudillo system in the 19th century); and (3) participation, understood as the real decision of the majorities of society over transcendental public issues (at the local levels).[68]

---

67 Heinz Dieterich, "El Socialismo del Siglo XXI," P49.
68 Heinz Dieterich, "El Socialismo del Siglo XXI," P48.

In this, the Bolivarians promote the destruction of the representative (or as they like to call it, substitutive) democracy for true popular, participatory and protagonist democracy, which encourages and facilitates the participation of the largest numbers of people possible. So how is this done? When Bolivarians think about participation, they are thinking of a few concrete activities: when they go to meetings; when they go out to the street to protest against or for something; when in a peaceful but public manner they refuse to buy, do or say something demanded by the majority; when they vote in electoral processes; when they carry out social activities like literacy campaigns or vaccination; when they have their voice heard in meetings; and when the people participate in decision-making[69] at the local level such as participatory budgeting, local needs assessments and allocation of local resources. The principal way this is done is through participating in decisions that affect the lives of others, and in the follow-up to the decisions taken. At the local (communal) level, it is a form of self-government by partisan committee, which is where Chavez (with the help of the Cubans) refined the idea of communes. This would be inextricably linked with the economy of equivalencies at a grassroots level.

As Dieterich explains, just as the economy of equivalencies will eventually do away with the need for military, for large companies, and even for national governments—as people interact with each other freely in a globalized society without coercion of capital or laws necessary to protect the profits of the elite—the same is true with direct democracy.[70] In direct democracy, a true decentralization will happen where the people at a local (municipal) level will be able to vote daily on things that affect their lives. This does not mean there will be no civil service; the functions of garbage collecting, of policing to control crime, of managing the public road system and delivering the mail are all still important within a direct democracy. The larger issues, however, such as the establishment of the budget, the setting of tax rates, the use of major investments resulting from taxes, and the election of the authorities to run the management of the system, will be done on a regular basis. This, as well as issues of national importance (before the nation-state disappears) such as the national budget, health care

---

69 Marta Harnecker, "De los Consejos Comunales a Comunas" 2009, P11.
70 Heinz Dieterich, "El Socialismo del Siglo XXI," P49.

legislation, immigration legislation, and others. This direct process of governance increases the power of a participating citizenry, and is able to be more responsive to the desires of the people than a senate or elected assembly controlled by special interests, campaign donations, and their own desire to perpetuate their careers. Direct democracy will achieve this by eliminating the need for a centralized location for governance and all elected officials will act ad honorum.

Again, just as in the economy of equivalencies, the technological advances brought by the information age will allow for the creation of a real, direct democracy. As we have seen in the advent of social media such as Twitter and Facebook, we can connect people across a wide geographic boundary, and there can be a debate in real time around issues of importance. Those without a computer will be able to use one set up by the government in their local village or municipality. The issues upon which they vote—for example, how much in tax to levy or how many police to hire—will have a direct bearing on their lives and will be immediately decided through a community vote, and on the list goes. The Bolivarians envision a responsive, flexible government answering immediately to the people, with an economy of equivalencies where profit and private land owning is outlawed, and that responds to the needs of the majorities, using technology as the grease to lubricate the entire process.

This has even extended itself to the military, where in the new constitutions (of the ALBA nations) defense of the nation becomes a duty and local militias are formed. Children are trained in asymmetric warfare (terrorism) and even armed. A law to draft people is passed. Of course, at the top, the leader/caudillo deals with macro issues while the new (Bolivarian) decentralization represented by the communes keeps people busy.

Regional Democratic Developmentalism
The third component of Dieterich's 21st Century Socialism is Regional Democratic Developmentalism (RDD). This idea holds that industrial capabilities, just like capital, concentrate in already developed nations and thereby leaves the nonindustrialized countries—countries that probably supply most of the natural resources—with a meager share of the "wealth pie." The industrialized nations in turn process the raw material and resell it to the

poorer extractive countries at a huge markup, further concentrating capital and relegating the poor countries to increased poverty in an endless cycle.

Therefore, the idea behind regional democratic developmentalism is an important component behind the creation of ALBA, through a type of economy of scale. Only as countries come together to exploit their own natural resources and form a block to stand against capitalism, and industrialize themselves without having to compete against cheap products mass-produced in already industrialized nations, are the poor countries truly able to develop. This concept has been presented as "south to south" cooperation, and is at the heart of the regional political project Hugo Chavez is attempting to build. This idea has formed itself into the "Consensus of Buenos Aires," juxtaposed against the "Washington Consensus" as a way for poor and less industrialized nations to unify their economies and emerge from underdevelopment[71] by denying the natural resources to the industrialized states while forming their own industrial capacity through solidarity and cooperation (referring back to the ALBA founding principles). Hence, the basis of the ALBA as the final opposition to the FTAA. According to the principle of regional democratic developmentalism, the FTAA represents the final victory of capitalist American imperialism over the poorer and less developed countries of Latin America, where no protection exists from the raw materials being sent abroad and cheap products flooding the markets. For this reason, the FTAA must be defeated at all costs.

In summary, RDD represents, in the terms of economies of equivalency, what economies of scale represent for a capitalist economy—for this reason, the attempt to bring together the most countries possible and exploit (and protect) the vast natural resources in the creation of their 21st Century Socialist block.

While discussing this important point, Hugo Chavez threw himself into the debate on RDD with his extensive promulgation of a development model called endogenous development (discussed previously): literally, development from within, the principle of developing a powerful national economy starting from the grass roots of production and working outward. The essential idea is to take stock of resources that are intrinsic

---

71 Heinz Dieterich, "Entre la barbarie y el desarrollismo," El Siglo, 27 de Octubre, 2003. http://www.elsiglodedurango.com.mx/noticia/15465.entre-la-barbarie-y-el-desarrollismo. html

to the country or region. It helps to see this through the eyes of a military man. Often, Chavez appears on national television poring over large maps of Venezuela or the region. Highlighted on the maps are areas where the nation can endogenously develop to meet the basic needs of the majority. "Here we have all these unused lands" Chavez will often say, "we can start farming maize." Or he will point to several bays that dot the two-thousand-kilometer coastline and say, "Here we can farm shrimp for local consumption." The same is true for the mountains, or the oil deposits on the coast or by the Orinoco River, or the gold deposits in the jungles of the southeastern section of the country. These all represent the military mind visualizing what "he" has in "his" country that can be taken advantage of to spur national growth. As a military caudillo, pouring over his war maps, Chavez sees the way to recreate the lands under his dominion through endogenous 21st Century Socialism while allowing the communes at the local level to self-govern. It's an audacious plan.

Ignoring the Japanese model of creation based upon the idea that ingenuity attracts resources, the idea of endogenous development is to better exploit the extractive industries of the nation through some Grand National Project. Following are seven principles of endogenous development as laid out in the manual written by Carlos Lanz Rodriguez for the Venezuelan Government strategic project called Vuelvan Caras or About Face. This project is one of the Venezuelan Government's "missions" to promote 21st Century Socialism within the country, and which have become the learning center for the Grand National Projects of ALBA. Carlos Lanz Rodriguez, a respected revolutionary thinker, is most famous for his role in the alleged three-year kidnapping of William Niehaus, an Illinois businessman who was allegedly abducted by guerillas led by Lanz in 1976, for the purpose of advancing revolution in Venezuela. Since the arrival of Chavez, Lanz has been participating with many branches of government, including allegedly the DISIP (now SABIN), Venezuela's political police. According to Lanz, endogenous development consists of the following:[72]

1. Understand the regional and national particularities that lend each country strength.

---

72 Haydee Ochoa Enriquez, "Gestión Publica y Desarrollo Endógeno en Venezuela," Marzo 2006.

2. Promote the transformation of natural resources, building value chains and localizing the production, distribution and consumption.

3. Take efficient advantage of the local infrastructure and capacity.

4. Incorporate the excluded population.

5. Adopt a new style of life and consumption.

6. Develop new forms of productive and social organization.

7. Build productive networks of differing sizes and technological structures such as microenterprises and cooperatives.

The Bolivian government of Evo Morales is also advancing endogenous development, as evidenced by their own work on manuals such as one on agricultural development funded by the Bolivian government.[73] Ecuador is another country seeking to transform its economy through the promotion of endogenous development, according to the Ecuadorian minister who coordinates economic policy, Katiuska King.[74] As such, this developmental model advanced by Dieterich is something being applied with increasing force in ALBA countries, upon the backs of their important natural-resource reserves. The Grand National Projects (discussed later), is the ALBA-wide application of endogenous development through RDD.

Grassroots Organizations

The fourth and final component—and the heart and soul of 21st Century Socialism, as well as of ALBA and the Venezuelan Bolivarian Revolution— are community-based organizations, grassroots organizations the ALBA calls Social Movements. Socialism of the 21st century proposes that the development of this model of socialism should become more flexible, allowing for the idiosyncrasies of social movements with their own agendas, cultures, histories, realities and ideas: as long as they embrace the general direction of a post-capitalist, post-market-economy world.

These grassroots organizations, part of ALBA's organizational structure as the "Social Movements of the ALBA"—have an important position,

---

73 Nelson P. Tapia, "Aprendiendo el Desarrollo Endógeno Sostenible," Cosmovision y Ciencias #3, Mayo 2008 ISBN: 978-99954-1-139-8.

74 "Ecuador Mira al Sur y Promueve Desarrollo Endojeno," Prensa Latina 29 de Marzo, 2011. http://ecuadorinmediato.com/index.php?module=Noticias&func=news_user_view&id=146582&umt=ECUADOR%20MIRA%20AL%20SUR%20Y%20 PROMUEVE%20DESARROLLO%20END%D3GENO

since they are relied upon heavily in the promotion of the values of ALBA and 21st Century Socialism across the geopolitical landscape of the region. Central to these is the creation of the new man. According to Dieterich, all attempts by ideological organizations—be it the capitalists through Ayn Rand-style objectivism, or the Taliban through their religious zealotry, or the Communists with their focus on work for the good of others—have failed. All these failures have led to "hell for others" in their respective efforts to socially engineer humankind. Therefore, what must be created must not be based on an ideological dream world but in a world, according to Dieterich, "whose creators are neither saints nor heroes, but mortals, who under the contradictory nature of misery and splendor of the human condition are willing to ethically change their destiny."[75] For Dieterich, it is also incorrect to equate a post-capitalist transition with a single-party system, such as exists in Cuba or has been discussed in Venezuela. In fact, the intellectuals of the Bolivarian Revolution have publicly encouraged Cuba to rethink its own half-century-old model—part of what they consider the antiquated and failed model of statist capitalism or totalitarianism of a bourgeois bureaucracy—to move to a more direct democratic system and democratically planned local economy, which will allow for a continuation of the Cuban revolution and avoid it falling back into capitalism.[76] And this, according to Steve Ellner, author and professor at the Universidad de Oriente in Puerto la Cruz, Venezuela, is where the Venezuelan and the ALBA revolution is failing. Unable to break the hold of what they call the "cultural optimists" on the revolution (those who are ideologically driven, most of them trained in Cuba with important connections to that regime), and embrace Dieterich's pragmatic values, too many people in Venezuela are still too busily engaged in an antiquated fight against capitalism to work pragmatically toward building the revolution. This is seen in the creation of the United Socialist Party of Venezuela (PSUV), where Chavez himself worked at cross-purposes with the model of the big tent he adopted in 2005. This battle is nowhere near complete, and has led to some of the rifts seen in Venezuela over recent years. It is noteworthy that it seems the "cultural optimists" have been increasing in authority, power and influ-

---

75 Heinz Dieterich, "El Socialismo del Siglo XXI," P49.
76 Claudio Katz, "La Democracia Socialista del Silgo XXI," P1.

ence within ALBA countries (people like Elias Jaua in Venezuela, Alvaro Garcia Linera in Bolivia and Ricardo Patino in Ecuador) which has caused some of the more authoritarian tendencies, for which traditional communism has become known, to increase. This has caused Dieterich himself to turn his back on the ALBA. In an article in April of 2011, Dieterich announced, "Neither Fidel, Evo, Correa or Chavez have made a serious attempt at building 21st Century Socialism."[77] He mentions that he offered his services to President Correa, who set up a commission to discuss the creation of this but has not given it the attention it needs. In Venezuela and Bolivia, Dieterich has received criticism from other revolutionaries for publicly stating that if these governments do not rectify their economic models, the ALBA will collapse. While Heinz Dieterich was an important godfather of 21st Century Socialism, he has entered communion with the long line of former friends who broke with President Chavez and his revolution out of disillusionment and frustration.

Last of all, and as the third side of the triangle, it's important to outline the role of the military in 21st Century Socialism. As Ceresole stated, the military is the only organization able to advance the new political project. The reason is obvious: the military takes orders. Anastasio Somosa relied on his National Guard, Fidel Castro on the Cuban military; Juan Peron was a military man; Rafael Trujillo made his son a general of his armed forces, and the list goes on.

In Venezuela, Hugo Chavez has always placed the military front and center in his Bolivarian Revolution. Upon winning the presidency and setting in place the new constitution in 1999, Chavez announced Plan Bolivar 2000.[78] This project foresaw the military delivering social services coordinated with the organized citizenry at the base in a so-called "civic-military alliance." In Bolivia, Evo Morales, not a military man himself, has used his relationship with Chavez to extend control over the military until it finally called itself "socialist." In Nicaragua, Daniel Ortega has passed a triad of national security laws in 2010, cementing his control of what had been a professional, non-political military. And in Ecuador, through his police

---

77 "Dieterich Evalua a Presidentes Socialistas," Diario Hoy, 17 de Abril, 2011. http://www.hoy.com.ec/noticias-ecuador/dieterich-evalua-a-presidentes-socialistas-470205.html
78 "Ministerio de Defensa, Plan Bolivar 2000." http://www.mpd.gob.ve/prog-gob/proyb2000.htm

kerfuffle in September of 2010, Rafael Correa has been able to replace the police chiefs with military generals. Correa has also worked extensively to promote a new group of revolutionaries into important positions within the military command structure. To obtain positions, in all these armies, soldiers are asked if they are loyal to the caudillo's political project, not the nation.[79]

The reason for the importance of control over the military is obvious. In Honduras, when then-president Manuel Zelaya attempted to carry out an illegal referendum, the military did not follow orders. When he insisted on his illegal course, they removed him from power under an order of that country's supreme court. Within ALBA, an independent military will always be a barrier to advancement of their political project. For this reason, they must be co-opted and controlled—or expelled.

The Bolivarian Alliance has as part of its regional political project a nascent military component. In January of 2008, during a meeting with President Daniel Ortega of Nicaragua, Chavez proposed the creation of an ALBA Defense Force.[80] "We are going to commission the elaboration of working papers. We must have a strategy for the joint defense of the ALBA." Ortega responded, "If they (the United States) pick a fight with one, they will be picking a fight with all of us. Touching Venezuela will ignite the region. Touching Venezuela is touching all of Latin America." As in all ALBA projects, development of the initiative is an organic process that advances only at the rate that is politically viable. With issues affecting the armed forces, this is especially complicated, and sensitive. There has been significant resistance in Venezuela with the presence of Cuban military advisors instructing their Venezuelan counterparts. Bolivia has experienced the same upheaval in its armed forces due to the presence of Venezuelan military on Bolivian soil. As Chavez well knows, the subversion of the military, while essential for the Bolivarian project, must be done slowly.

The first step toward the regionalization of the ALBA's armed forces has been the creation[81] of a Defense School for the ALBA. Due to its embryonic nature, little has been written about the ALBA defense school. In

79 Author interviews with confidential sources.
80 "Chavez propone creación de fuerza armada del ALBA," EFE, 27 de Enero, 2008. http://www.esmas.com/noticierostelevisa/internacionales/698504.html
81 "Escuela de defensa del ALBA avanza," 4 de Diciembre 2010. http://www.alba-tcp. org/contenido/escuela-de-defensa-del-alba-avanza-04-de-diciembre-de-2010

2010, during the Summit of Defense Ministers of the Americas that took place in Bolivia, the ministers of defense of ALBA nations took a side trip. Led by Bolivian Defense Minister Ruben Saavedra, the ministers visited the site in Santa Cruz that would host the new defense school. According to Doug Farah, award-winning investigative reporter, "ALBA views itself as a movement toward the Bolivarianization of all of South America, and the support for the FARC, MRTA, etc. are clear signs the group supports armed movements, even in countries with democratic governments. So creating a military base to expand the military integration of those state (and possibly nonstate) armed actors follows as a logical step in that process. Bolivia is by far the most aligned with Venezuela in the ALBA process. It may be Chavez's way of creating a sort of military outside Venezuela that could defend the revolution even if he were attacked or were to fall."

"In 2011 we will have important news regarding this topic," Saavedra told reporters. This prediction came true. On May 31, 2011, President Evo Morales inaugurated the Defense School. The special guest participating in the inauguration was Ahmad Vahidi, Iran's defense minister. His presence on South American soil caused a diplomatic row between the governments of Argentina and Bolivia due to the open INTERPOL arrest warrant against him for the bombing of the Jewish Center in Buenos Aires in the early 1990s.

The ALBA military doctrine that will be taught at this base is what President Chavez consistently calls "asymmetric warfare." Chavez himself has spoken extensively about this issue. In April of 2008, he announced the creation of the Military Reserves, a parallel military force that reports directly to him (bypassing the Ministry of Defense) and is responsible for preparing for "asymmetric war."[82] Much has already been written on Chavez' strategy of asymmetric warfare. To begin, Dr. Max Manwaring, Professor of Military Strategy who holds the Douglas MacArthur Chair of Research at the United States Army War College, has written extensively on the subject.[83] According to Manwaring, Chavez is attempting to: (1) radically change the traditional politics of the Venezuelan state—and

---

82 "Hugo Chavez crea reserve military," La Republica, 15 de Abril 2008. http://www.larepublica.com.uy/mundo/307190-hugo-chavez-crea-reserva-militar

83 Max Manwaring, "Latin America's New Security Reality: Irregular Asymmetric Conflict and Hugo Chavez," August 2007 ISBN 1-58487-303-5.

other Latin-American states—to that of direct (totalitarian) democracy; (2) destroy North American hegemony throughout all of Latin America by conducting an irregular Fourth-Generation war super insurgency; and, (3) country-by-country, building a great new Bolivarian state out of a phased program for the liberation of Latin America.

But what is a super-insurgency? Immediately, historians think of Mao, or other proponents of irregular war. What makes ALBA's insurgency warfare different?

To answer that question, we look to the ALBA's theoretician in asymmetric war, the Spaniard Jorge Verstrynge. In 2005, Verstrynge was invited to Venezuela to teach courses in asymmetric warfare to the Venezuelan military, and that same year thirty thousand (or 127,000, depending on the source) copies of his book[84] were printed[85] for distribution to officials in the Venezuelan army. This book is titled, *Peripheral War and Revolutionary Islam*. In an interview[86] in 2007 while in Venezuela, Verstrynge defended the linkage between asymmetry and Islam thusly: "Actually let us say that this is the way in which Islam defends itself against the new crusades, fundamentally North American, because it cannot any other (way). Every time a Muslim country has tried to attain the (atomic) bomb, they have been stopped. It's what Arafat said when they said to him, 'You carry out terrorist attacks' and he responded, 'Give me Israel's air force and I wouldn't do terrorist attacks.'"

As Doug Farah notes, "Revolutionary Islam, through the prism of the Iranian revolution, provides a framework for defeating the 'empire.' While Iranians and Muslims (at least Shiites) view the Iranian revolution in religious terms, Carlos [the Jackal], Verstrynge and Chavez view it in 'revolutionary' terms, a methodology for attacking the United States and changes the overall global political dynamic that leads to a country being able to develop nuclear weapons, etc. Verstrynge's book is the most complete articulation of that idea: Iran stood up to the United States and is entitled to WMD [weapons

---

84 Jorge Verstrynge, "La Guerra Periferica y el Islam Revolucionario," El Viejo Topo. 2003.

85 "Un libro de Jorge Verstrynge sobre el Islam sera editado por el ejercito Venezolano," Webislam, 18 de Agosto 2005. http://www.webislam.com/?idn=1900

86 http://www.noticias24.com/actualidad/noticia/7979/verstrynge-el-chacal-y-la-guerra-asimetrica/

of mass destruction] in order to defend itself and inflict further damage on its enemy. This means that any nation opposing the empire is entitled to the same in order to free not Muslims, but the oppressed of the earth. It is the repackaging of the Islamist world view as part of the traditional Marxist view (the proletariat rising up against the oppressor) that makes the book so attractive, I think, to Chavez and other Bolivarian leaders."

This theory explains the ALBA nations' closeness with terrorist groups and Iran. Before outlining some of Verstrynge's ideas, one must understand the link between Verstrynge and Hugo Chavez. This link comes, as Farah states, through the international terrorist (of Venezuelan birth) Carlos the Jackal. "Carlos, as evidenced by Chavez's early letters to him in prison, seems to have been an early influence on Chavez and his military strategy. He views Carlos as a freedom fighter, unjustly imprisoned, and thereby endorses the concept of the use of terrorist methods to achieve political ends. Just as importantly, Carlos' ability to merge radical Islamist thinking with Marxism and a call to war against the imperialist powers seems to have resonated deeply with Chavez and provided a framework, later expanded on, by Verstrynge, for confrontation with the United States and a rationale for the close ties to Iran."

Carlos' original name was Ilich Ramirez Sanchez, born in Venezuela to a family of Syrian origins. He is the cousin to Rafael Ramirez, the Chavez Administration's current minister of oil. His father was a member of the Communist Party and he grew up with those influences, including training in Havana and attending Patrice Lumumba University in Moscow. After being expelled from that university, Carlos found his true revolutionary nature in the activity of the Popular Front for the Liberation of Palestine. According to Carlos, the atheistic nature of communism did not allow for a full appreciation of the metaphysical and spiritual aspects of revolution—these were found best in revolutionary Islam. Carlos himself appeared to merge Islam with Marxism based upon his relationship with Abu Akram of the Iranian People's Mujahidin (PMOI or MEK)—who were at that time fighting the Shah. The MEK is a Marxist Islamic organization whose philosophy appears to provide the marriage (in the minds of Carlos and Chavez) between what would seem mutually exclusive principles (as Farah says above). According to Carlos himself, his conversion to Islam was not found in academic study but, "the brotherhood of arms is the origin of my conversion."[87] The relationship between Islam and revolution, according to Carlos, was indivisible: "I am and remain a revolutionary fighter. And the revolution today is, above all, Islamic[88] (…) revolutionary and communist I was, I am and so I shall remain."

Carlos has been an important influence on both Verstrynge and Chavez, and continues to actively promote his ideology and his organization from his prison cell in France. Carlos includes Chavez among his admirers. Chavez said this about the imprisonment of Carlos:

"Carlos Ilich Ramirez, some of you will remember him, is sentenced to life in prison in France. They accuse him of being a terrorist, but Carlos, what he was, was a revolutionary fighter. I re-vindicate him, what do I care what they say about me in Europe tomorrow, I don't care, I don't care (…) A few years ago I sent him a letter, that was intercepted and it came out on the first page of Le Monde, 'Chavez talks to terrorists' but I don't care. (He was) condemned unjustly—that's what I believe—to life in prison."

According to Verstrynge, "Ilich Ramirez 'Carlos' is the authentic synthesis between Marxism and Islam."[89] Verstrynge summed up and added Carlos' thoughts to his seminal work, *The Peripheral War and Revolutionary Islam—Origins, Rules and Ethics of Asymmetric War.* According to this work, and using Occam's razor as a guide, Verstrynge states that asymmetric warfare (1) uses rules or strategies different from traditional warfare, and (2) exploits the weakness of the adversary especially those who accompany the difference in size, weight and power. This is important, according to Verstrynge, because the United States (and the west) has conspired to take away the ability of the "peripheral countries" to fight on a level playing field. This is done using dissymmetry in sanctions, technology and economic power. The ultimate dissymmetric weapon was the nuclear bomb: against which there is no defense.

---

87 Ilich Ramírez Sánchez, dit Carlos (with Jean-Michel Vernochet), *L'islam révolutionnaire*, Monaco, Editions du Rocher, (2003): P24.

88 Ilich Ramírez Sánchez, dit Carlos (with Jean-Michel Vernochet), *L'islam révolutionnaire*, Monaco, Editions du Rocher, (2003): P23.

89 "Verstrynge, el Chacal y la guerra asymetrica," Noticias 24, 14 de Septiembre, 2007. http://www.noticias24.com/actualidad/noticia/7979/verstrynge-el-chacal-y-la-guerra-asimetrica/

The concept of dissymmetry was also used in the creation of a fixed set of rules of war through the Geneva convention, which assured that the peripheral countries would never be able to overthrow western control. These laws were written by the west and served as propaganda tools against terrorists or others using different rules of warfare. Yet, Verstrynge states, "It is possible to conceive of a war without borders and without methods to confront the enormous power of the United States."[90] And again, "The great innovation in today's war is the end of the monopoly on the state's use of violence that requires fighting political organizations, irregular militias, and fundamentalist networks that are not under the control of any state."[91] In this, "State military power looks to have lost a large part of its utility, not only in the case of nuclear war, or conventional intrastate war, but also above all in the war against nonstate actors."

Verstrynge outlines six types of asymmetry: (1) use of concepts and rules different from the adversary, for example guerilla warfare; (2) technology; (3) use of critical will when one believes their survival or way of life is threatened; (4) groups organized in networks, not hierarchically; (5) patience and a longer sense of time horizons; and (6) the will to fight (for example, suicide bombers). It seeks to wear the traditional forces down in terms of time and energy. It [asymmetry] does not seek traditional victories but instead to test the patience of the opponent. It seeks to use "unpredictable forces, free of suspicion (for example civilians) with weapons it is hard to defend against and alternative tactics (guerillas, terrorism) to the conventional ones, in improvised theaters of operation (cities) and using the effect of surprise."[92] Verstrynge patently rejects international humanitarian law (IHL) and the rules of war.

All of this is evident in the Bolivarian ideology of asymmetric warfare. Chavez has called on each civilian to be prepared to defend the revolution; he has called for the arming of civilians and distributed Russian-made weapons; and he has made common cause with terrorists. His evolving

90 Jorge Verstrynge, "La Guerra Periferica y el Islam Revolucionario," El Viejo Topo, (2003): P22.
91 Jorge Verstrynge, "La Guerra Periferica y el Islam Revolucionario," El Viejo Topo, (2003): P23.
92 Jorge Verstrynge, "La Guerra Periferica y el Islam Revolucionario," El Viejo Topo, (2003): P38.

understanding of this type of warfare (along with his close relationship with Carlos) explains his contact with terrorist organizations such as Hezbollah, ETA, ELN, IRA, MRTA and FARC. As the Defense School of the ALBA advances, it is clear that they will be studying Verstrynge and Carlos and will most probably have important lecturers from the terrorist organizations across the world.

Before closing this chapter, and as can be seen, 21st Century Socialism is an attempt to break with the "current world order" to create a "new world order." However, none of the tenets of ALBA's new plan are, technically or wholly, legal—in that they violate international law and the covenants and conventions to which ALBA countries have agreed. The below table demonstrates the differences with what we would call the current world order and the new world order.

In the economic sphere, the focus on endogenous development has led Venezuela, Bolivia and Ecuador to violate contracts with dozens of international companies. These range from oil services, oil exploration, fertilizer, bottle makers, agriculture, livestock, mining, telecommunications, electricity, and many others. These contracts are legally binding, and the ALBA's arbitrary abridging of these contracts has led to billion-dollar lawsuits pending in international arbitration mechanisms. In Venezuela, the right to private property has been violated as Chavez has expropriated more than six hundred businesses and more than 2,500,000 hectares of private land. In Ecuador, Correa defaulted on sovereign debt, money that the Ecuadorians received but simply refused to pay back. Internally they have seized even more companies, disrespecting private property while distributing companies and land to their cronies or seizing assets from political opposition.

Politically it has been even worse. The ALBA countries, through their attempts to destroy their opposition, have run afoul of almost every treaty and obligation the "current world order" has set up to protect individuals from predatory governments and individuals from other individuals within society, to protect businesses (to safeguard their investments), and to protect nations from each other. Ceresole's and Dieterich's assertions that the opposition must be destroyed flies in the face *of all* the human-rights agreements ALBA countries have signed. Their attempts to do away with Liberal Democracy violate the progressive rights that acknowledge individual civil and political rights—they go backward, something that is not allowed in civil rights jurisprudence. The use of constituent assemblies to rewrite the laws of the land is of dubious legality itself. As Javier El-Hage of the Human Rights Foundation states[93]:

The United States and the Bolivarian Alliance — A Comparative Analysis	
"Illiberal Democracy" — Dr. Bruce Bagley, Miami University	
• "Dictatorship with Popular Support" — Juan Bosch, President of the Dominican Republic	
• "Post-Democratic Model" — Norberto Ceresole	
• "21st Century Socialism" — Heinz Dieterich	
• "Popular and Protagonist Democracy" — Bolivarian Alliance Countries	
Current World Order	New World Order
Life, Liberty and the Pursuit of Happiness	Fatherland, Socialism or Death
Universality of Rights Trumps All	National Sovereignty Trumps All
Representative Democracy	Participatory and Protagonist Democracy
• Legitimacy of government derived from the consent of the governed	• Legitimacy of government derived from the ongoing approval of the "permanent majorities" demonstrated through constant plebiscites or elections
• Opposition must be nurtured and protected	• Opposition must be destroyed
• Separation of powers	• "Separation of powers weakens the state"
• Hard (legal) separation between government, party and state	• Blurring of the lines between government, party and state
• Political tolerance	• Conflict serves to cement permanent majorities
• Term limits for the executive	• Presidents for as long as the permanent majority allow
• Professional/nonpartisan civil service administrating the nation for the benefit of all	• Partisan civil service at the service of the revolution and the permanent majorities
• Increasingly transparent, decentralized governments more responsive to the people	• Centralized, secretive government

93 Author interview of El-Hage, March 2011

The United States and the Bolivarian Alliance — A Comparative Analysis	
Civil and Political Liberties	Economic, Social and Cultural Rights
• Nucleus of hard rights: life, speech, assembly, religion, property, fair judicial process	• The right to read is more important than the right to speech, the right of a job is more important than assembly
• International treaties serve as guarantors of progressive rights (International Covenant on Civil and Political Rights, UN Declaration of Human Rights, etc.)	• International treaties are mechanisms of imperial control by the developed world to maintain their exploitation and domination of the poorest
• Rights are universal, progressive, irreversible and un-renounceable	• Rights are subject to the will of the permanent majority via referenda
Liberal Economic Order	Socialist Economy
• Market-based provision of the needs and desires of a diverse citizenry	• State responsible to provide for the basic needs of the permanent majority
• State serves as a arbiter over disputes	• State is actively involved in service provision
• Preeminent right of private property	• Property not a right but a privilege granted by the state
• Protection of intellectual property rights	• Sovereignty above international rule of law, international arbitration is a mechanism of "imperial domination"
• Conflict resolution through international mechanisms such as WTO, ICJ, international arbitration	• State cooperation for the provision of the basic needs of the permanent majority
• Free trade agreements	
Rules of War	Asymmetric Warfare
• Geneva convention, international humanitarian law and rules of war guarantee a world with decreasing conflict	• Rules of war and international humanitarian law are mechanisms of imperial control to wrest from the peripheral countries their only mechanisms of legitimate defense
• Terrorism, irregular militias, arming of children, arming of the general population, and guerilla warfare are illegal and prosecutable by the ICC	• Terrorism, militias and guerilla are legitimate mechanisms of defense for peripheral countries, as Arafat once said, "Give me an air force like Israel's and I wouldn't use terrorism"
• Professional armed forces to "provide for the common defense" of the nation	• Partisan armed forces at the service (internally and externally) of the revolution

A constitutional convention always entails the great peril of allowing a small set of individuals to do away with democratic institutions, along with the rights and liberties of their citizens (most commonly, dissenting citizens). This is why constitutional conventions have been the preferred method for tyrants of all political persuasions, especially in Latin America during the 19th and 20th centuries. With the stroke of a pen and under the guise of a legitimate call for change, caudillos and dictators have periodically convened partisan constitutional conventions that have dismantled institutional checks on their governments, and trumped the rights and liberties of their opponents. From the perspective of international law, however, an all-powerful constitutional convention is yet another state organ whose actions may make the state responsible for violating its obligations under international law. For example, a peace treaty establishing a specific borderline may be violated either by a presidential decree, a statute of congress, or a constitution that doesn't recognize the terms of the treaty. If the UK were to withdraw its consent from the 1783 peace treaty that legally settled the war with the American states (that, in 1787, would legally unite under the US Constitution), and tried to physically reclaim its former territory, the United States would see this as a unilateral attack that violates international law—i.e. the 1783 treaty. Thus, the United States would be entitled, under international law, to retaliate and wage war against the aggressor.

The governments of ALBA countries have closed down media outlets, interfered with the right to assemble, the right of free speech, the right to a free and fair trial, the protection from arbitrary detention, and even freedom of religion. They are in violation of the International Covenant on Civil and Political Rights, the Universal Declaration of Human Rights, the Kimberly Process (from which Venezuela was expelled), and the Inter-American Democratic Charter, the International Covenant on the Rights of the Child, nonproliferation treaties, drugs, and crime, and many more. The mechanisms to protect ALBA's citizens, such as the Inter-American Commission on Human Rights and its associated court, have continuously issued rulings against ALBA countries. These rulings have been summarily dismissed by ALBA nations. Under the guise of sovereignty, they state that these treaties and covenants were established by rich and powerful countries to control the developing world. And using this argument, they walk away from what Oscar Arias calls, "the nucleus of hard rights." Again El-Hage states:

Just like it, the rights to privacy or to freedom of expression, recognized under international human rights law, may be violated either by a decree, a statute or a newly-enacted constitution. For instance, if a supreme court decision (from any country in the hemisphere) were to ratify the constitutionality of certain censorship statute, those affected by it may find international remedy in the Inter-American Court of Human Rights, pursuant to the American Convention on Human Rights. The Inter-American Court would rule the State's actions wrongful under international law and order the State to repeal them and restitute its citizens' rights. The exact same thing would happen if it was a Constituent Assembly that approved the censorship provision. In other words, international law imposes limitations on the power of States (and its domestic organs, including constituent assemblies) to rule at will, and imposes penalties on those that disregard previous international commitments. Under an international framework that put the right to State sovereignty above the individuals in the State, Hitler's Third Reich was able to enact laws that curtailed the rights of many Germans, and succeeded in mass-murdering its own population. Filling this huge and inhumane vacuum in international law was precisely what western democratic nations had in mind after WWII, as they promoted the adoption and approval of the numerous human rights treaties and declarations now in force, under the UN and the OAS umbrellas.

Internationally, the ALBA countries are in violation of the Vienna convention as they pay their Social Movements to interfere in internal affairs and internal elections of neighbor states, and attempt to swing other countries into their sphere of influence—something at which they have been successful in the past.

Perhaps the most dangerous is the ALBA's military doctrine. Asymmetric warfare brings the ALBA countries in violation of the Geneva convention and International Humanitarian Law. By arming civilians, by arming children, by setting up irregular militias and supporting terrorism, they are in violation of the rules of war, the UN Convention on the Rights of the Child, and all the terrorism agreements signed by the OAS, the UN and Interpol, and all other mechanisms that seek to end global terror. More concerning, this military strategy has brought them into compromising collaboration with the FARC, ELN, ETA, MRTA, Hezbollah and even Al Qaida. As the former US Assistant Secretary of State for Western Hemisphere Affairs unwillingly confirmed in a House Foreign Affairs Committee hearing in early 2011, Venezuela has become a state sponsor of terror. Asymmetric warfare stemming from revolutionary Islam has brought the ALBA in close contact with Iran—and has led them to break UN and US sanctions against Iran, as well as making the ALBA nations sponsors of terrorists placed at the behest of Iran. As El-Hage states on this:

> Under the same reasoning, international humanitarian law is violated by States and State-sponsored armed groups that use or endorse so-called asymmetrical warfare as a legitimate means to wage war. Their domestic statutes or constitutions may praise or even legally establish the legitimacy of these methods, but they will still be considered wrongful under international humanitarian law. The leaders from these States may be prosecuted and found liable at the International Criminal Court.

Finally, the FARC's support has made the ALBA run afoul of the global fight against illicit drugs, and both Venezuela and Bolivia (and probably soon, Ecuador) have been decertified as being allies of the United States in the fight against universally recognized illegal narcotics.

For these reasons, Chavez and his ALBA are keen to bring about a new world order. The current world order is one of law, of rules, an order from which they are realizing it is difficult to break. It does not allow for the philandering of the ALBA, and Chavez knows that eventually he will try the patience of even the exceedingly long-suffering United States government. Only seeking a world where the rules established in the 20th century are no longer relevant will allow Chavez and his ALBA to get away with 21st Century Socialism.

This brings an important question. Faced with the very real facts of increased criminality, increased violence, collapse in well-being, decrease in freedoms, increase in authoritarianism, and the apparent failure of the model they so energetically supported to bring about the changes they so desperately wanted, why does the international left continue to support Hugo Chavez? Dieterich himself said about past attempts at Marxism,

"The project has become hell."[94] He, again, has spoken. In his September 28, 2010 article, "Change the model or collapse,"[95] Dieterich argues that the model the cultural optimists have imposed upon the Venezuelan system will lead to the collapse of Venezuela in full within eight months and will lead Chavez to lose the elections in 2012—effectively ending the ALBA and 21st Century Socialism. The reason, he states, is that Chavez has failed to eliminate the opposition and now the components he counted on for a total victory—high oil prices, full supreme executive and legislative control, and a collapsed opposition—are now things of the past. Dieterich has been saying similar things since 2007 when Chavez, driven by the cultural optimists within his administration who have embraced wholeheartedly the Soviet Union's model of State Capitalism, a one-party system, and ushered into power a new bourgeois bureaucracy that controls Venezuela's revolution. According to Dieterich, in essence, the Bolivarian revolution has fallen into the trap that destroyed the USSR. It remains to be seen if he is correct—as of this writing, there is still one year until the presidential elections and things could change. However, the challenges for the Bolivarian leadership are piling one atop the other.

The second question is, in the face of the failure of Chavez' model, why does Socialism of the 21st Century retain such support internationally? The answer to this is simple. Despite its limitations, Hugo Chavez' project remains, nonetheless, the last, desperate gasp of global communism. China and Vietnam have embraced the free-market economy with a vigor that has disheartened the remaining communists the world over. The new Russian government is much less an ideological single-party structure than a return to a Tsarist model, with Vladimir Putin at the center. The dictatorships that still plague the world are not—outside of Latin America—attempting to promote these old and discredited ideologies. This leaves the ALBA, as it were, as the only game in town. It is the only place where staunch adherents to the failed vision of global communism can still engage with their antiquated ideas and visit their disastrous experiments upon an unwitting people, adapting and changing and attempting their models and

---

94 Heinz Dieterich, "El Socialismo del Siglo XXI," P49.
95 Heinz Dieterich, "Venezuela: Cambia el modelo o colapsara como el modelo Cubano," Kaosenlared, 28 de Septiembre, 2009. http://www.kaosenlared.net/noticia/venezuela-cambia-modelo-colapsara-como-modelo-cubano

ideas as they see fit, with support and funding from the governments. It is their last, although perhaps worst, hope. This reality makes the Bolivarians more dangerous, not less. The left that so desperately support this failing model understand that upon the failure of the Bolivarian experiment, their raison d'être will come to a spectacular end. For the Bolivarians, the struggle is more existential still. Their mere survival is gleaned from their ability to keep their model propped up and moving forward. Bolivarians see the fantastic natural resources as the platform upon which they will build their new dictatorial model and influence friends across the region. But this can only be done if they keep their people happy, and keep winning elections, something that looks increasingly difficult. This makes them more dangerous. They are wounded by their own model and trapped in their own incompetence. It is a deadly cocktail. For this reason the ALBA careens recklessly ahead. Should they slow, they will, indeed, collapse.

CHAPTER 4

ALBA as a Trade Agreement?

We fully agree that the ALBA will not become a reality based upon mercantilist interests or desire for personal gain through business, or in the increase in national benefit at the expense of other countries. Only a broad pan-Latin-Americanist vision, that recognizes the impossibility that our countries can develop and be truly independent isolated from one another, will be capable of achieving what Bolivar called "in America the greatest nation in the world, less so by its expanse or riches than by its freedom and glory" and what Marti conceived as "our America" to differentiate it from the other America, expansionist and with imperial appetites.

> —Joint Declaration for the creation of the ALBA,
> Havana, Cuba, December 14, 2004

The advance of the Bolivarian Alliance of the Americas (ALBA) across the geopolitical landscape of Latin America has been both unprecedented and stunning. The bold idea, which would become the central component of Hugo Chavez' foreign policy agenda, was introduced by President Hugo Chavez during the Summit of the Americas in Quebec in 2001, and elaborated upon at the Third Summit of Caribbean Presidents and Heads of State, which took place on the Venezuelan island of Margarita in December of 2001. The newly reelected President Chavez who stood before the other heads of state was flush with victory. Less than three years before, he won the presidency virtually unopposed; his main challenger collapsed in the polls weeks before the election. Taking his oath of office with his hand placed upon "this moribund constitution," a veiled reference to the Constituent Assembly he was advocating, he set about recreating Venezuela. He immediately embarked upon a wide and sweeping rewriting of the constitution via a Constituent Assembly, which had also been successful. Only six months before his momentous announcement, he had re-competed for the job of president, and in the corresponding "mega-elections" saw his followers take a majority of every institution of government across the country, including mayors, council members, parliamentarians and judges. With this, he was prepared to advance his Bolivarian project.

In the tumultuous years that followed, President Chavez worked consistently to consolidate his control over the institutions of the Venezuelan state and, most importantly, the Venezuelan oil sector.[96] [97] By August 2004, following his victory in a recall referendum where the political opposition attempted unsuccessfully to remove him from office using a mechanism set in place in the 1999 constitution, the chess game of Bolivarian advance across the region was set to begin. On December 14, 2004, President Chavez and Cuban President Fidel Castro signed into law the formal creation of ALBA.[98] The agreement had twelve fundamental principles, which continue today to be the guiding principles of the ALBA.[99]

1. Commerce and investment are not ends in themselves, but should be mechanisms to advance just and sustainable development and true Latin-American integration. This requires effective participation of the state in the economy as regulator and coordinator.

2. There should exist special and different treatment (for weaker countries), which takes into account the development of different countries and the

---

96 This is a fantastic story in and of itself, and has been the focus of many notable books and manuscripts. For those wanting greater insight into this period, Venezuelan lawyer Alan Brewer Carias has recently completed an outstanding blow-by-blow.

97 "Dismantling Democracy in Venezuela," Alan Brewer-Carias, Cambridge University Press, September 20, 2010. 9780521145572.

98 "Declaracion Conjunta entre el Presidente de la Republica Bolivariana de Venezuela y el Presidente del Consejo de Estado de la Republica de Cuba para la creación del ALBA," 14 de Diciembre, 2004. http://www.alianzabolivariana.org/modules.php?name=Content& pa=showpage&pid=2060

99 I am translating and paraphrasing for brevity. You may read the original document for the exact language.

dimension of their economies, as well as guarantee to all participating states of the benefits derived from the process of integration.

3. Economic complementarily and cooperation among countries and products allows for the promotion of a productive and competitive specialization which is compatible with each country's economic equilibrium and with their strategies for poverty alleviation and cultural preservation.

4. Cooperation and solidarity expressed in special plans for the least developed countries of the region, in the areas of literacy, health care and regional scholarships are deemed to be most important for economic and social development.

5. Creation of an emergency social fund.

6. Integrated development of the systems of communication and transport between Latin-American and Caribbean countries, including telecommunications, railway, airlines and ship lines, and others.

7. Actions to promote sustainable development with norms which protect the environment, stimulate rational use of resources and impede the proliferation of patterns of consumption which are foreign to Latin America.

8. Energy integration between the countries of the region, by the creation of PetroAmerica.

9. Foment investment capital within Latin America, with the objective of reducing the dependence upon foreign investments. This is to be done through a Latin American Investment Fund and a Development Bank.

10. Defense of Latin-American culture with particular respect for indigenous cultures, and the creation of the Television station TeleSUR as an alternative service for the diffusion of our (Bolivarian) realities.

11. Norms for intellectual property rights which protect the Latin-American heritage from voracious transnational businesses and assure that they (trans-national companies) don't become a roadblock to the necessary cooperation between our countries.

12. The coordination of positions within multilateral institutions and in negotiations with all other regional blocks, including for the democratization of international institutions, particularly the United Nations.

Following these twelve guiding principles, the ALBA as an institution grows, morphs and adapts itself organically to the economic and geopolitical realities of the region and the world. It is also able to modify itself to fit the needs of new member countries, proving a source of support for member countries that extends far beyond a simple trade agreement. This has allowed the ALBA, over the last six years, to develop into a cohesive and in fact, exceedingly responsive political block, able to deal somewhat effectively with crises, achieve successes both developmental and political, and come to each other's assistance during times of instability. Due to the internal discipline within the membership, it has also been able to serve as an obstacle for projects, regional and even global, that it believes goes against its interest. Finally, it has been able to dominate the narrative of an entire continent. While the United States refuses to accept it, every other country in the region, from Mexico to Chile, is talking about Hugo Chavez and his ALBA.

The most important principles of the ALBA are: opposition to the United States; opposition to free-market economics; integration through statist cooperation and solidarity; the importance of state-run communications (read propaganda); what Chavez calls "petro-indebtedness" (the linking of member countries' economies using the energy sector, and the use of energy as a political lever or weapon); and a cohesive international block able to stand together in opposition to the United States' interests. For all of this, it's best to see the ALBA not as a static organization guided by an all-inclusive document like the free trade agreements, which negotiate product by product to establish clear rules and guidelines, but instead as a political alliance among countries working to support each other and advance their political agendas. It is best viewed through the optic of the Big Tent, which allows many different and divergent interests to unite and build support amongst each other—so long as they support the general tenets of "21st Century Socialism."

In recent history, Latin America has made many attempts to unify. Examples of this include the Community of Andean Nations (CAN), Southern Cone Common Market (MERCOSUR) as a trade agreement between the Southern Cone countries, the Association of Caribbean Countries (CARICOM) and the Central American Integration System (SICA), among others. Generally speaking, these organizations have sprung up to attempt to address trade challenges, or as forums for political discussion. Each one has had varying degrees of success. The ALBA is wholly different. It is not a mechanism for conflict resolution or for political negotiation; it represents the interests of Venezuela and Cuba to bring about the re-founding of Simon Bolivar's Great Colombia, under the ideology of 21st Century Socialism. The ALBA is an imperialist, often predatory construct that uses the veneer of democracy and social justice to create mechanisms to undermine other governments, supplant representative democracy with a "participatory and protagonist democracy" and enshrine President Chavez' power across the continent. It is working.

But what gave President Chavez the idea to form an Alliance in the first place? Latin-Americanists who have watched Chavez morph over the years have witnessed the reactionary nature of Chavista policies. Chavez has often used reactionary posturing to advance his agendas. It has been the mark of his government to draw lines in the sand, to divide, to set himself and his projects on the contrary side of an ideology—apart from viewpoints of others—and to rule from that vantage point. The ALBA is no different, and emerges as a reaction to a proposal by, naturally, the United States of America. The seeds of his ALBA were planted in 1994, while he was still in jail, in the Venezuelan prison of Yare near Caracas, doing time for his failed coup attempts. That year, the United States hosted the first Summit of the Americas, in Miami. There, the US delegation unveiled its plan for a Free Trade Agreement of the Americas (FTAA): one great economic block from Alaska through the Patagonia. According to the plan presented, the conclusion of negotiations was set for 2005[100] (a date that would become fundamental for Hugo Chavez and the ALBA). However the Clinton Administration, as would President George W. Bush after him, underestimated the opposition to the FTAA across wide sectors of Latin-American society. Sensing a fight, the Clinton Administration instead focused on the creation of a much more palatable NAFTA. This was seen as more politically viable than an agreement encompassing over thirty countries, and the larger trade area was left for the subsequent administration.

By the time FTAA was revived by the Bush Administration late into his first term, the situation in Latin America had already changed. By the

---

100 "Mandatos de la Cumbre de las Americas: Miami 1994." www.summit-americas.org/esp/cumbremiami.htm

early 2000s, the political tides across the region—a region frustrated by what they considered the "abandonment" of America after the fall of communism—began to turn. Angered by income inequalities, rampant unemployment, perceived economic stagnation and the exclusion of most of the population to the economic (if not political) benefits of American-style democracy, the Latin-American poor were ready for revolt. The natural focus of this revolt, led and exemplified by Hugo Chavez' rise to power, was against free trade and against what an increasing number of Latin-American countries were willing to publicly call the hegemonic intentions of their mighty neighbor to the north. It was into this toxic political environment that President Chavez introduced the ALBA.

The ALBA was at first conceived as the Bolivarian *Alternative* of the Americas—an alternative to the unpopular free trade agreement pushed by an even more unpopular American President. The word "Alliance" was added later, as part of the organic growth of this organization.[101] Seen as a counterproposal to the American savage capitalist trade agreement, many of the initial written discussions regarding the ALBA focused on the distinction between the FTAA and the ALBA. These discussions have been succinctly summarized in the following tables by Josette Altmann of FLACSO, an intergovernmental think tank based in in Costa Rica.

According to Altmann's analysis, the alternative offers are as shown in the table on page 91:[102]

As is demonstrated in the above table, and through the founding articles of the ALBA, the initial focus of the Alliance was designed to combat what was seen as the desire of the United States, through the FTAA, to exert increasing authority over the region through unfettered access by American transnational companies into local economies. Whatever your personal opinion on this matter, in Latin America there has been—and continues to be—significant fear of and opposition to free trade agreements with the United States. This distrust was made painfully obvious by the extraordinarily close result in the Costa Rican referendum

---

101 Rafael Correa (Diputado), "Construyendo el ALBA: Nuestro Norte es el Sur" Ediciones del 40 Aniversario del Parlamento Latino, Mayo, 2005.
102 Josette Altmann y Tatiana Beirute, "Dossier ALBA," 1ª ED., Facultad Latinoamericana de Ciencias Sociales (Secretaría General) Dossier ALBA / ed. Jossette Altmann; comp. Tatiana Beirute. – 1a. ed.—San José, C.R., 2008.

on their joining CAFTA, which, despite wide popular support for President Oscar Arias (who pushed Costa Rica's CAFTA as a personal project of his administration) only passed with a two percent margin.[103] With this change in public support for the United States, an aftereffect of decades of perceived meddling and neglect, President Chavez had his golden moment to advance his plan for regional integration.

In April of 2005, the first operational meeting of the ALBA took place in Havana. Specific activities were adopted and the Alliance became a functional institution. Most of the agreements dealt with social initiatives, in the areas of medicine and education, perceived by Latin Americans (and some in the United States) as Cuba's strength—and also in the areas of creation of what are called endogenous development projects in both countries. According to Webster's Dictionary, endogenous means "produced from within, derived internally." This idea of endogenous development, taken from 1960s academia, would stay with Chavez until the present day as he seeks a way to make the ALBA countries mutually self-reliant and self-sustainable. In a globalized world, this seems less than plausible; nevertheless this remains an important part of Bolivarian ideology.

President Chavez on many occasions will appear on television, poring over a large map of Venezuela and the continent, outlining in true military fashion how he would organize the national territory through endogenous development projects to become self-sustainable and break their reliance upon the outside world. Most recently, in the last several years Chavez has passed laws focused on the reorganizing of the national territory, which intend to allow the maximum efficiency for the endogenous development projects, managed communally, which will lead Venezuela into developed-world status. None of these projects has been successful. Of the hundreds of nuclei for endogenous development spread across the Venezuelan landscape, the only one that appears functional is called Fabricio Ojeda, which makes revolutionary paraphernalia.

While this first ALBA Summit gave the Alliance a framework and a narrative to sell across Latin America, it wasn't until the Fourth Summit of the Americas in 2005 that the ALBA began to gain traction. In December

---

103 "Costa Rica Referendo," La Nacion, Octubre 2007. http://www.nacion.com/ln_ee/ESPECIALES/2007/octubre/referendo/mapa/index.html

of 2005, the leaders of the Western Hemisphere met in pomp and circumstance at a resort in the Argentine city of Mar de Plata. Also present were the inevitable anarchist protesters, who meet at these events to throw stones and reject the presence of politicians they don't like. Security was tight, the summit relatively uneventful. The initial topic for the summit was to be "Creating Jobs to Fight Poverty and Strengthen Democratic Governance."[104] An important topic, but too stale for the vision of Hugo Chavez; this was to be his coming-out party. The Clinton Administration had set 2005 as the original date for the conclusion of discussions for the Free Trade Agreement of the Americas, a date that coincided perfectly with the Summit of the Americas. The Bush Administration had decided that a Free Trade Agreement of the Americas would be its legacy for the region, and pushed the project aggressively prior to the meeting. In their minds, the meeting would serve as a breakthrough for the FTAA. It was not to be. The discussions at the summit degenerated into arguments about free trade. The four MERCOSUR countries—Argentina, Uruguay, Brazil, Paraguay—plus Venezuela, were the harshest critics, MERCOSUR because of potential damage to their economies from American access to their markets, and Venezuela for ideological reasons.

The summit came to an inglorious close with no agreement adopted and an improvised date of 2006 set to renew discussions: without MERCOSUR and Venezuela. This date was to pass unnoticed and unsung. Upon this defeat, the Bush Administration decided to change its tactics and focus bilaterally on individual free trade agreements on a country-by-country basis.

Upon conclusion of the summit, President Chavez drove across town to preside over a massive "counter-summit." His Social Movements, which would become so important to the ALBA, had spent weeks preparing a massive rally, paying off participants, lining up the media, and getting ready for Chavez' victory dance. There, in front of forty thousand people and beside other leaders such as Evo Morales, Hugo Chavez ceremoniously and graphically declared the death and burial of the FTAA.[105]

---

104 "Fourth Summit of the Americas: A New Challenge for the Hemisphere," Organization of American States. http://www.summit-americas.org/newsletter/newsletter_Feb05_eng.htm
105 "Maradona y Chavez encabezan una gran protesta contra Bush," El Paiz, 11 de Mayo, 2005. http://www.elpais.com/articulo/internacional/Maradona/Chavez/encabezan/

FTAA	ALBA
Purpose: Promote prosperity through economic integration and free trade	Purpose: Promote the fight against poverty and social exclusion
Objective: Promote improved quality of life through stable and sustained economic growth	Objective: Preserve the identity and autonomy of Latin America through a new integration mechanism
Increase pressure to eliminate barriers to foreign investment	Condition the lifting of barriers to the transfer of technology and development of human resources
Agriculture Policy	
Demand the elimination of domestic subsidies and agricultural controls	Priority on food security and agricultural production as seen through the lens of sovereignty
Intellectual Property	
Reduces the ability to patent traditional knowledge and share technology and access to medication and education	Should not get in the way of people's right to advance technologically, and in access to medicine, food and education
Access to Markets	
Elimination of tariffs as a mechanism for the defense of national production	Defends tariffs, quotas, licenses, and other mechanisms and political tools to promote and protect domestic agriculture and industry.
Services	
Promotes the liberalization of delivery of services, removing the state's ability to serve as regulator	Countries can liberalize their services in accordance with their national development priorities.
Government Purchases	
Desires to open the public market to foreign companies	Domestic companies retain priority in the delivery of services procured by the state.
Competition	
Total elimination of anticompetitive practices through legislation.	Anticompetitive practices will be looked at on a case-by-case basis, no foreign company should be able to take the government to court
Conflict resolution	
The installation of a supranational system for dispute resolution	Favors using the national judiciary to resolve individual issues.

gran/protesta/Bush/elpepiint/20051105elpepiint_3/Tes

"Bush insists on setting in place the pieces of his domination of the continent. He comes to Mar del Plata with the pretension to revive the cadaver of the FTAA, when the peoples have clearly expressed their rejection to integration subordinated to the United States."[106]

This was a moment of significance for Chavez' international persona: and his Bolivarian Alliance. At that moment the Alliance was only a few signed documents, agreements between two revolutionary countries, and a grandiose idea. The six years since, unfettered by opposition either at home or abroad—and with almost unlimited oil wealth—Venezuela and Cuba have gone about quietly building upon this idea the essential infrastructure for an active organization, one they hope will finally unite Latin America against the United States.[107]

---

106 "Discurso de Hugo Chavez en Cumbre de las Americas," Mar del Plata, 11 de Mayo 2005. http://www.taringa.net/posts/downloads/7541770/Discurso-Hugo-Chavez_-ContraCumbre-Mar-Del-Plata-2005.html
107 Josette Altmann, "Integracion Latinoamericana: Cronica de una Crisis Anunciada," FLACSO, 15 de Septiembre, 2006.

CHAPTER 5

ALBA, More than a Trade Agreement

We from Caracas continue promoting the Bolivarian idea of achieving the political integration of our states and our republics. A Confederation of Latin-American and Caribbean states, why not? Why don't we have a plan for a decade? We don't have a medium-term plan, it is imperative that we make a plan ... if not we will continue making strides forward, backwards, and sideways, losing the definitive and defining direction. Yes, we believe that it is possible, that we can build a union or a confederation of republics from this part of the world.

—Hugo Chavez, III Conf. of Caribbean States, 2001

As seen in the previous chapter, the initial discussions of the ALBA focused on the trade issues and the differences between proposals for the region. However, the moment Hugo Chavez was able to announce the symbolic burial of the FTAA at the counter-summit in Mar Del Plata in December of 2005, he succeeded in a propaganda victory which has allowed him to take the simple idea of a counterproposal and with it, form a broad political alliance. This alliance, as I will present below and in the following chapters, has been successful beyond the wildest dreams of the Chavistas and beyond the ability of the ever-reactive US Government to understand the rapidly morphing dynamics in the region where we spend so little of our attention and time.

So, if the ALBA is not a trade agreement seeking to open up the markets of the member countries, what does it consist of and what is the direction?

Reclaiming the project of unification and independence of the liberators, the ALBA is presented today as the concrete chance to bring into reality our dream of the Great Nation. When we understand that the Latin-American and Caribbean territory comprises one sole nation, it is easy to see that the unionist idea is finding itself in the fullness of time.[108]

—from *Cuadernos de la Imancipacion,* #35

The idea of the ALBA is the re-assembly of the Gran Colombia of Simon Bolivar, under the present-day leadership of Hugo Chavez and under the ideological banner of 21st Century Socialism. It is to be a confederation of Latin-American states. According to Oxford English Dictionary, "A confederation in modern political terms is a permanent union of sovereign states for common action in relation to other states. Usually created by treaty but often later adopting a common constitution, confederations tend to be established for dealing with critical issues such as defense, foreign affairs or a common currency, with the central government being required to provide support for all members."

We will discuss this latter topic in the future, focusing now on what the ALBA has become to the members of the Alliance.[109]

The ALBA is unlike other trade agreements, such as NAFTA and CAFTA, MERCOSUR and the European Economic Community, where the importance of the activities emanate from the carefully scripted, debated and negotiated details in the final documents. ALBA's agreements are shell statements: political declarations given structure by the efficiency and political will of those involved. The Alliance is a political and ideological alliance meant to form a common front in the establishment of an anti-American block in the region.

The idea emerges from the 1826 Congress of Panama, in which Bolivar attempted to set up a confederation able to unite Latin Americans to contain the economic and military advance of the United States across the region.

---

108 Cuadernos de la Imancipacion, #35, ISSN 0328-0179, April, 2009.
109 I have decided to decline from a blow-by-blow narrative of the formation of the Alliance. This would require an analysis of each agreement signed, a rundown of the participation at each summit and translation of the final declarations as well as activities that saw the advance of the Alliance across the region. This would be tedious for me to write and for the reader to read, and I do not believe it would add significant value to the end product of my research.

The Congress sought, as one of its primary goals, to serve as a buffer that could minimize the power of the United States.[110] As Bolivar so realized, Chavez also has understood that with a unified block supporting his agenda, the power of his ideas contains more weight. In true Latin-American fashion, the ALBA is being assembled while looking with longing into a distant, romanticized past, with its ultimate prize being a utopian future. Achieving this future is ALBA's greatest challenge; and according to experts such as Josette Altmann of FLACSO, the ALBA model is unsustainable in the long term.

Name	Size (square Km)	Population	GDP (in $ Millions)	Date Joined
Antigua and Barbuda	442	85,632	1,522	24-Jun-09
Bolivia	1,098,581	9,775,246	45,560	29-Apr-06
Cuba	110,860	11,451,652	110,000	14-Dec-04
Dominica	751	72,660	744	20-Jan-08
Ecuador	283,561	14,573,101	108,800	24-Jun-09
Nicaragua	130,370	5,891,199	16,510	23-Feb-07
St. Vincent and the Grenadines	389	104,574	1,069	24-Jun-09
Venezuela	912,050	26,814,843	349,300	14-Dec-04
ALBA Totals	*2,537,004*	*68,768,907*	*633,505*	
Non-voting Observer Nations: Haiti, Iran and Syria				

For the reasons stated above, it is clear that one of the most important tenets of the ALBA alliance is what they call "Anti-Imperialism," a desire to serve as a block against what they see as the hegemonic power of the United States. As they state, in their own words, the ALBA imperialists refer incessantly to the project as a fight between Monroeism vs. Bolivarianism. In their opinion, the power of the United States emerges less from its military might than economic power, especially in the Latin-American region where invasion from the US military is decreasingly plausible. More concerning is the economic advance, described as the new manifestation for

---

110 Geoensenanza Vol. 9-2004, P57, ISSN 1316*6077.

the Monroe Doctrine, through the vehicle of the FTAA.[111] In this scenario, the FTAA is seen as the substitute for the Monroe Doctrine. Through this vehicle, the United States will exert its control over other countries in the region. For this reason, it is important—in the mindset of Bolivar and his modern acolytes—for the poor and formerly colonized countries of the new world to unite: to form a common bond against imperialism and use their joint strength to cushion themselves against imperial aggression. This age-old battle has been reborn in the mind of Hugo Chavez and those who feel that the advances of the United States are made in bad faith. For them, the ALBA has emerged as the main alternative to ward against unwanted imperialist advances. If the FTAA is the new face of Monroeism, the ALBA is the final emergence of a viable Bolivarian-ism.

As demonstrated in the table below, the ALBA (through the People's Trade Agreement) views itself as organized quite differently from the principles of FTAA. From the point of view of the member-states, the basic principles of the ALBA vis-à-vis the FTAA are as follows:112

FTAA (Basic Principles)	ALBA (Basic Principles)
Competition	Cooperation
Free Trade	Just Trade
Expansion of transnational companies	Fight against poverty and inequality
Exploit resources and labor of our (their) countries	Complement capacity and share resources
Uneven development of our (their) countries	Joint development of our (their) countries

These principles are important, and are in marked divergence with the American approach to development. As such, the ALBA is founded at least rhetorically on what they call social justice and equality between the states. This is why the ALBA is naturally a political animal, because to invest in the development of each other is a political decision. They seek to break with the market approach to the supply of stated needs of the population. In their opinion, the markets only create injustice, and income inequalities

---

111 Geoensenanza Vol. 9-2004, P59, ISSN 1316*6077.
112 Encuentro Regional Sobre la Flexibilidad Laboral Managua 3 y 4 de Abril de 2008, Presidente de la Central Sandinista de Trabajadores, José Benito Escobar "Que Es el ALBA?"

are wrong on moral grounds. They see their role as the political leaders to legally (and illegally when necessary) interfere with market-driven economics in favor of the poorest, using the power of the state to replace the market's role in the provision of the basic needs of the majority.[113] Naturally, this strategy sounds good on paper and has won the ALBA friends and influence among the "socialists" of the developed world. Unfortunately for them, centrally planned and managed economies have never worked and the ALBA experience appears to be no different.

Nevertheless, the Washington consensus has brought both positive results and significant challenges (due mostly to the lack of correct implementation of the recommendations) to a region unprepared and unwilling to embrace market economics.[114]

This unwillingness of the region's governments to correctly enact the market-based economic model—due in large part to the populist approach to electoral politics in too many Latin American countries—caused economic stagnation.[115] With the economic model of the past years wearing down due to bureaucracy and corruption in too many countries of the region, the political model followed in short order, causing a crisis of both confidence and governance across the region. In his book, *The Mystery of Capital*, Peruvian economist Hernando de Soto outlines the problem of "dead capital" as residing in the extra-legality of most economic activity across the region. In this hallmark book, de Soto painstakingly lays out the unending procedures that make it nearly impossible for a person of little means to register a company and own their home. Because such a significant part of national capital is held in extralegal economies such as homes with no titles and businesses with no papers, it is impossible for the poor to advance. Conversely, without the legality of these items, it is impossible for the government to collect taxes on them.[116]

This system was accompanied by government red tape, rampant corruption and an antiquated legal system and made it impossible for the majority

113 Geoensenanza Vol. 9-2004, P59, ISSN 1316*6077.
114 J. Rosenau, (1997). "Demasiadas cosas a la ves: La Teoria de la complejidad y los asuntos mundiales. En: Nueva Sociedad, Caracas, Venezuela #148.
115 *Left Behind: Latin America and the False Promise of Populism*, Sebastian Edwards, University of Chicago Press, 2010.
116 *The Mystery of Capital: Why Capitalism Triumphs in the West and Fails Everywhere* Else, Hernando de Soto, Basic Books; 1st edition (July 8, 2003), ISBN 9780465016150.

poor to participate in the new economic model as sold by the United States. While the rich became richer, the resentment of the poor grew. This same problem caused a crisis of capital, since the government has been unable to collect property tax on title-less homes or capital gains tax on unregistered companies. The resources of the state dried up, causing the countries to become more reliant upon the World Bank and IMF and the dictates of the Washington consensus. And the downward spiral continued.

According to some of the ALBA thinkers, this has been exacerbated by the neo-liberal solution sold as a panacea for all the ills of these countries.[117] While governments were told to decrease their spending and social support—to balance their budgets, privatize state resources and industries— capitalism itself had entered what they call its imperialist phase: pushed by the transnational industries and financial institutions after the perceived collapse of the Keynesian model in the 1980s.[118]

As these Latin-American countries became mired in the intransigent problems generated by stagnant economies, exploding populations and social ills, an increasing resentment and suspicion grew of the Washington consensus and the IMF's structural adjustment packages, especially from emerging leaders at the time. It was this hostile climate the ALBA took advantage of. They espouse a wholesale rejection of this model for a new (or, in point of fact, old) statist approach to economics. To be sure, their proposed model has been tried and failed in the past, but the ALBA countries are counting on something the old models did not: the massive natural resources of the region in a world where commodities are in increasingly short supply. To gain full use of these resources, the large transnationals would have to be expelled and new political agreements forged to protect them and advance a new model of exploration, exploitation and exchange. This is what PetroAmerica has set out to do. First, the ALBA had to become an ideological alliance, to better defend member countries from the assault they were sure would arrive from the developed world while they illegally dismantled legal frameworks and agreements.

---

117 Geoensenanza Vol. 9-2004, P59, ISSN 1316*6077.

118 Carmen Chinas Salazar, "El neoliberalismo y el deterioro de las condiciones de vida de la clase trabajadora en America Latina." 3 de Abril, 2008. http://revistaintereconomia. blogspot.com/2008/04/el-neoliberalismo-y-el-deterioro-de-las.html

CHAPTER 6

ALBA: From Integration to Ideological Alliance

Look how on all sides the flags are trembling, the flags of our peoples, who at the bottom are one sole flag, the flags of Bolivar, of Artigas, of San Martin, of Sandino, of el Che, of Camilo, of Torrijos, of Morazan, Farabundo Marti, the flag of Tupac Katari, Bartolina Sisa; they are our flags of struggle, of battle and of victory.[119]

—Hugo Chavez

What began as an alternative to the Free Trade Agreement of the Americas morphed rapidly into a mechanism to support Latin-American integration. Nevertheless, the integration proposed by Hugo Chavez was not sufficient.

While this mechanism for integration has been important, as they state, to "reinforce the self-determination"[120] of member countries, it was only sufficient to support an active defense. According to FLACSO, the collective weight of the organization has allowed it to *affect* policy, but not yet to *set* policy.[121]

This as well explains that, on occasions, when measures and actions promoted by a member state are not adopted within another integra

---

119 "Con El ALBA, Despiertan Los Pueblos," Hugo Chávez Frías, Junio, 2008. Depósito Legal: 1f87120083202647, Impreso en la República Bolivariana de Venezuela.
120 "Integracion Regional: Un Proyecto Politico y Estrategico," III Informe FLACSO, P16.
121 Josette Altmann, "La Alianza Bolivariana para los Pueblos de Nuestra America," Foreign Affairs LatinoAmerica, Volumen 10, Numero 3, Julio-Septiembre 2010. P2.

tion mechanism, that country seeks support within the ALBA and, generally speaking, receives strong support.[122]

—Josette Altmann

This was evident in Copenhagen where the ALBA served as a mechanism to thwart the Obama Administration's attempt to make a deal on climate change. It also serves as a loud voice in opposition to what they called the US militarization of the Haiti relief effort. The ALBA has been able to mobilize their collective weight due to an extreme discipline: They consistently vote together on issues that affect them as a whole or member-states individually (especially at Venezuela's behest), allowing the countries individually to count upon the unqualified support of ALBA member countries in any international or regional assembly.

However, according to the thinkers behind the ALBA movement, the time has come to move the organization from an integration mechanism to a broad-based ideological alliance, to take the organization on the offensive.[123] The confederation was about to become itself imperialist. According to Carlos Malamud, "In that sense, the existence of a hegemonic ALBA Project, synthesized in the so-called 21st Century Socialism and the Bolivarian Revolution, coordinated and directed by Cuba and Venezuela for the entire continent, not only weakens the possibility of a joint Latin-American position but also makes dialogue with Europe more difficult."[124]

The tipping point for the ALBA countries to understand their power in not only opposing the agendas from the western, developed countries but also in setting the agenda on key issues came, paradoxically, at their moment of greatest weakness. This moment occurred during the Honduras crisis.

Led by Hugo Chavez, the ALBA member-states believed that if they sat by and allowed the opposition within Honduras to stop the efforts of Zelaya to remake his country according to the ALBA's package of democratic subversion, it would have a domino effect in their own countries.

---

122 Josette Altmann, "La Alianza Bolivariana para los Pueblos de Nuestra America," Foreign Affairs LatinoAmerica, Volumen 10, Numero 3, Julio-Septiembre 2010. P4.
123 Fernando Bossi, "Cuadernos de Emancipacion," N35, ISSN 0328-0179, P26.
124 Carlos Malamud, "La Cumbre ALCUE de Madrid y el Estado de la Relacion Bilateral Europa-America Latina," Real Instituto Elcano, June 16, 2010.

This would lay bare their weakness (both internally and abroad) and limit the future addition of new members. They responded following the age-old adage; the best defense is a good offense. They realized quickly that the Obama Administration was weak and would not attempt to counter the ALBA's influence in the region. With broader issues to worry about and no desire to tussle with Hugo Chavez over an inconsequential piece of Central America, they allowed the Organization of American States (OAS) to lead the response. Under the backdrop of this vacuum, the ALBA effectively orchestrated the suspension of Honduras from the OAS by invoking the Democratic Charter—a suspension that lasted two years.[125] Their not-insignificant propaganda tools, beginning with TeleSUR, were able to rapidly define and control the information regarding the situation and turn world opinion against the interim government.

Honduras is seen by many in the ALBA as their one failure. As Evo Morales, President of Bolivia, recently stated in his November 2010 speech at the opening of the summit of the Defense Ministers of the Americas, "The United States won in Honduras, but we the people of the Americas won in Venezuela, Ecuador and Bolivia."[126]

While unsuccessful in their attempts to carry out a Constituent Assembly or bring former President Zelaya back to power, the ALBA countries realized they had succeeded in proactively managing the situation and setting the agenda for the Organization of American States. Through their aggressive response, they were able to turn their defeat into victory and speed the advance of the ALBA. Using Honduras (and Ecuador in 2010), they defined a new "democratic charter" from the Union of South American Nations (UNASUR) which is meant to replace the OAS's Inter-American Democratic Charter. They congealed the discussion around an ALBA military force, which would be the next big project for the Alliance starting in 2011. Things were moving forward.[127]

---

125 Honduras was re-admitted to the OAS on June 1, 2011, after a meeting between President Chavez and President Lobo brokered by Colombian President Juan Manuel Santos.
126 Evo Morales, "Discurso de Evo Morales en el IX Cumbre de Ministros de Defensa, 22 de Septiembre, 2010. http://www.lostiempos.com/diario/actualidad/po-litica/20101122/discurso-del-presidente-de-bolivia-evo-morales-ix-conferencia-de-minis-tros_100256_194768.html
127 Josette Altmann, "Integracion Latinoamericana: Cronica de una Crisis Anunciada,"

I believe in the strength of the people, in the unity of the people, the way we relate in transparency, in complementarity to liberate not only one, two, three, four, five countries but all South America and all America. I feel that in South America at least with conscientious, permanent work with a tight relationship with Social Movements, it's possible to free all of Latin America—that is the goal.

— Evo Morales, Speech to the Sixth ALBA
Summit on June 5, 2009 in Caracas

It is important to note that this alliance has not abandoned its initial tenets of opposition to the free trade agreements and to capitalism and the advancing of endogenous development through 21st Century Socialism (we will discuss this in a later chapter) as the means to advance the development in the region. It has, however, continued to grow and expand and deepen as new thinkers arrive with their visions of the direction the Alliance should take, and with their passion for individual projects under the umbrella of the ALBA.

The skeleton of the ALBA remains the same, outlined in the agreement signed in Havana between Fidel and Chavez and the strategic plan of April 2005.[128] This has not changed. However, upon this skeleton people have been building organs and muscles. These components are being developed with varying degrees of success. Some are atrophied due to mismanagement, some are overly strong, others exist only in name. While the ALBA claims to centrally plan these components, more than that, they occur as recommendations from the Social Movements[129] or member-states. However, they all fit within the skeleton, the overarching framework that can be defined as Venezuela's foreign policy imperatives.[130] Much more than simply Venezuelan largesse, the principles of the ALBA and 21st Century Socialism exist as a plan pushed by President Chavez, with significant

---

FLACSO, 15 de Septiembre, 2006. P6.

128 United Nations University—Comparative Regional Integration Studies, Working Paper W/2008-4, P34.

129 Rafael Correa, "Construyendo el ALBA: Nuestro Norte es el Sur," Parlamento Latinoamericano, Mayo 2005.

130 United Nations University—Comparative Regional Integration Studies, Working Paper W/2008-4. P33.

logistical support and know-how from Cuba.[131]

This brings us to address the issue of the increasingly ideological nature of the ALBA and, by reflection, their member-states. Case in point, the instability in Ecuador in September 2010. In a country that was seen as ALBA-lite, the increasing pressure of ideological dialogue has brought about serious instability in the country. Much of this occurs due to the pressure caused by the implementation of 21st Century Socialism, specifically, the limitation of certain freedoms, the authoritarian nature of the Correa regime, and what appears to be a wanton disregard for private property and dissent.

The ideological nature of the Alliance should not be seen as peripheral to the ALBA, but at the core of the Alliance. At the outset, this seems almost counterintuitive. Powerful, influential countries in the region are walking back from ideological positions and confrontations in favor of a more nuanced and pragmatic approach to international relations and local governance. The perfect case-in-point is Brazil, which despite the radical past of Luis Ignacio "Lula" da Silva, former president of Brazil, or Dilma Roussef, current president of Brazil, has adopted fairly orthodox economic approaches with a healthy portion of social democracy. Even Colombia, coming out of a four-decade ideological battle with guerillas-turned-terrorists, is moving away from its policy of democratic security to democratic prosperity.

This causes the ALBA's increasingly ideological approach to regional integration to have the opposite effect: that of fragmenting the region.[132] According to FLACSO, this confrontation has brought two consequences, one positive and one negative.

The positive consequence is the increased support for regional integration among the countries within Latin America.[133] The discussion the ALBA countries are having has spilled over into the mainstream, which has catalyzed countries such as Brazil and Mexico to look at other mechanisms for integration. The first of these has been the Union of South American

---

131 Josette Altmann, "La Alianza Bolivariana para los Pueblos de Nuestra America," Foreign Affairs LatinoAmerica, Volumen 10, Numero 3, Julio-Septiembre 2010. P3.
132 Josette Altmann, "La Alianza Bolivariana para los Pueblos de Nuestra America," Foreign Affairs LatinoAmerica, Volumen 10, Numero 3, Julio-Septiembre 2010. P3.
133 Josette Altmann, "La Alianza Bolivariana para los Pueblos de Nuestra ," Foreign Affairs LatinoAmerica, Volumen 10, Numero 3, Julio-Septiembre 2010. P5.

Nations (UNASUR), which has had an important protagonist role in re-
solving a 2010 crisis between Venezuela and Colombia, which led to rupture of relations and the closure of the border, as well as the Ecuador
situation wherein Colombia bombed a FARC rebel camp inside Ecuadoran
territory. The second is the first summit of Latin-American and Caribbean
leaders in Cancun, Mexico in 2010 (CELAC). This was an effort on the
part of Mexico to take leadership in the region, a leadership that should
naturally be theirs due to language, population size and economy, but due
to their close and complicated relationship with the United States has left
them out of regional Latin-American discussions.

Nevertheless, fragmentation has occurred as the demand for increased integration exposes the effect that the new integration mechanisms will have on the mechanisms that currently exist—namely, the OAS.
Chavez and the ALBA countries have made explicit their hope that the
OAS be destroyed. In their mind, it represents the hegemonic past—one
of American interference in the affairs of the hemisphere—and in their
minds is linked to Monroeism. Specifically, the ALBA countries refute the
OAS's Democratic Charter, the agreement signed by thirty-four Western
Hemisphere nations in Lima on September 11, 2001 that cemented the
democratic nature of the continent. The ALBA sees this as less important
than a Social Charter that would reflect more the values of the member-
states of the ALBA. Also, they have serious concerns with the Inter-
American Human Rights Commission and Court, with which they are
constantly and publicly at odds. Venezuela, for example, has on various
occasions declared that the rulings of the Court (based in San Jose) are a
violation of their sovereignty and must pass through the domestic court
system to be validated. The OAS has not helped their situation, capitulat-
ing repeatedly.

The second, and negative consequence of the ALBA's ideological nature has been the confrontation of the ALBA's heads of state with the
heads of state of other Latin-American nations. Contrary to promoting integration, these confrontations have caused considerable unease in
the region. Examples of this have been President Chavez' confrontation
with President Fox of Mexico, President Arias of Costa Rica, President
Toledo of Peru, President Garcia of Peru, President Calderon of Mexico,

President Uribe of Colombia, President Santos of Colombia, King Juan Carlos of Spain and Secretary General Insulza of the OAS. President Correa has fought with President Uribe. President Ortega has fought with President Laura Chinchilla of Costa Rica. President Morales has fought with President Lugo of Paraguay, and President Garcia of Peru, and with President Pinera of Chile. They have all fought quite publicly with Presidents Micheletti and Lobo. And the list goes on. Contrary to creating Latin-American integration, this constant bickering has instead caused significant problems in attempts to build regional harmony. Sometimes this bickering turned ugly, with Venezuelan threats of military action against Colombia, Guyana and Honduras; with Nicaraguan seizure of Costa Rican territory; and the rupture of relations between Ecuador and Colombia, Venezuela and Peru, Nicaragua and Colombia, all of them with Honduras, and so on.

Yet, while the ideological nature of the Alliance has brought friction to the region, it has also, in the minds of ALBA member countries, served to institutionalize the radical conflict that is an important component of Venezuelan foreign policy[134] and the ALBA Project. According to Fernando Bossi, the ALBA is the next phase of the "ancient and permanent confrontation between the Latin-American and Caribbean peoples and imperialism."[135] In this new phase, countries are placed under intense pressure to choose sides, to select whether they are on the side of Venezuela (and by extension the ALBA) or the United States.[136] For countries still economically interlinked with the United States, this represents a fool's choice. However, for increasingly politically independent governments that can count on the important support of Hugo Chavez—economic, political, ideological and motivational—this alternative to the Washington consensus and what they see as the hegemonic influence of the United States (and the strict limitations of representative democracy) is a welcome breath of the proverbial fresh air. Mixed with the burgeoning authoritarianism in ALBA countries, some countries have found a longed-for ally.

---

134 UN University—Comparative Regional Integration Studies, WP W/2008-4. P33.
135 Fernando Bossi, "Cuadernos de Emancipacion," N35, ISSN 0328-0179. P21.
136 Josette Altmann, "Integracion Latinoamericana: Cronica de una Crisis Anunciada," FLACSO, 15 de Septiembre, 2006. P7.

Ironically, as the new Honduran government found out, these countries might be replacing one unwanted hegemonic power for another. According to some, the ALBA represents the final manifestation of the hegemonic tendencies of Hugo Chavez's imperial plan.[137] More than even Venezuela, the ALBA is a deeply personal project that places Mr. Chavez at the center of this ever-widening group of nations. He is, in the mind of himself and others, the final figure of Bolivar, who is able to succeed where that liberator was unable—to unify the Gran Colombia under the power of his persona and the significant resources he brings to the table through petro-dollars. This is the heart of the ALBA, the political project of President Chavez to exert personal control over a greater swath of Latin-American territory and usher in 21st Century Socialism, placing his model of governance in opposition to the great hegemonic influence of American capitalism and remaking the mechanisms of integration in his own image.

Yet, besides being an alternative to the FTAA, an integration mechanism founded on 21st Century Socialism, and an anti-American, hegemonic alliance, what exactly is the ALBA? What are its foundations philosophically? What agreements have they signed, and what organizational components allow them to operate and to demonstrate the benefits of the Alliance—the famous social initiatives—to the majority poor within the member countries?

Fernando Bossi, one of the revolution's thinkers and a member of the Bolivarian Congress of the People, an ALBA Social Movement, has encapsulated the spirit of the ALBA into ten principles.[138]

1. *The ALBA is a historic project:* with roots in the conflict between Monroeism and Bolivarianism, the ALBA countries believe they have been victims of a two-century-long American conspiracy to deprive them of their natural resources, while relegating them to poverty and underdevelopment. They see this as their moment. They have finally woken up to their true governance mechanisms: popular and protagonist democracy, which will save them from their subjugation. Naturally, this project is not homogenous. The ALBA has succeeded in assembling a coalition that represents a

---

137 Carlos Malamud, "La Cumbre ALCUE de Madrid," Real Instituto Elcano, 16 de Mayo, 2010. P5.
138 Fernando Bossi, "Cuadernos de Emancipacion," N35, ISSN 0328-0179. P21.

broad range of actors. Anticapitalists, anarchists, environmentalists, gay and lesbian activists, communists, authoritarians and many others amass under the umbrella of the ALBA. Through their joint membership, through the "Social Movements of the ALBA," these widely antiestablishment groups have found their historical moment in the weakness of a world on fire.

2. *The ALBA is a new creation:* Unlike many of those who see the ALBA as a renewal of the USSR's failed model of communist, one-party central planning or the political extension of the Cuban revolution with a veneer of direct democracy, those building the ALBA from the ground up insist it is a new animal altogether. They reject the idea that the ALBA is a copy of some other mechanism, and are adamant that the act of building the ALBA must be without formulas. As they say, "Or we invent, or we err." They also reject the idea that they are attempting to build a Latin-American Union modeled after the European Union, or a United States, stating that these are intercapitalist and interimperialist organizations that still respond to the dictatorship of the capitalist model. It is for this reason that they emphatically insist that they must build their own organization, listening to "voices from the past that show the way to the future." In reality, this explains the chaotic improvisation that has led many to believe that the ALBA has no plan or direction. The builders of the ALBA would argue that it is in the very nature of their model of building the ALBA that allows for modification and experimentation, and that encourages failure as part of the process.[139]

3. *The ALBA is sustained by the potentials of Latin America and the Caribbean.*[140] The ALBA countries have woken up to the fact that they are some of the most naturally rich countries on the planet. From oil to bauxite, gold and silver, diamonds, timber and water, and agricultural land, these countries

---

139 Marta Harnecker, "Latin America & Twenty-First Century Socialism: Inventing to Avoid Mistakes," *Monthly Review*, July 28th, 2010.

140 This is probably the most important component of the ALBA. Arguably, the ALBA would not exist except for the economic support of Venezuela's oil sector. It is through the windfall profits that Chavez is able to subsidize the expansion of his regional agenda and deepen his 21st Century Socialist project. Through the nationalization of significant local industries, they have been able to seize important quantities of natural resources. And through complicity in the drug trade, they have been able to secure important off-budget resources for the Social Movements and other components of their political project.

possess untold riches. Too often these riches, like the chocolate of the Barlovento region of Venezuela, Ecuadorian oil, or Bolivian silver, are transferred to other countries for processing and commercialization. The markups represented for these goods are exorbitant, and the local producer, too, often remains in poverty. For the ALBA countries, this is the legacy of underinvestment by government after government too keen upon acts of corruption. Frustrated by underinvestment, local leaders such as Evo Morales declared at the IberoAmerican Summit in Madrid in May of 2010, "Bolivia will never negotiate the looting of our natural resources."

4. *The ALBA is based on anticapitalistic values:* Market capitalism is the global norm. After the collapse of all other economic systems, it is the unchallenged way in which people interact to meet their needs. Understanding this, the ALBA countries, despite moving forward in their ideological and political alliance, are still unable to make any headway in creating a new economic model. Their economic model proposed by intellectuals, 21st Century Socialism, has not been implemented. This has caused them to fall instead into state capitalism and statism. While they continue to say they want "an independent development model which prioritizes regional economic complementarity, brings into reality the desire to promote the development of everybody and strengthens genuine cooperation based on mutual respect and solidarity,"[141] they have been unable to advance this in any real way.

5. *The ALBA is an organization of popular construction:* Popular participation has been at the root of radical change in Latin America for decades. The argument is that the poor, uneducated and excluded sectors of society are finally, through these revolutionary movements, being given their opportunity to accede to the goods, services and resources from which they have been excluded. For this reason, in revolutions such as the Bolivarian Revolution in Venezuela or the Sandinista Revolution in Nicaragua, they talk about forming communal councils and of popular power, and of building their new societies from the ground up. This is from where the authority of the Social Movements of the ALBA comes (I will address this in another chapter). This is also where the idea of the permanent

---

141 IV Informe del Secretario General de FLACSO, Integración Regional, P37.

majority has emerged to co-opt historical representative democracy.[142] For this reason, the ALBA countries are exceedingly sensitive when it comes to majorities. They hold elections and plebiscites ad infinitim to demonstrate they are still a majority; they reject any suggestion that they could lose this majority; and they aggressively continue to work at the grass roots in communities to shore up their permanent majority. When this doesn't work, as has been suggested in Venezuela, they seek alternative methods to containing their majority such as lowering the voting age. They pad the voting register—there are reports that in Venezuela there are as many as one million ghost voters. They threaten, cajole and intimidate, and buy vote after vote. As their only remaining vestige of true democracy, they must at all costs continue to win elections.[143]

6. *The ALBA is one chapter in global revolution:* In this assertion, the ALBA countries align themselves with global revolutionary forces attempting to overthrow the current world order. These alliances seem to be indiscriminate, crossing ideological and religious bounds. Hugo Chavez has been accused of supporting ETA, IRA, FARC, Hezbollah, NFLP, MRTA, MEK, the Mapuches, and others such as the independence of Western Sahara, South Ossetia and Puerto Rico. This is also where the ALBA's counterintuitive relationship with Iran emerges. As energy exporters, they are natural competitors. They both have atrophied industrial sectors. Add to this the fact that Iran is suffering under crippling US and UN sanctions, and that makes them an illogical commercial partner. They are united only in their ideological attempts to confront the West and the United States. This principle also recognizes and enshrines the role of conflict in the building of the ALBA—a conflict that manifests itself both internally and externally.

---

142 Heinz Dieterich, "El Socialismo del Siglo 21," (2005): P1.

143 Yet, why is being a majority so important? This is where the Bolivarians find their defense of their radical agendas. Using direct democracy and the vote, they rewrite their constitutions to eliminate private property, protection of the minorities, and important freedoms such as speech and assembly. Upon any challenge by other democratic countries, they simply fall back upon their argument of the permanent majorities and cry vociferously that American representative democracy is in fact a conspiracy imposed upon poor, resource-rich countries to continue "the north's" pattern of perpetual domination. As they say, "Individuals die, governments pass, but the people remain forever."

7. *The ALBA is integration that is not based upon market economics:* Departing from the need to create a new world order, what the thinkers behind the ALBA believe is that this new order must not be grounded on market-based capitalism. That is to say, not upon consumption or profit. They use the old communist adage of "the greatest sum of happiness, of social security and political stability."

8. *The ALBA is a political tool:* The ALBA believes it is in their ability to interact together, to prop each other up in difficult moments, to use the joint power of their votes to avoid criticism within the OAS and the UN that they find power. This has been apparent in more than one case. When President Chavez has been in trouble due to issues of insecurity, incompetence or student movements, he has relied on support from Cuban intelligence. Morales, for his part, relied heavily upon Venezuelan support during the crisis of the "half moon" prefectures that were threatening to secede in 2009. During the recent 2010 crisis in Ecuador, Correa called upon support from the ALBA countries (and expanding from there to UNASUR) to assure that he remained in power. Their only failure came in their inability to keep, or return, Mel Zelaya to power in Honduras. That failure has haunted the ALBA, and has caused them to accelerate and increase their cooperation to assure that setbacks like that one will never happen again.

9. *The ALBA is the program for the Latin-American and Caribbean Revolution:* There is no other. This is vitally important to understand. Before, there were many revolutionary groups with affiliations: the Shining Path, the MRTA, the FARC, the ETA, the ELN, the FMLN, the FSLN, the EZLN, all with benefactors from Libya to Iran to North Korea, Syria, Cuba, the USSR and many other places. Now, Caracas is the center of continental revolution. President Chavez is not tied too closely to any individual revolutionary ideology. As long as people are attempting to cause chaos, upset the apple cart to build a new world order, he is content to let them work, and will finance whatever political project they might have. With support from Venezuela, they are engaged in three important revolutionary tasks: (1) educate and convince people about the need for the ALBA; (2) propagandize the good news of the ALBA to all the people of the region; and (3) start to organize and build links between groups

in member countries, and among social movements in countries that are not members yet.

10. *The ALBA is a strategic leap:* This is Chavez' project. As seen below, through this project he has spent tens of billions of dollars, brought other countries under the banner and created important links with terrorists. They are betting their mutual survival on the success of the ALBA. The future is unsure; they know this more than anybody. For this reason, they are aggressive.

What model are they pushing? And, how do they believe they will be able to achieve success in the face of such a powerful world market system? Any good leader knows that before one starts pushing forward with a plan, it's important to explain that plan well to one's followers. If they are participants in the discussions and understand clearly the direction—and believe in it—then they will be energetic foot soldiers in the task. Chavez' ALBA revolution is no different. Mr. Chavez has been remarkably flexible in allowing large groups of thinkers, philosophers, civil society organizations and social movements to drive the discussion and debate as to what the ALBA will eventually look like. In doing so, he has been able to tap into the large global movements such as the Foro de San Paulo, the world socialist fora, anarchist and communist movements, environmental movements and countless others.

As mentioned above, since the ALBA is now the only place in Latin America where these misfits can find a home, they have flocked to Chavez' ALBA revolution. Chavez didn't have to build this discussion; it has been going on for decades. He just had to name it. He called it 21st Century Socialism. This is the name under which Chavez has been advancing his agenda with the unwitting support from millions of global foot soldiers who, not understanding the reality of Venezuela or the true plans of Mr. Chavez, have fallen prey to his charisma and of their own delusional desire to see the world changed.

CHAPTER 7

The ALBA in Their Own Words

The previous chapters were based upon analysis and understanding of Venezuela and the ALBA, the political project behind 21st Century Socialism. However, it is also important to review what the Bolivarians say about themselves. An important component of the Bolivarian project is propaganda. Taken from the principles listed earlier, presidents of the ALBA member countries have understood the importance of organizing their message to assemble the groups they use to defend themselves. They do this exceedingly well; it is done through extensive use of the rhetoric of social justice. Those committed to the principle of *Esse Quam Videri*—To Be Rather Than To *Seem*—find objections to the propaganda that claims things are, even if they are not. That is the case for the ALBA. Like the Soviet Union before, the Bolivarians believe it is more important for people abroad (and at home) to think something about them, than to actually deliver, the hard work of service delivery a nuisance to the act of building a Revolution.

Through adept management of the terminology, the Bolivarians are able to purchase and hold friends who defend them abroad while they consolidate power at home. To do this, they have developed a sophisticated vocabulary which, coupled with an overpowering populism, has been able to camouflage the true intentions of the ALBA leaders.

On January 30, 2005, at the fifth World Social Forum sponsored by the Foro de Sao Paulo (FSP) in Porto Alegre (shortly after the creation of the ALBA), Hugo Chavez announced the new direction of Venezuela's

Bolivarian Revolution: 21st Century Socialism. The venue was important; the FSP has become important as one of the ALBA Social Movements that most successfully provides cover and support to the nouveau authoritarians of the 21st century.[144]

Only with a model that we are inventing of a 21st Century Socialism will there be true democracy, economic productivity, egalitarian distribution of resources, and we will succeed in providing equilibrium to a system that is still dangerously unequal.

So said Hugo Chavez on one of his weekly television shows, *Hello President*, in May 2005 following the forum.

Hugo Chavez, who met Dieterich in 1998 as Chavez was planning for his run for office and studying what approach to use for governance, took a while to arrive at socialism. He made the way there from what he claimed early on was a Tony Blair-styled third way. He had been told in his campaign to avoid the word revolution, to not appear too radical.[145] Yet, as time moved along he has radicalized, arriving at 21st Century Socialism in his second term.

However, it is important to see what the Venezuelan Bolivarian Government says about its own socialist model (and that of the ALBA). It is important to understand what they are trying to do, and how they describe their own process and how that process responds to some of the concerns about "totalitarian bourgeois bureaucracies" that led to the USSR's collapse. Based on their own document entitled "21st Century Socialism—The Force of the Small," from the ministry of Propaganda in Caracas, the authors take issue with Francis Fukuyama's comment about "The End of History" in his famous book, "The End of History and the Last Man"—rather, in their minds, the process has only just started. Folowing are the self-proclaimed tenets of the Venezuelan model:[146]

It's easy to see how the Bolivarians have been so successful in building their coalitions. Their big tent is broad and deep, and with the funding

---

144 Alejandro Pena Esclusa, "The Foro de Sao Paulo: A Threat to Freedom in Latin America" Alejandro Pena Esclusa, February 2009, Mary Montes, Editors, Bogota, Colombia.

145 Author interviews with confidential sources.

146 "Socialismo del Siglo XXI: La Fuerza de los Pobres," 2007 Ministerio de Comunicacion de Venezuela, If87120073201165.

from the Venezuelan government through the Social Movements and the permissive environment within the ALBA to experiment with socialist projects, they have assembled an army of defenders.

Tenet	Description
Egalitarian and Communal	All the riches in a territory should be distributed equally among members.
Property of the Means of Production is Collective	Majorities should own the means of production and the land to avoid the abuses of capitalism.
No Exploitation	Exploitation is eliminated slowly as the people become the owners of means of production who don't have to sell their "vital energy" to others.
Reform of the Market	The new market system should be guided by cooperation, complementarity and communal interests, not devastating competition leading to an amassing of capital.
State Participation	The government participates protagonistically in the defense of the will of the masses as an actor in itself.
Principles	
Learning from its Ancestors	While the new socialism does not break with Marx and Engels, it recognizes that in the past the USSR was abusive and destructive. The new socialists must learn from the issues that caused the collapse of this model.
An Ecological Socialism	New socialism should not try to subordinate human beings and the environment to an unlimited development of great industry. Instead, the model should advance alternative development, such as small industries, small farmers and more ecologically light footprints.
A Respectful Socialism that Believes In Its People	Must not impose criteria, or limit freedom and the fundamental rights of the populations — which deny the traditional substrate, which are the people.
An Amalgam of Many Socialisms	Not only Marxism, but learning from the Cuban socialism, indigenous socialism, and other small socialist streams that lead to the "great socialist river." Many of these are the revolutionaries of the continent including Sandino, Marti, Sucre and el "Che."

Tenet	Description
A Feminist Socialism	"21st Century Socialism, if it isn't feminist, isn't socialist." Must vindicate the rights of the excluded—and this includes women.
A Wise Socialism	"21st Century Socialism is an open window to see the panorama of responses by those who wish to eliminate injustice." It is an inclusive process that learns from the idiosyncrasies of all revolutionary socialist movements and becomes instead, "…the socialisms of the 21st Century."
Tailor-made Socialism	Each country understands the needs, benefits and requirements of their country to overcome "injustice" and create a socialist world.
A Christian Socialism	Rejecting the atheism that in part led to the collapse of the USSR, 21st Century Socialism embraces the "Liberation Theology" of the Catholic Church as taught by priests such as Paulo Freire.
A Healthy Socialism	A vibrant body of communal creation which allows the model to work and grow.

CHAPTER 8

Dictatorships of the 21st Century

There are those who minimize, through ignorance or interest, the expansionism of the ALBA group, saying it is limited to the governments of Venezuela, Cuba, Ecuador, Nicaragua and Bolivia. However, they forget that this group is only the most radical of a much larger group integrated by governments and parties into the much larger Foro de Sao Paulo. (…) The strength of the ALBA group is that they surround themselves and advance protected by numerous and diverse partners in the journey, like during the Cold War. (…) If Chavez' project triumphs in the region we will witness the end of the third wave of democracy that started toward the end of the 1970s. We will return to the era of dictators, but this time with the ideological sign called Socialism of the 21st Century.…[147]

With these words, Oscar Alvarez Araya, a well-respected Costa Rican diplomat and thinker, expresses the fundamental concern democrats have about 21st Century Socialism. Below are outlined some of the fundamental tenets of this new socialist plan.

Political Constitutions: The Bolivarian political package begins with the rewriting of their constitutions. We have witnessed this in Venezuela, Bolivia and Ecuador, who called constituent assemblies. Honduras was able to keep their 1982 constitution only through the early departure of Zelaya. In Nicaragua, Ortega is first attempting to consolidate his power. Should

147 Oscar Alvarez Araya, "Valores, Humanismo y Democracia," Lara Segura Editorial, (2010) ISBN: 978-9968-930-29-1. P 191.

he win the absolute majority of the Nicaraguan Congress in the 2011 elections, a constitutional reform will most probably ensue. Ollanta Humala, Peru's Bolivarian President has already said, only days into his presidency, that his government will be attempting constitutional reforms. These constitutional reforms are critical to building 21st Century Socialism. They allow the governments to eliminate institutions of government, with a constituent assembly governing for a period of time. When the constitution is finally approved, the new texts allow the increase in the power of the executive, eliminate or loosen term limits, and rewrite the nuclei of hard rights allowing language to dismantle these rights. They also place restrictions on speech and private property. Most importantly, these reforms set in place the "protagonist and participatory democracy" used to progressively limit rights and co-opt the institutions of state.

Increase Conflict: Those who witness the conflict in Bolivia on the issues of decentralization; or in Ecuador due to the constant struggle between the executive and with the police, the National Assembly, and the judiciary; or in Venezuela between the Chavistas and the private sector, business and opposition; or in Nicaragua between Ortega and the judiciary, business, the congress and the opposition, see a pattern—the creation of hostility between sectors of society. This conflict is used as an excuse to accelerate radical change. As Dieterich explained in his comments on permanent majorities, it is important to use the presence of the millions of people, through their incessant voting processes, to create a war at the grass roots—a war they know they can win. This war seeks to destroy the opposition, as advocated by Ceresole and Dieterich. As Alvarez says in his book,[148] Chavez and the ALBA use electioneering and populism to deepen their majorities and to build and keep their permanent majorities on their side. The conflicts are not only internal. Ecuador and Venezuela have created conflicts with Colombia; Nicaragua has engaged in a border conflict with Costa Rica; Bolivia has fought with Chile and Peru; they all increase their conflict with the United States.

The conflict with the United States is particularly important. As can be seen in the decibels of rhetoric against US imperialism, juxtaposing the

---

148 Oscar Alvarez Araya, "Valores, Humanismo y Democracia," Lara Segura Editorial, (2010) ISBN: 978-9968-930-29-1. P 191.

images of an imperial tyranny motivates the diehard Bolivarians. For the revolutionaries—the fight against a goliath is part of the joy of the fight. And blaming the United States is an effective scapegoat for internal problems as well.

Establish New Leaderships: In ALBA countries, the idea is to establish the citizens power into the body that controls national decision-making. This is done by placing the leader (read Morales, Ortega, Correa, Chavez, and so on) at the center of the people-leader relationship and weakening any institutionalism that would place limitations on their power. This eliminates the need for local government through the creation of communes in Venezuela, Committees for citizens Power (CPCs) in Nicaragua or Committees for the Defense of the Revolution (CDRs) in Cuba. As Dieterich would say, this is the ideal state of self-governing locally, with an important "caudillo" watching over the affairs of the state from above.

Transform State Institutions: The institutions must be fundamentally reorganized, from bureaucratic entities to organizations promoting the political ideology of the revolution. Diplomats are fired from the Venezuelan embassy in Washington, told they were not wanted because, "all the employees must be pulling in the same direction (...) have the same Bolivarian vision." Before promotions (military or civilian) in Ecuador[149] (and all ALBA countries), public servants are asked if they are willing to defend the revolution. The democratic idea of a professional, non-partisan bureaucracy is shoved aside at the expense of an activist government seeking to advance a partisan political project.

Control the Media: This becomes essential, to reduce the voice of other actors so the debate for the creation of the "new nation" is only one of degrees. They do not allow the debate on alternative mechanisms of economics or government. As Dieterich said, "The debate about capitalism must fall to the side." Free speech, as such, is only allowed within the bounds of the new revolutionary doctrine. For this reason, as Andres Izarra—president of the ALBA television network TeleSUR—said, "It is important to gain communicational hegemony in order to build the plans of the president (Chavez)." The old Soviet Union was also a master of propaganda, and considered propaganda a mechanism to build the communist state.

---

149 Author interviews with confidential sources.

Within degrees, the ALBA countries have also adopted state-sponsored propaganda mechanisms. While the debate is much more rich than it was in the USSR, it is still only permitted within the loose confines of the revolution. Counter-revolutionary debate is punished by seizure, censure or closure. This is evident in Bolivia by the September 2010 antiracism laws, that provide the Bolivian government the opportunity to close media outlets; the closure of RCTV in Venezuela; and the purchase of Chanel 8 by Ortega's ALBANISA in Nicaragua (through the use of ALBA funding from Venezuela). Ecuador closed TV stations and has sued the main opposition newspaper for millions for defamation of character of the president. In all these countries, dozens of radio stations have been closed.

The setup of these "Dictatorships of the 21st Century" has come with a price, and the cost can be counted in the currency of freedom. As the revolutionary ALBA governments attempt to socially reengineer the fabric of liberal society, hard-fought and hard-won, they have found that success lies only in their ability to eliminate the "truths we hold self-evident," Oscar Arias' "nucleus of hard rights."

Over the years the international community set in place, through its vibrant civil society organizations, many objectively verifiable indicators that are used to evaluate the democratic performance of countries. However, there is also an important principle to follow, which is to go with what works. For those without ideological bent, the recognition is that any system increasing well-being, and allowing its citizens to live in greater freedom in societies more responsive to their wants and needs, is fine. For this reason, below, here are some of the statistics on freedom inside ALBA countries in areas of: human freedom, transparency/corruption, economic freedom, press freedom, and competitiveness (as an indicator of the health of the free market).

Hugo Chavez and the ALBA countries obtain some of their success through their ability to control the dialogue surrounding their revolutionary processes (effective use of propaganda). In doing this, they continue to provoke a broad debate on capitalism and market economics, and how best to meet the social needs of the poorest. While they keep us debating this ad nauseam, they use the cover provided by the debate to set in place their dictatorships. Here are three things one must remember while examining the charts below:

1. Venezuela is the end goal of the Bolivarian countries. Therefore, the fact that Venezuela is far worse than the other countries is because they are further (twelve years) down the path toward 21st Century Socialism than the others.

2. This is a gradual process. Unlike past revolutions that were fast and bloody and brutal, the setting up of these new dictatorships usually happens bit by bit.

3. The ALBA itself is only six years old, and some countries (such as Ecuador) have only been members for a little over two years. The process of dismantling democracy takes time.

Human Freedom: The negative progression of human freedom in the ALBA countries has been gradual; most notably in Honduras and Venezuela. Take below the table from Freedom House's annual Freedom in the World Survey[150]. This survey rates countries from 1 to 7, 1 being totally free and 7 totally unfree.

Freedom House "Freedom in the World"											
(Note: "CL" stands for civil liberties, "PL" for political rights.)											
Country	2005		2006		2007		2008		2009		2010	
	CL	PR	CL	PR	CL	PR	CL	PR	CL	PR	CL	PR
Antigua	2	3	2	2	2	2	2	2	2	2	2	3
Bolivia	3	3	3	3	3	3	3	3	3	3	3	3
Cuba	7	7	7	7	7	7	7	7	6	7	6	7
Dominica	1	1	1	1	1	1	1	1	1	1	1	1
Ecuador	3	3	3	3	3	3	3	3	3	3	3	3
Honduras	3	3	3	3	3	3	3	3	3	3	4	4
Nicaragua	3	3	3	3	3	3	3	3	3	4	4	4
St. Vincent	1	2	1	2	1	2	1	2	1	2	1	2
Venezuela	4	3	4	4	4	4	4	4	4	4	4	5

150 Freedom House Table on Civil Liberties and Political Rights. http://www.freedomhouse.org/template.cfm?page=15

Corruption: The political projects of these countries advance upon corruption. Secretive, centralized government is never very responsive to the people, and politicized bureaucracy where people are chosen not by their merit but by ideology provides fertile ground for corruption. Simultaneously, these projects use government resources for partisan projects and require soft money, for which they must not be accountable, to fund the propaganda and people movements—and electoral events—upon which rests their direct democracy. The indicators below rank countries against each other, with 1 being the most transparent and 190 the least[151].

Transparency International Index						
Country	2005	2006	2007	2008	2009	2010
Antigua	n/a	n/a	n/a	n/a	n/a	n/a
Bolivia	117	105	105	102	120	110
Cuba	59	66	61	65	61	69
Dominica	n/a	53	37	33	34	44
Ecuador	117	138	150	151	146	127
Honduras	107	121	131	126	130	134
Nicaragua	107	111	123	134	130	127
St. Vincent	n/a	n/a	30	n/a	n/a	n/a
Venezuela	130	138	162	158	162	164

Economic Freedom: For those of us who believe the free market is the only way to assure freedom in the supply of the diverse needs and wants of people, the collapse of the ALBA countries in this area is emblematic of the ills these economies suffer. It must be noted, again, this is a gradual process but the end game is manipulation of member countries' free market (as I demonstrated above through the essays of Dieterich). This index uses 1 as most economically free, and 0 as economically unfree. The countries are rated against themselves[152].

---

151 Transparency International table on perceptions of corruption. http://www.transparency.org/policy_research/surveys_indices/cpi/2010
152 Heritage Foundation Index of Economic Freedom. http://www.heritage.org/Index

Heritage Foundation Economic Freedom Index						
Country	2005	2006	2007	2008	2009	2010
Antigua	NR	NR	NR	NR	NR	NR
Bolivia	58.4	57.8	54.2	53.1	53.6	49.4
Cuba	35.5	29.3	28.6	27.5	27.9	26.7
Dominica	NR	NR	NR	NR	62.6	63.2
Ecuador	52.9	54.6	55.3	55.2	52.5	49.3
Honduras	55.3	57.4	59.1	58.9	58.7	58.3
Nicaragua	62.5	63.8	62.7	60.8	59.8	58.3
St. Vincent	NR	NR	NR	NR	64.2	66.9
Venezuela	45.2	44.6	47.9	44.7	39.9	37.1

Freedom of Speech: One of the most important components of a democratic society is the ability of a free press to shine a light on issues and hold government accountable. Governments that are corrupt by design do not like this—and believe that only as they have "communicational hegemony"[153] are they able to build their revolutions. As those of us who study democracy know, dissent fosters freedom. In the ALBA, as demonstrated by the table below, this is the first human right sacrificed. In the below table, countries are rated against each other with 1 being the country with the freest press environment and 190 the least free[154].

Reporters Without Borders Press Freedom Index						
Country	2005	2006	2007	2008	2009	2010
Antigua	NR	NR	NR	NR	NR	NR
Bolivia	45	16	68	115	95	103
Cuba	161	165	165	169	170	166
Dominica	NR	NR	NR	NR	NR	NR
Ecuador	87	68	56	74	84	101
Honduras	76	62	87	99	128	143
Nicaragua	68	69	47	59	76	83

153 "Andres Izarra: El socialismo necesita una hegemonía comunicacional," Boletin Digital Universitario, 8 de Enero, 2007. http://www.boletin.uc.edu.ve/index.php?option=com_content&task=view&id=4990&Itemid=38

154 Reporters Without Borders Press Freedom Index. http://en.rsf.org/spip.php?page=classement&id_rubrique=1034

St. Vincent	NR	NR	NR	NR	NR	NR
Venezuela	90	115	114	113	124	133

Competitiveness: The World Economic Forum, recognizing that a competitive economic environment is most healthy for economic growth, provides an annual index. In this index, they compare countries to each other, with again 1 being the most competitive and 190 being the least competitive.[155]

World Economic Forum Global Competitiveness Report						
Country	2005	2006	2007	2008	2009	2010
Antigua	NR	NR	NR	NR	NR	NR
Bolivia	101	100	105	118	120	108
Cuba	NR	NR	NR	NR	NR	NR
Dominica	NR	NR	NR	NR	NR	NR
Ecuador	87	94	103	104	105	105
Honduras	97	90	82	83	89	91
Nicaragua	96	101	111	120	115	112
St. Vincent	NR	NR	NR	NR	NR	NR
Venezuela	84	85	98	105	113	122

As demonstrated above, in key areas of democratic and economic freedom, the ALBA nations are heading in the wrong direction. During a moment when most countries are advancing in freedom and prosperity, the ALBA shines by its resolute march into the past.

Below, is the UNDP HDI, which stands for the United Nations Development Program Human Development Index, the organization's premier tool to measure the advance of countries on social issues. The tool isn't perfect. One limitation is that the United Nations HDI only includes basic items such as health care, food, water; it does not pretend to quantify personal freedoms.

The ALBA countries state that their end goal is greater well-being of the majority. To do this more efficiently, they say, they must dismantle the infrastructure of representative democracy, which they claim is limiting their

---

155 World Economic Forum Global Competitiveness Index. http://www.weforum.org/en/initiatives/gcp/Global%20Competitiveness%20Report/PastReports/index.htm

ability to do their work. As Maripili Hernandez, former Under-Minister of Foreign Affairs for North America, said in her speech at the UN Human Rights Commission in Geneva, "We need to place emphasis on social and cultural rights, which is why Venezuela has focused on promoting the Social Charter of the Americas."[156] And in the same meeting, she declared, "What good is free speech, if you can't read?" For this reason it's important to evaluate whether the ALBA nations have increased in HDI since joining ALBA and beginning their 21st Century Socialist project. The trajectory is quite apparent. As is demonstrated in the below chart, the ALBA country ratings have collapsed. This collapse is shown below in real numbers (in order for the reader to evaluate the ALBA only against its own performance) as well as in country comparisons.

Year	2000	2001*	2002*	2003*	2004*	2005	2006*	2007*	2008*	2009*	2010
Bolivia	80	82.4	84.8	87.2	89.6	92	92.6	93.2	93.8	94.4	95
Cuba	..	..	..	..	..	..	..	..	..	..	..
Ecuador	63	65.4	67.8	70.2	72.6	75	75.4	75.8	76.2	76.6	77
Nicaragua	92	96.21	100.4	104.6	108.79	113	113.4	113.8	114.2	114.6	115
Venezuela	65	67.6	70.2	72.8	75.4	78	77.4	76.8	76.2	75.6	75

				HDI value			
	2000	2005	2006	2007	2008	2009	2010
Bolivia (Plurinational State of)	0.593	0.631	0.631	0.625	0.632	0.637	0.643
Cuba	..	..	..	..	..	..	..
Ecuador	0.642	0.676	0.681	0.685	0.691	0.692	0.695
Nicaragua	0.512	0.545	0.55	0.555	0.56	0.562	0.565
Venezuela (Bolivarian Republic of)	0.637	0.666	0.677	0.689	0.697	0.696	0.696

---

156 http://www.vtv.gov.ve/noticias-nacionales/5503

Finally, according to Barclay's Research,[157] Venezuela's performance in well-being creation is dismal. According to their analysis, over the last twelve years Venezuela earned more than $480 billion in oil revenues (other sources put the income at over one trillion dollars). However due to the steady stream of politically motivated nationalizations, foreign direct investment has collapsed and as a result Venezuela has been unable to keep up with their population in job creation. Between 2000 and 2009, only 2.1 million jobs were created, half in the public sector, which is only fifty-one percent of the jobs necessary to keep up with demand. Furthermore, real salaries dropped twenty percent over this time due to inflation. In other social areas, such as access to water, Venezuela only improved two percent over the ten-year period while Mexico and Brazil have doubled this improvement. The same is true for infant mortality; Brazil improved three-fold, and Colombia has outperformed Venezuela by two hundred percent, even based upon less-than-trustworthy government statistics. Such poor performance, after such an unprecedented flood of oil money ($35,000 per citizen), demonstrates the utter failure of the Bolivarian Revolution in Venezuela to provide a better life for its citizens, in either basic freedoms or in social advances.

It is clear that the ALBA justifies its dismantling of representative democracy and the corresponding civil rights as necessary to rapidly improve well-being. Nevertheless, (as demonstrated by Venezuela), countries asked to sacrifice in their gateway rights for the possibility of an economic, social or cultural right soon become aware they are being asked to make a fool's choice. The other ALBA countries would be wise to take note of the only possible end at which these destructive policies will arrive.

---

157 "Venezuela, Evaluating the Bolivarian Revolution," November 4, 2010, Barclays Emerging Markets Research. www.barcap.com

CHAPTER 9

The Infrastructure
of the Bolivarian Alliance

Over its short six-year history, the ALBA has been extraordinarily active politically, economically, and socially. On the political front, the ALBA has carried out sixteen presidential summits and a myriad of other technical and ministerial meetings. These summits serve to add new members, to define key joint positions for upcoming international events (like the Summits of the Americas summarized in the following table, or the UN General Assembly meetings), and to offer each other political support. The latter is especially important due to the instability that radical political changes bring about internally.

During the Seventh ALBA Summit, which took place in Cochabamba, Bolivia on October 17, 2009, the ALBA agreed upon a skeletal structure that allowed for staffing and organization to provide follow-up to the ALBA-TCP (People's Trade Agreement) projects and activities. The infrastructure is overseen by a presidential council, to which social, economic and political and Social Movements councils and respective commissions report. An executive secretariat was created, with a leadership structure and an Executive Secretary. The executive secretary's office is in Caracas, and the current Secretary is Amenhotep Zambrano. The staffing structure of the office is as follows:

First Summit	Havana, Cuba	Dec. 14, 2004	· Joint Declaration Establishing the ALBA between Cuba and Venezuela
			· Twelve Founding Principles Agreed upon
Second Summit	Havana, Cuba	27-Apr-05	· Strategic plan to promote the ALBA is signed
Third Summit	Havana, Cuba	28-Apr-06	· Bolivia joins the ALBA
			· Bolivia proposes the creation of the People's Trade Agreement
Fourth Summit	Managua, Nicaragua	11-Jan-07	· Nicaragua joins the ALBA during the inauguration of newly elected President Daniel Ortega
Fifth Summit	Tintorero, Venezuela	27-Apr-07	· Introduced the idea of Grand National Projects and Companies
			· Energy Agreement Signed
Sixth Summit	Caracas, Venezuela	26-Jan-08	· Dominica joins the ALBA
			· Grand National Projects and Companies are defined
First Extraordinary Summit	Caracas, Venezuela	23-Apr-08	· Agreements to support food security
			· ALBA declares political support for Bolivia
Second Extraordinary Summit	Teguc, Honduras	25-Aug-08	· Honduras joins the ALBA
			· Agreements signed to support social projects in Honduras
Third Extraordinary Summit	Caracas, Venezuela	26-Nov-08	· Agreed to create the regional trade currency SUCRE
Fourth Extraordinary Summit	Caracas, Venezuela	2-Feb-09	· Agreed upon strategic objectives in the social arena
			· Created a Grand National Project and company to support food production

Fifth Extraordinary Summit	Cumana, Venezuela	16-Apr-09	·Created ALBA Cultural Fund, Grand National Energy projects, and a Grand National medicine and drug project
			·Agreed to fund projects in Haiti
			·Agreed upon the position of ALBA countries during the upcoming Summit of the Americas
Sixth Extraordinary Summit	Maracay, Venezuela	24-Jun-09	·Ecuador, St. Vincent and the Grenadines and Antigua and Barbuda join the ALBA as newest members. Creation of a joint commission to organize the celebration of the bicentennial
Seventh Summit	Cochabamba, Bolivia	Oct. 17, 2009	·Establish the principles of the Peoples Trade Agreement
			·Approved a plan of action for the development of trade between ALBA countries
			·Modified the structure of the ALBA
			·Special declarations on: Environment, Climate Change, Honduras and the demand to end the Cuba embargo
Eighth Summit	Havana, Cuba	Dec. 13, 2009	·Approved the work of the ALBA Peoples Trade Agreement
			·Approved the Structure and Funding of the ALBA Peoples Trade Agreement (including the ALBA Bank)
Ninth Summit	Caracas, Venezuela	19-Apr-10	·Reiterated the principles of the ALBA
Tenth Summit	Otavalo, Ecuador	25-Jun-10	·Summit focused upon indigenous issues

ALBA Executive Secretariat
Av. Francisco Solano, Esq.
Calle San Geronimo, Edif. Los Llanos, Piso 8. Sabana Grande, Parroquia El Recreo.
Caracas, Venezuela
Phone: 011-58 (212) 905 93 55
Fax: 011-58 (212) 761 13 64
Amenhotep Zambrano
Executive Secretary
Adjunct Secretary to the Executive Secretary
Coordinator for Social Issues
Coordinator for Social Movement Issues
Coordinator for Grand National Projects and Companies
Coordinator for Economic Issues
Coordinator for Economic Issues
Coordinator for Economic Issues
Coordinator for Communication and Information
Coordinator for Communication and Information
Coordinator for Statistics
Secretary

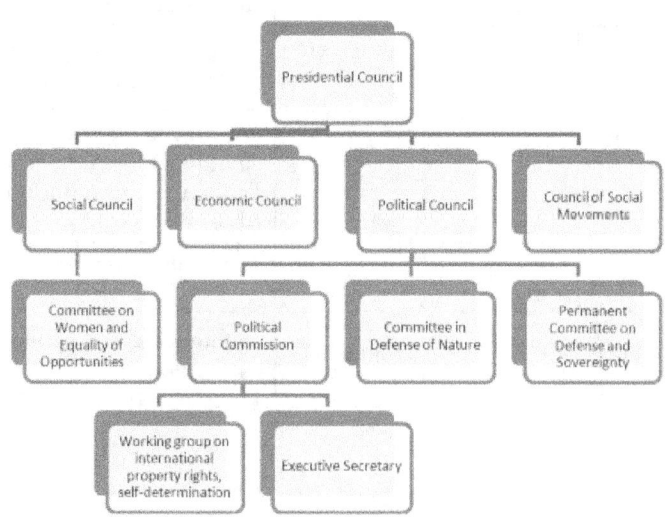

This skeleton seeks to institutionalize, stabilize and thereby rapidly advance the ALBA's advancement across the region. To do this, they needed to have the mechanisms and staff (as outlined above). ALBA projects are, by nature, bilateral assistance (unless they are carried out by the Social Movements), so the funding and initiatives are driven by host governments. Each ALBA member country has designated ALBA coordinators based upon the relevance and importance they give to the ALBA relationship. For example, in Nicaragua the Ortega regime has realized that the ALBA's political and economic support is essential for it to continue its bid to rule Nicaragua indefinitely. For this reason, Daniel Ortega has placed Rosario Murillo—the first lady—as point person for the ALBA there.

ALBA Coordinators by Country		
Venezuela	Maria Jacqueline Mendoza	Vice-Minister for Latin America and the Caribbean
Cuba	Rogelio Sierra	Vice-Minister for Latin America and the Caribbean
Bolivia	Huascar Ajata	National Coordinator for ALBA in Bolivia
Nicaragua	Rosario Murillo	National Coordinator for ALBA in Nicaragua (and Nicaraguan First Lady)
Dominica	Aaron Philberth	National Coordinator for ALBA in Dominica
Ecuador	Jose Rafael Serrano	National Coordinator for ALBA in Ecuador
St. Vincent and the Grenadines	Ellworth John	National Coordinator for ALBA in St. Vincent and the Grenadines
Antigua and Barbuda	Joan H. Underwood	National Coordinator for the ALBA in Antigua and Barbuda

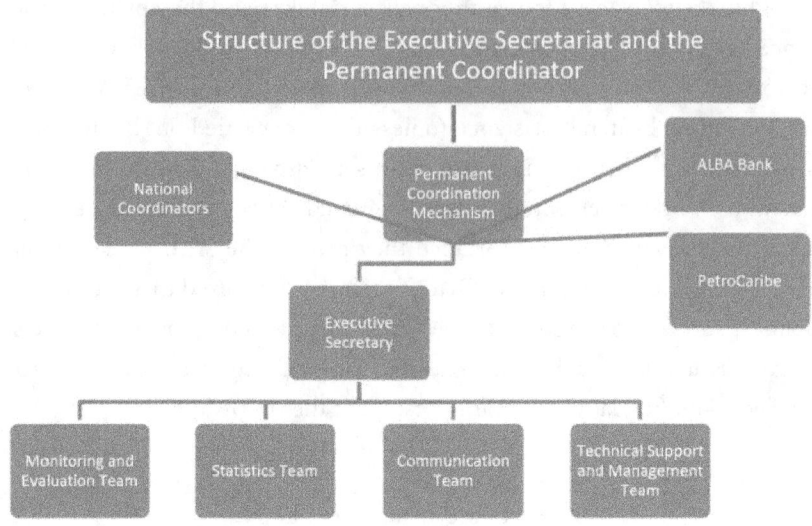

The ALBA knows that the rapid provision of social services to the poor is their niche activity that will provide them political cover and internal/international support. To this end, the ALBA has established Grand National Projects to provide these services. These projects are in varying degrees of development and, at least for now, lean heavily upon the support and discipline of Cuban community workers and mobilizers. There are more than forty thousand official Cubans in Venezuela, eighteen thousand Cubans and thirteen thousand Venezuelans in Ecuador. There are also many Venezuelan and Cuban military and social workers in Bolivia, although the number is difficult to ascertain. To a lesser degree Nicaragua, which already has its foot soldiers in the FSLN, receives support from ALBA member countries. For this reason, when it comes to ALBA health or the "Yes I Can" literacy program, the progress is much more significant than in other ALBA projects such as tourism. In the advancement of the ALBA, they created Grand National Businesses as corporate structures to advance their statist projects such as tourism, trade, agriculture and energy. They also quickly realized that they needed a way to fund these Grand National projects, and envisioned an ALBA Development Bank, which could assume financing operations. They have set in place a regional trade currency, and have developed a sophisticated communications infrastructure to deliver their messages to the grass roots across the region. Following are specific descriptions of the sixteen different ALBA projects currently contemplated.

Grand National Concept

In brief, the Grand National concept as laid out by the ALBA has the following characteristics:[158]

1. Geopolitical and historic—focusing on the unification of the countries of the ALBA. Essentially, the idea of a "mega-state," or as Ceresole, Dieterich and Chavez called it, the "Patria Grande" (great fatherland). Simon Bolivar called it the Gran Colombia and the Congress of Panama.
2. Socioeconomic base—the development of the economies should be for the satisfaction of the basic needs of the majority, and this cannot be done if limited to local geography
3. Ideological—these projects are a natural expression of the rejection of neoliberal ideas such as globalization and capitalism, focused instead on sustainable development and social justice (this is where the principle of conflict enters).

Within the Grand National concepts, there are two components: the Grand National projects and their corresponding Grand National companies.

Grand National Projects are the operationalization of the aforementioned philosophy in a specific area of economic, social, cultural or political life. These projects must be carried out in at least two ALBA countries, but do not necessarily require the participation of the entire ALBA confederation. At times, participation takes a phased approach such as the "Yes I Can" literacy program, which was first implemented in Venezuela, then Bolivia, then Ecuador, and has now moved to Nicaragua. Nevertheless, the projects must support the ALBA philosophy and ideology as a whole and be agreed upon by the relevant technical council and then by the Presidential Council. There are currently twelve Grand National projects in various stages of development.

Grand National companies are in essence the operational arms of Grand National projects. They emerge in opposition to capitalism's

---

158 "Conceptualización de Proyecto y Empresa Grannacional en el Marco del ALBA – Documentos del VI Cumbre," 30 de Octubre, 2009. http://www.alianzabolivariana.org/modules.php?name=Content&pa=showpage&pid=2074

transnational companies. The eventual idea of the Grand National companies is to create a huge network of industries involved with what the Bolivarians call "just trade" across Latin America. Grand National companies are state-owned enterprises. Grand National companies are organized around the ideas of solidarity, complementarity, cooperation and sustainability. They can only be successful insofar as they emerge from the activity of Grand National planning (read central planning, or Dieterich's Regional Democratic Developmentalism through a democratically planned economy), and through the control of the raw goods and natural resources.

Grand National Projects	Updates & Status of Project
Food Security	Grand National Project and Company created
	ALBA of Nicaragua selling food to Venezuela, now Nicaragua's second most important customer
Environment	ALBA opposition to climate change agreements in Copenhagen
	Bolivia holds a climate summit in 2010 calling for the reation of a climate court
Science and Technology	Inactive
Fair Trade	Inactive
Culture	Three Olympic- style ALBA Games held in Cuba (300 athletes, 23 countries in 37 different sports) (Update: A fourth ALBA Games was held in the summer of 2011 in Caracas)
	Establishing a "Casa del ALBA" in Havana, set to be established in La Paz and Managua
	Magazine and other publications
	In Bolivia supported the creation of a government magazine "Identities"
	Host for coordination of diverse activities related to the bicentennial year of the independence of Venezuela (which is close to other ALBA countries, making a continent-wide celebration)
	Literature competition
	A regional fellowship program affording ten fellowships a year
	191 organizations across member-states formally affiliated

Grand National Projects	Updates & Status of Project
Education	"Yes I Can" Cuban literacy program declared the region "free of illiteracy"
Energy	Energy is the lifeblood of the ALBA
	PetroAmerica includes one large petroleum company from Argentina to Mexico. A gas pipeline from Venezuela to Argentina. PetroAmerica is inactive
	PetroCaribe works as part of PetroAmerica. Manages Fondo ALBA Caribe which has planned many projects across the Caribbean (which has morphed into the ALBA Bank)
	Provides oil at a discounted rate (not to people, but to foreign governments)
	It is unclear as to the advances of these projects — one would have to visit each country in question. It is, however, important to note that the only refinery project completed of more than 30 promised by President Chavez has been Cien Fuegos in Cuba. The storage facilities are completed for Nicaragua and El Salvador.
	ALBA Energy has assisted in supplying hundreds of electric generators to Ecuador, Nicaragua and Venezuela — along with Cuban experts — to produce additional megawatts into the national grid
Mining and Industry	Joint mining company was created. Rumors that Iran is searching for uranium through this company
Health	Pharmaceutical project based out of Cuba's State Center for the Quality and Control of Medicines supplies drugs to ALBA countries
	Handicap project, seeking to reduce discrimination toward handicapped people and take a census of the number of handicapped people, 72,000 social workers visited 2,000,000 homes and worked with 900,000 handicapped people and 1,100,000 non-handicapped people to reduce stigma
	Miracle Mission Eye operations have operated on more than 1,100,000 people from twenty different countries
	Latin-American School of Medicine has trained 1,700 doctors from ALBA countries
	Haiti Humanitarian Assistance manages five internally displaced persons (IDP) camps in Haiti for 17,000 people

Grand National Projects	Updates & Status of Project
Tele-communications	Purchased the Simon Bolivar Satellite for $430 million from China (and announced the purchase of another for spying)
	Completed the project of laying an underwater fiberoptic cable from Venezuela to Cuba
	Established regional television news station TeleSUR with affiliates in more than ten countries
	Established news wire services, a network of hundreds of community radio stations
	ALBA Multi-Channel website with links to thousands of interviews, movies, programs, and documentaries down-loadable for free for community TV stations
	ALBA Radio of the South with live-feed access for community radios
	ALBA Ciudad Radio with live-feed access for community radio stations
	Radio stations, thousands of websites and an army o f bloggers
Transport	Envisions a regional airline and ship line, but is currently inactive
Tourism	Has held various tourism fairs in Caracas. Seeks to establish a "liberators route" but to-date mostly inactive

Grand National Project ALBA Culture

An important component of the Bolivarian project is belief that the weight of traditional western culture and media, represented mostly by Hollywood and the US entertainment industry, has crushed the richness of Latin-American revolutionary culture. Many Latin Americans from across the political spectrum lament being unable to make their cultural heritage felt and respected. This has certain merit. As in other regions of the world, Hollywood has permeated Latin America as US-created movies, books and television shows are perceived to dominate the airwaves. Superior techni-cal and programmatic ability and substantially more financing has allowed US media to outperform media from other regions of the world. The ALBA countries have taken this as a personal insult. In their mind, looking back upon their past in idyllic images of peasant perfection, Hollywood is destroying their cultural heritage; they even blame Hollywood for the high levels of violence in their countries. As Oscar Arias said in his article "Culture Matters" in *Foreign Affairs* magazine, "Latin Americans glorify their past so ceaselessly that they make it almost impossible to advocate change."[159]

The ALBA countries, led by Hugo Chavez, understand this. Through the process of assembling the Bolivarian ideology from a hodgepodge of different authors, President Chavez found Antonio Gramsci.

> Therefore I'm going to resort to the thought, to some of the ideas of this great Italian revolutionary thinker, Antonio Gramsci, to make an observation about the moment that we are living. A truly historic crisis occurs when something is dying ... but has not finished dying, and at the same time there is something that is being born but which also hasn't finished being born. In the time and space where this occurs, an authentic organic crisis unfolds, an historic crisis, a total crisis. Here, in Venezuela, let's not forget that for several years we have been right in the middle of a true organic crisis, a true Gramscian crisis, a historic crisis. That what is dying refuses to die and doesn't finish dying and that what is being born has not yet been completely born either. We are in the epicenter of the crisis, a good number of the years to come are part of this historic crisis as long as the IV Republic has not yet definitely died and the V Republic, the Socialist and Bolivarian Republic of Venezuela, has not completely been.[160]

Such are the interpretations of Gramsci by Hugo Chavez. Of course, one of the powers of Gramsci's ideology was the vision of blocks of society, political society and civil society. These were not meant to be separated, but should all be unified through the state's use of the unifying power of culture.

More than any others, the ALBA governments are able to see the powerful political tool that culture can play in the unification of their disparate countries and the advancing of their revolutionary agendas. For the ALBA countries, that very culture has been marinated in revolution since the beginning. The values, the stories, and the history itself can only be

---

159 Oscar Arias, "Culture Matters," Foreign Affairs, January-February 2011 Edition, P3.
160 Antonio Maira, "Hugo Chavez presents Gramsci to hundreds of thousands of people," Axis of Logic, June 28, 2007. http://www.axisoflogic.com/artman/publish/article_24813.shtml

seen through the optics of Latin-American revolution. And the culture of revolution is a powerful unifying and motivating force in Latin America.

It's important here to understand the love affair many Latin Americans have with revolution. This love affair with romantic revolutionary activity comes as a reaction to multiple external sources. One of these is religion.

The Catholic Church in Latin America has come to be seen, over time, as an organization dedicated to the protection of the upper class and the privileges of the elite. Instead of following the doctrine of the Irish Catholic Church in the early centuries, the Latin-American Catholic Church, led by the Jesuits (and the extremely brutal Spanish Catholic missionaries), have come to be associated with instruments of repression. And rightly so, since Latin-American Catholicism was the ideological tool of the conquistadores to justify their rape, pillage, destruction—and conversion—of the locals. The Catholic Church itself has flirted with revolution, namely through the liberation theology espoused by priests such as Paolo Freire, Bishop Romero in El Salvador, and current Paraguayan president (and former priest) Fernando Lugo. These liberation theologians talked of social justice, equity, and veiled references to the Marxist motivation of Jesus Christ through the social gospel. The heavy-handed repression of the Church on the Latin-American people is second only to the predatory repression of the "oligarchs," who supported by the Church have ruled, and continue to rule, since the arrival of the conquistadores.

Income inequality in Latin America is the highest in the world. A small upper class enjoys immense privileges, while most live under the poverty line. Another motivation for the revolution is that so many Latin Americas see their exclusion as permanent; they don't feel they can ever advance. In Peru, Ecuador, Colombia, and up through Central America, entire generations of communities live on "fincas"—estate-plantations owned by rich elite—and serve in what resembles modern-day feudalism.

In Venezuela, the nature of extractive industry—in this case, oil—is unable itself to provide a broad employment base. While a tiny group of elite, highly educated engineers earn salaries comparable to the United States, live in camps and vacation in Europe, a vast majority of people crowd together in barrios and *favelas* that cling precariously onto the hillsides. Oil checks swell the national coffers and maintain lazy and corrupt leaders, providing them with almost unlimited income and proving a disincentive to the types of reforms that would facilitate a more fluid economic movement and increase the tax base of the economy as well. This "Devil's Excrement"[161] reduces investment in other sectors, such as agriculture, services and tourism, which provide most countries with their job markets. This causes a significant percentage of consumables (eighty percent at last count) to be imported—deemphasizing local production and job creation and keeping the poor in poverty and dependent upon the welfare programs of the moment and reliant upon odd jobs found in the informal sector.

These policies have caused huge migration to the cities between the 1960s and the 1980s. For example, currently approximately ninety percent of Venezuelans live in six major cities, which exacerbates problems faced by the poor as they huddle in their orange brick structures on hillsides overlooking the country clubs, swank apartment buildings and fantastic malls that line the valleys. This is the same in other countries in Latin America. This is a recipe for social disaster, inspiring more than one of the ALBA nations to engage instead in forceful, violent redistributive revolution. Many Latin Americans vicariously live their anti-US beliefs through a tolerance of the Castro's regime.

Finally, this revolutionary spirit is brought out by Latin-American love of ideology. This ideology is both reactionary and proactive. The constant feeling of inferiority and personal powerlessness, coupled with the lack of geopolitical power, fosters an affinity with the underdog. Many revolutionaries across the continent find their power from portraying themselves as holding the line against titanic forces. They see themselves in a quixotic sense as the last, lone stragglers fighting against an enemy far greater than themselves. And their fight is always noble, epic and ultimately futile.

For this reason, even leaders at the pinnacle of their power strive to portray themselves in this fashion. It is always important for them to find a greater foe to keep them in the profile of a fighter, an underdog, and an ideological revolutionary against this foe. There are many examples of this, but probably the most significant in Latin-American lore is Fidel Castro.

---

161 Moises Naim, "The Devil's Excrement," Foreign Policy Magazine, September 2009. http://www.foreignpolicy.com/articles/2009/08/17/the_devil_s_excrement

The vision of him, vastly outnumbered by the US-supplied and trained Batista regime forces, emerging from his hideout in the Sierra Maestra Mountains to take control of the country, has captured the hearts of Latin Americans (and not a few North Americans) for generations. Even after his victory and half-century of brutal repression while he and his family live in opulent luxury, in the minds of Latin Americans he is still in the Sierra Maestra Mountains, fighting the true evil behind the Batista regime: the United States. Ergo, even while he sits at the pinnacle of power and wealth, he retains the image of a beleaguered revolutionary fighter.

In the minds of Latin-American leaders, there exist multiple reasons for the necessity of revolutionary ideology. The first: the enemies of the people have, for the most part, been internal. Like most in the United States or Europe, these leaders have not had significant international conflicts. Even the periodic wars that flare up between countries are often portrayed as internal, insomuch as the countries of the region so often consider themselves as brothers. Second, the ethnic, religious, and historic differences from one country to another are minute, hindering the ability to demonize a regional enemy and neutralizing many of the elements of conflict. Third, the generally weak and corrupt governments have never spawned a militarily expansionist regime—a stark difference from the European nations—and this has mostly kept armies within their own borders and focused on local control. These bored militaries often start to conspire against their elected governments, bereft of any real enemies and with the prospect of thirty years of guarding tollbooths. These issues (or their absence) have led to a people motivated by ideology and class warfare—and who emphasize the otherness within their midst, and against which they must fight to achieve well-being. This has caused internal conflict over the centuries.

Part of the problem stems from the Latin-American people's zero-sum mentality, a limited-good worldview that leads them to believe wealth is a finite commodity and that attaining it is a zero-sum game; the more one possesses, the less the other can. This mentality is as true for the wealthy as well as the poor. It probably emerges from the collective historic memory of the conquistadores loading up gold, silver, wood, and other riches and shipping it away to the increased impoverishment of the locals. Nevertheless, these are some of the historical idiosyncrasies of Latin-American society. Therefore, following upon this worldview, if one decides to increase his share of the wealth pie, it is perceived to be at the expense of another; and those with the greatest power to take from others were born into that power, as were their parents and going back in time to the colonial days.

The revolutionary mindset is even enshrined in the selection and preservation of the national heroes across the continent. Unlike in Europe or America, they are not usually great warriors of even greater wars. In Latin America they instead immortalize their poor, people who stood up against the rich "oppressors" and "colonials" and struggled against the titanic odds: usually futilely. This is the case in Cuba, with Fidel Castro; in Nicaragua with Augusto Sandino; in El Salvador with Farabundo Marti; in Mexico with Pancho Villa; Salvador Allende in Chile; and of course Che Guevara, a figure who stands above the others as the international symbol for revolution. While many of these people were from the middle or upper classes themselves, they have nevertheless captured the rhetoric of the pro-poor fight and made it their own.

Notwithstanding, and much to the chagrin of would be revolutionaries, a revolution can never be carried out for revolution's sake—it must have a cause. And most often, this cause is galvanized by a warped but powerful view of social justice. The issues outlined in the previous paragraph have bred into Latinos a deep sensitivity for social injustice that plagues society. The prevailing theory (which has so hampered the creation of well-being) is that social justice and advancement are not achieved through peaceful, democratic means or economic growth, but through violent social revolution and the subsequent redistribution of the illegitimately attained wealth. This yearning for that violent version of social justice is immortalized and glorified in the romantic arts of Latin culture; in poetry and literary authors, such as Pablo Neruda, Ruben Dario, Gabriel Garcia Marquez, and Isabel Allende; and in music, with the "*trova*" or "*protesta*" (protest) singers such as Pablo Milanes, Silvio Rodriguez, Mercedes Sosa, Soledad Bravo, Ali Primera, and others. This artistic bent feeds off high levels of literacy and education and is accentuated by equally high levels of unemployment (especially in college-educated youth), as well as relative isolation from the international community.

ALBA Culture was created to harness this spirit.[162]

Cultural ALBA has as its objective to contribute to the unity of the creators, artists and intellectuals, institutions and Social Movements of our America to confront the pseudo cultural currents promoted by the so-called entertainment industry, whose products are generated fundamentally in the United States. ALBA Culture encourages the promotion of our values of Latin-American and Caribbean literature and art, and the work of recuperation, preservation, promotion, development and appreciation of the culture of the peoples of Latin America and the Caribbean, conserving its rich cultural identity.[163]

The ALBA Cultural Project has promoted a variety of activities meant to deepen the revolutionary spirit of the participating countries. Again, like other ALBA Grand National Projects, the advance of ALBA Culture varies across countries. In Bolivia, due to its rich cultural heritage and the focus that President Evo Morales has given to indigenous majorities in the country, ALBA has funded the creation of a magazine called *Identities*.[164] This magazine was produced monthly through calendar year 2009, before ending production in 2010. As discussed previously, not only do ALBA projects depend upon the member countries, due to the lack of a disciplined institutional nature, they also depend heavily upon the people in those countries able to move the projects forward. The exception of this is Cuba, which has a much more disciplined ideological bureaucracy.

In fact, most of ALBA Culture activity takes place in Cuba, where in Havana exists the most significant *Casa del ALBA* (House of the ALBA)—offices meant as living museums where member governments and Social Movements can promote cultural activity. In Peru, with support of the ALBA, domestic Bolivarians have set up almost two hundred of their own ALBA houses to spread ALBA propaganda in the successful operation to swing the presidency toward Ollanta Humala: who was elected in June 2011 as Peru's president. In Havana, the ALBA office provides ten fellowships a year for cultural research, provides financing for movie producers to work at the large, sophisticated film institute outside Caracas (in the satellite town

---

162 ALBA Cultural. http://www.albacultural.org
163 ALBA Cultural. http://www.albacultural.org/quienes.php?lang=1
164 "Identities Magazine." http://www.albacultural.org/__admin/imagenes//libros/
Revista%20Identidades/IDENTIDADES%2019.pdf

of Guarenas), conducts literary contests, produces theater productions and offers coveted prizes and sponsored scholarships. Besides the contests and scholarships, ALBA Culture has set up the coordination of various networks across the ALBA countries. These are, for example, networks of magazines, training organizations, cultural institutions, cultural promoters for Social Movements, and others. ALBA Culture offers training for audiovisual and documentary designers, research, creative writing, and other artistic programs. The Project office also has a directory of 191 organizations across the countries affiliated with ALBA Culture.

ALBA Culture holds important annual events, including the aforementioned Olympic-style games called the ALBA Games.[165] Held the first three years in Havana, the 2011 ALBA Games took place in Venezuela and were well attended, although they did not receive significant press coverage from the international press. Also, among its annual cultural festivals, art festivals and movie festivals, ALBA Culture recently held their annual music celebration and awarded the 2011 prize to Silvio Rodriguez, an important revolutionary singer.

In 2011, ALBA Culture is hosting the 200th celebration[166] of the liberation of Latin America, to commemorate the first Simon Bolivar battles against Spain. Multiple downloadable materials and photos serve to promote the cause across the continent, and ALBA Culture provides funding and coordination of the Bicentennial in countries across Latin America, with marches in Caracas, festivals in Ecuador, special musical events in Bolivia, and dozens of events in countries across the region, all coordinated from Havana. As of this writing, celebrations are occurring across the length and breadth of the ALBA nations through festivals, festivities, military parades, marches, and other cultural events.

The richness of Latin-American culture has been important for and to the region, and the world. There exists in that fantastic continent a wealth of artistic, literary, historical and gastronomic culture, as demonstrated by fantastic works of literature by people like Mario Vargas Llosa, winner of the 2010 Nobel Peace Prize; incredible "protest music" written to decry the military dictatorships of the 20th century, and wonderful cuisine emanating

---

165 ALBA Games. http://www.juegosalba.cu/2009/Home/DefaultPage.aspx
166 ALBA Bi-Centennial. http://www.bicentenario.gob.ve/

from Peru and Mexico. Even cinematographically, movies such as *Express Kidnapping*, locally made in Venezuela and on its way to win international awards—except that the government of Hugo Chavez believed it offended the country and hence should be censored. The irony is, all this culture which Chavez and the ALBA so resolutely promote and defend represents the two-hundred-year-old cry of an ever-oppressed people seeking their own freedom—freedom from poverty and tyranny and voicelessness. Yet this cultural heritage is used within the ALBA not as positive reinforcement to promote national pride and reconciliation, but as another weapon to foment intolerance and conflict within their countries, and in their neighbors. And these Latin-American values, values that the United States shares—values such as freedom, democracy and diversity—are vilified in the attempt to use culture as yet another control mechanism. For those who know and love Latin America, it is ironic that the supposed promotion and protection of this fantastic culture is used to prop up the crushing, dictatorial mediocrity of the ALBA's revolutionary vision.

ALBA Communications

Probably the most advanced of the ALBA projects is the Grand National Project for Communications. Andres Izarra, president of TeleSUR, the ALBA's cable news station and current Venezuelan Minister of Communication, put it best[167] in a 2007 interview: "We have to elaborate a new plan, and the one we propose is the communicational and informational hegemony of the state. Construct the hegemony in the Gramscian style." Gramsci, the Italian Marxist, advocated for the deepening of the state's control of the cultural expressions of a society, to use them to advance the unification of the sectors of society. This can only be done, according to the Bolivarians, through the control of communication and information.

In Honduras (during their brief membership in the ALBA), the important public television Channel 8 was seized by Zelaya by the use of decree.[168] TeleSUR technicians assisted Zelaya in the redesign. In Nicaragua,

---

167 "Andres Izarra: El Socialismo Necessita una Hegemonia Comunicacional," El Boletin Universitario, 8 de Enero, 2007. http://boletin.uc.edu.ve/index.php?option=com_content &task=view&id=4990&Itemid=5

168 "Canal de television del gobierno comenzó a emitir," 4 de Agosto, 2008. http://

Daniel Ortega used proceeds from the ALBA to purchase Channel 8. In Ecuador, President Correa has closed down three television stations as part of the Government of Ecuador's ongoing effort to control information.[169] Morales has gone on the offensive against the media, using the anti-racism law against several Bolivian television stations for their coverage of the case of former Drug Tsar Sanabria's involvement in drug trafficking (see Chapter 10). Morales has increased his government's harassment and manipulation with threats of canceling government advertising (a tactic that Venezuela's Chavez has used well). In Venezuela, freedom of expression has been difficult for years. Venezuela closed RCTV, the most important television station in the country, replacing it with its own government-run station and seizing the production equipment and repeaters to fulfill the political promise that, "the second RCTV goes off the air, TVES (a new government-run channel) will emerge," a promise the Venezuelan government would have been unable to keep without the equipment. Venezuela has purchased other stations and manipulated many through direct threats. Currently, the vitriol is targeted against Globovision, the only opposition station left in Venezuela. Chavez has said that the station managers should, "Take a tranquilizer and back off. Because if you don't, I will (take over). You and any other station that demonstrates it is manipulating feelings (against the government)."[170]

The situation for radio and print media is similar, with an ongoing effort by the governments of the ALBA countries to set in place judicial, financial and criminal restrictions that obstruct a free press. In Venezuela this has led to the outright closing of thirty-four radio stations across the country.[171] President Ortega has closed several dozen stations, and has increased attacks against La Prensa. President Correa sued the main opposition newspaper, El Universo, for defamation. The paper was fined tens

---

legislaciones.item.org.uy/index?q=node/732

169 "Correa cierre canales de Television," 9 de Julio, 2008. http://www.diariocritico.com/bolivia/2008/Julio/noticias/85677/correa-cierra-canales.html

170 "Chavez amenaza ahora a Globovision," 30 de Mayo, 2007 EFE. http://www.cadenaser.com/articulo/internacional/Chavez/amenaza/ahora/Globovision/unico/canal/privado/critico/gestion/csrcsrpor/20070530csrcsrint_2/Tes/

171 "AIR condena cierre de 34 emisoras de radio en Venezuela," El Nacional, 1 de Agosto, 2009. http://el-nacional.com/www/site/p_contenido.php?q=nodo/92617/Internacional/AIR-condena-cierre-de-34-emisoras-de-radio-en-Venezuela

of millions of dollars and four editors and owners were thrown in jail for several years.

These attacks, as demonstrated in statistics in the previous chapter, have thrust the ALBA countries into a free fall in relation to freedom of speech. It is important to note here that this 21st century mechanism of controlling information does not follow 20th century patterns. In the last century, authoritarian governments, such as China or the USSR, attempted to limit the peoples' access to information. However, with the rapid advance and globalization of the information age, this is no longer possible. The Bolivarian governments have realized this, and Bolivarian countries also have adopted a policy of saturation to go along with intimidation and regulation. Using ALBA Culture and their Social Movements, they fund millions of bloggers, tweeters, Facebook experts and others to generate a stream of propaganda attacking and repudiating and challenging anything said that is opposed to their Bolivarian vision. The idea is that those bold enough to write or talk about issues of concern will be so put off, or simply drowned out, by the army of social networking Bolivarians they will stop or back down, or their ideas will remain unheard in the manufactured babble of opposing views.

The governments of the ALBA have surged to fill the communication void left by the closed radio and television stations and self-censorship that is often the media community's response to government threats.[172] They have also gone about setting necessary infrastructure in place to control the social networks in support of their revolutions. From the most macro level to the most micro, from the cable-television airwaves to community bars and taverns, the Bolivarian governments' propaganda allows them to influence the discussion in their favor.

Contrary to the aforementioned isolation of people in authoritar ian regimes from information, the Bolivarians have adopted instead the Gramscian approach of saturating local populations with revolutionary information from as many sources as possible. Their hope is that the multiplicity of messaging will allow the states to consolidate their control over the media by providing different sources and simultaneously discrediting

---

172 "Venezuela: Situacion de Libertad de Expresion e Informacion" Informe 2010, Espacio Publico. ISBN 9801218274.

any other sources (such as private media programs) and slowly strangling them via regulation, financing and harassment. To support this initiative, the Venezuelan government, at a cost of $420 million and in the name of the ALBA, has purchased a Chinese satellite designed and launched by the China Great Wall Industry Corporation.[173] According to the Venezuelan government, this satellite will:

Cover all the national needs which have to do with telephone, transmission of information, access and transmission of messages by Internet, especially in all those places which because of low population density are not covered by commercial telecommunications companies. Equally, it will seek to consolidate the programs and projects carried out by the state, guaranteeing to arrive in the most remote locations, installing at those places satellite-connection points so as to guarantee in real time the education, diagnostic and information to that population which perhaps has no access to any means of information (…) as well as consolidation of social programs linked to education and health.[174]

Parallel to the functioning of the satellite, the Venezuelan government has laid a fiber optic cable from Havana to Caracas, which will soon extend to Jamaica and Managua.[175] This cable cost Venezuela $70,000,000 to install. Between the cable and the satellite, the Bolivarian Alliance will be able to share information quickly and cheaply across its member-states. In 2007, the governments of Venezuela and Cuba set up a Grand National Company called Telecommunications Gran Caribe SA, sixty percent owned by the Venezuelan government and forty percent by the Cuban government. Initially the companies were CVG Telecom (an offshoot of Venezuela's public mining company) and Cuba's Telecommunications Company. Antonio Pascuali, a Venezuelan expert in communications, believes that the purpose of the fiber optic cable is to allow the Cuban government access to fast communications (up to three thousand times the current satellite connectivity). Cuba has only had satellite access to the Internet, due to the unwillingness of telecommunications companies to work on the island because

---

173 http://www.skyrocket.de/space/doc_sdat/venesat-1.htm
174 "El Satelite Venezolano Simon Bolivar," 26 de Mayo, 2006. http://www.lapatria-grande.net/04_opiniones/attilio_folliero/satelite_simon_bolivar.htm
175 "Fiber Optic Cable Linking Venezuela to Cuba, Jamaica to come Online," *Latin American Herald Tribune.* http://laht.com/article.asp?ArticleId=370928&CategoryId=14510

of Cuba's statist economic model. This will let the Cuban government manage information from the various control rooms they have throughout the island (through the use of the Venezuelan satellite—including the new spy satellite being purchased by Venezuela from the Chinese). The Cuban state company ALBET Engineering and Systems has been hired by the Venezuelan government to manage the following government functions: Administrative Services for Identification in Migration and Foreigners, Administrative Services for Notaries and Registers, Integral System for the Management of Emergencies and Citizen Security, and the Management System for Police Information.[176] The Cubans will be able to use this cable to manage in real time these Venezuelan government activities. There is also fear within the Venezuelan opposition that the Cuban authorities will use this infrastructure to assist Venezuelan, Ecuadorian, and Nicaraguan immigration officials and electoral councils in the management of their national databases[177] and electoral processes.

Simultaneously, and as previously mentioned, the ALBA countries are acquiring through coercion a large network of partner television stations around the region. In Venezuela alone, the government controls TVES, ANTV, Vive TV, VTV, and several others and has co-opted the Cisneros family's Venevision with threats of closure. Regionally (at the state level) the panorama becomes more convoluted, with the Chavez government controlling a network of local television stations through purchase, threats or outright closure. The same has happened in Honduras, Nicaragua, and Ecuador, with powerful governments seizing and co-opting previously independent TV stations.

The ALBA has also worked tirelessly to assemble a network of community radio stations. The exact number of community radio stations is unknown, though in Venezuela alone, it is in the hundreds, and in 2006, Bolivia's President Evo Morales spoke of thirty community radio stations and a television station.[178] The reality is probably far greater by now. In Nicaragua, the process has a head start. Many of the community radio stations the Sandinistas established in the 1970s and 1980s are still

---

176 Author interviews with confidential sources.
177 "Un cable bajo control," May 8, 2011, El Nacional.
178 "Bolivia tendrá 30 Radios comunitarios y un Canal de TV," Voltairenet.org, 22 de Junio, 2006. http://www.voltairenet.org/article141096.html

functioning, with many new radio stations formed since President Ortega's return. In 2007 in Ecuador there were twenty-six community radio stations, an amount that has likely increased. The Bolivarians continue to fund millions upon millions of dollars for the creation of community radio stations through their ALBA cooperation mechanisms—funded bilaterally through the ALBA Bank as well as off-project support through PDVSA, Venezuela's state oil firm, and the Venezuelan embassies.

The ALBA has understood that it must produce quality products. The days of a local communist leader screaming into a microphone are over. The revolutionaries know their young people are confronted with sophisticated western media and information. They must provide their youth with at least as high-quality information if they are to continue to win the war of ideas.

On the backbone of their high-tech infrastructure, the ALBA has established online mechanisms for transmitting high-quality information, live feed as well as downloadable. These include ALBA Multi-Channel,[179] which has live-feed links to ten television stations, thousands of documentaries, movies, interviews and music videos, and links to eight important radio stations across the region.

The ALBA has also set up the ALBA TV Channel,[180] a regional television channel available to all television stations through live feed and whose focus is to air locally produced television spots by community journalists to increase awareness across the ALBA nations of grassroots revolutionary activity in other countries.

Similar to this channel, they also have ALBA Radio of the South,[181] similarly a live-feed radio program with high quality content. Both ALBA TV and Radio include interviews, documentaries and special programs. Another radio is ALBA Ciudad,[182] which connects the satellite ALBA countries to events in Venezuela. There is an ALBA wire service as well, which provides up-to-the-minute information.

From a massive, high-tech movie studio in Guarenas, outside Caracas, the ALBA produces movies with revolutionary themes featuring figures from across the continent. Danny Glover is completing an ALBA movie

---

179 ALBA Multi-Channel. http://www.multicanalalba.org/
180 ALBA TV. http://www.albatv.org/
181 Radio of the South. http://laradiodelsur.com/
182 ALBA City. http://albaciudad96.org/wp/

on Haiti, for example.

Naturally, there are hundreds of magazines, newspapers and online print editions for download that provide revolutionary information. The quantity of high-quality information produced is massive.

Perhaps the most important component of ALBA Communications is TeleSUR.[183] This television channel is the Bolivarians' cable news outlet, as they seek to compete against CNN and other private news enterprises. It is similar to Russia Today or (perhaps less so) Al Jazeera, in that it follows an ideological line dictated by their ALBA governments. TeleSUR has eleven sub-offices (including one in Washington), and is seen in countries across the world on cable, Internet, and open television. The governments of Nicaragua, Bolivia, Ecuador and Venezuela are forcing local cable service providers to carry TeleSUR, upon threat of closure.[184]

Going beyond traditional media, TeleSUR is often at the forefront of the "attack groups" attempting to push events in a specific direction. The best recent example of this occurred during the 2009 events in Honduras. TeleSUR served as a megaphone for the supporters of ousted president Mel Zelaya, who were seeking to create a negative opinion of the government of Interim President Micheletti. TeleSUR newscasters and journalists participated in pro-Zelaya marches, were onboard the Venezuelan airplane as it tried to land in Tegucigalpa (with Zelaya on board as well) and publicly confronted pro-Micheletti supporters. The same was true during the September 2010 Ecuador situation; TeleSUR was the only station allowed to operate after the government's takeover, effectively making it the main news source for those outside the country. Overall, TeleSUR has carried out its alternate role effectively.

More recently, TeleSUR sent its reporters to Tripoli during the Libyan government's crackdown, where they showed only peaceful scenes and made statements like, "There is nothing going on here, the reports of Libyan repression are just western propaganda."

Not only is ALBA Communications important to alert and inform ALBA nations, jockey for position and confront those of opposite opinions, the station is also vital as one of the principal tools in the workbox

---

183   TeleSur TV. http://www.telesurtv.net/secciones/canal/index.php
184   Author interviews with confidential sources.

of the ALBA Social Movements. These Social Movements are charged with defending the revolutions in member-states and recruiting new Social Movement members to the ALBA cause in hopes of swaying their own governments through unrest and/or the ballot box.

ALBA Medicine

The project with perhaps the greatest impact for the ALBA nations has been ALBA Medicine. One of the paramount challenges in the lives of the poor across the region has been access to even basic medical care. The Cuban government has been using health care as a political tool for decades, in all corners of the world. Many excellent analyses and studies have been done of these programs, the quality of Cuban health care, the value of their model, its limitations and other issues. This brief review does not attempt to qualify and quantify the value of Cuban medicine. It is, nevertheless, important to mention that support from Cuban doctors has been of immense political value to the ALBA countries.

In the years following the Soviet Union's demise, Cuba's extensive overseas operations involving medicine and health care (as well as political ideological training and intelligence work that accompany the doctors) were suspended as the Cuban government focused all its effort on survival. With the arrival of President Chavez in Venezuela, Cuba was able to use Venezuela's oil revenue largesse to reactivate many of its overseas activities. The most famous of these is the "Inside the Barrio" (Barrio Adentro) program whereby the Cuban government sent over forty thousand doctors to live in the poor areas of Venezuela in exchange for oil in an "oil for doctors" scheme seen by many as distinctly one-sided. Despite its detractors in the political opposition, the "oil for doctors" scheme can arguably be credited with saving the Chavez presidency during the difficult moments of 2003 and 2004, and is an essential piece of the ALBA.

The projects themselves fall, like others, under the supervision of the Social Council, comprised of the different ministers of social development or health from ALBA member countries. Together, the ministers form working groups in their respective areas such as health, housing, water/sanitation, sports, culture, and others. Naturally, ALBA Medicine[185] is led

---

185 ALBA Health. http://www.salud.alianzabolivariana.org/

by the ministers of health from the ALBA member countries and relies heavily upon its institutional partners in each country's ministry of health. The greatest support comes from the Cuban Ministry of Public Health. The Social Council's function is to: (1) define the strategic direction for the Social Council, (2) establish priorities for the execution of programs, (3) evaluate the social council's effects, and, (4) promote the follow-through of selected Grand National projects.

Five projects are carried out under the support of ALBA Health.

Pharmaceutical Project: This project, under guidance of the Cuban State Center for the Quality and Control of Medicines,[186] seeks to harmonize and centralize the registers for essential medicines exported via the ALBA Grand National Import-Export Company.

Handicap Project: This project seeks to reduce discrimination against handicapped people. In six member countries, seventy-two thousand ALBA social workers have visited two million homes and worked with nine hundred thousand handicapped people and 1,100,000 non-handicapped people to reduce the stigma.

Mission Miracle: This project supports eye operations for those unable to afford them, in public hospitals in Cuba and Venezuela. So far, eye doctors have carried out over 1,100,000 eye surgeries for people from over twenty different countries.[187]

Latin-American School of Medicine: One of the projects has been the creation of this medical school, to train doctors from across Latin America. As mentioned previously, to date, over seventeen hundred doctors have been trained.

Haiti Humanitarian Assistance: The ALBA is also managing five Internally Displaced People's (IDP) camps in Haiti (an ALBA observer state). These camps hold a total of seventeen thousand people, and the ALBA has also provided sixty thousand doctor's visits.

---

186 Cuban State Center for Quality Control of Medicines. http://www.cecmed.sld.cu/
187 I talked to a poor Nicaraguan man who had participated in this activity, who had gone to Caracas, stayed in a nice hotel and spent time as a tourist before his operation. He left quite impressed with Venezuelan solidarity.

It is clear that for an organization with a short five-year history, the ALBA Medicine program's success has been impressive, directly affecting the lives of millions. Nevertheless, participation comes with a price. Recent information has revealed the concern of government officials from neighboring (non-ALBA) countries, which outline fears that the operations or assistance come with political and ideological proselytizing.[188] This should not surprise readers of this book; the fundamental reason for the social support is to deepen the feeling of attachment between the maximum "strongman" Hugo Chavez, and his people across the hemisphere.

ALBA Energy

The most far-reaching, ambitious and by far the most costly ALBA initiative is the ALBA Grand National Energy project. The master plan behind this Grand National project is the formation of an ALBA Energy block which controls a significant amount of the hemisphere's energy supply and uses this primary resource as a mechanism for economic growth, political support and international power. According to the US Department of Energy,[189] Venezuela has 99.4 billion barrels of proven oil reserves, making it the largest reserve in South America. On top of this, Venezuela has[190] 176 trillion cubic feet of natural gas reserves. Bolivia is an important energy producer in its own right,[191] with 27 trillion cubic feet of proven natural gas reserves. Ecuador, which under the instigation of Venezuela rejoined OPEC in 2007, also has[192] 4.5 billion barrels of oil reserves. Should the initial assessments[193] of a 20-billion-barrel reserve of oil in an offshore oil discovery in Cuban territorial waters be correct (the Cuban government won't know the exact quantity of reserves until REPSOL, the Spanish agency, finishes its assessments), ALBA will possess enough energy reserves to influence the global market.

---

188 Author interviews with confidential sources.
189 US Department of Energy. http://www.eia.doe.gov/cabs/venezuela/oil.html
190 US Department of Energy. http://www.eia.doe.gov/cabs/venezuela/oil.html
191 US Department of Energy. http://www.eia.doe.gov/country/country_energy_data. cfm?fips=BL
192 US Department of Energy. http://www.eia.doe.gov/country/country_energy_data. cfm?fips=EC
193 Roy Carrol, "20 billion barrel oil discovery puts Cuba in the big league," The Guardian October 18, 2008. http://www.guardian.co.uk/world/2008/oct/18/cuban-oil

As it is, Venezuela has been successful in its attempts to manipulate the price of oil. When President Chavez arrived in power, oil was hovering at roughly $10 per barrel. Chavez' permanent campaign to push and keep oil above $100 per barrel has been working. "We've been thinking about that [the range between $80 and $100 a barrel], and we believe that price would be a fair price for oil,"[194] Chavez has said on many occasions. Oil prices have moved higher throughout Chavez' presidency, providing much-needed financing for the expansion of the Bolivarian project.

An essential component of Grand National companies is the control of natural resources. It is not a secret that, historically, Latin America has been used as a source of raw material—which has forced Latin-American economies into the role of major suppliers of extractive industries. Since the days of the Spanish Empire, gold and other raw materials have flown between a resource-rich, personally poor Latin America and the wealthy nations of the now-industrialized world. The ALBA Grand National projects and companies are seeking to reverse this trend. And in no sector of the economy is their strength more evident than in the energy sector. Understanding the political and economic power represented by their control over this important natural resource, Presidents Chavez, Correa and Morales have all warred against the transnational energy companies, which they blame for the ongoing pillage of Latin America. In Venezuela the government unilaterally renegotiated the contracts with the oil sector and declared every business working in the sector a public utility. Ecuador has done the same. Bolivia took over the Brazilian state oil company PetroBras' operations, running the natural gas extraction industry in Bolivia by sending in the military (and at the behest of Chavez). The takeover of the raw materials has moved forward.

With the energy industry firmly in the hands of the revolutionaries, the ALBA countries have proceeded to use energy as a mechanism for integration, protection and ideological advancement. This plan, according to President Chavez, is called "PetroAmerica" and comprises one large energy cartel from Mexico to Argentina. Initially, this ambitious plan even included a natural-gas pipeline from Venezuela to Argentina at a cost of $17 billion,

---

194 "Chavez reconoce crisis por caída de petróleo," 25 de Noviembre, 2008. http://www. infobae.com/mundo/417061-101094-0-Chavez-reconoce-crisis-caida-del-petroleo

a plan that was counterintuitive because it proscribed Bolivia's role as gas supplier to the Southern Cone. The pipeline project was scrapped; nevertheless, the Bolivarians pushed forward with PetroAmerica. As always, Chavez has had greater success working with hardline ALBA member countries than he has manipulating other Latin-American nations.

On January 26, 2008, five ALBA countries (excluding Ecuador) formed a Grand National energy company.[195] This company will have eight specific activities: (1) assemble a matrix on the energy balance of the region; (2) develop a map of alternative energy possibilities in the ALBA; (3) study the refining capacity of the ALBA; (4) build a strategic vision of energy in the ALBA region; (5) create an

Oil Price per Barrel	Percentage to Finance	Interest, repayment and grace period
≥ $15	5%	
≥ $20	10%	2% interest, repayment in 15 years with 2 years grace period
≥ $22	15%	
≥ $24	20%	
≥ $30	25%	
≥ $40	30%	
≥ $50	40%	1% interest, payment in 23 years with 2 years grace period
≥ $80	50%	
≥ $100	60%	
≥ $150	70%	

ALBA Energy-training center; (6) study the internal energy cooperation of the ALBA countries; (7) create elaborate maps of possible electric routes and a database of future projects; and finally, (8) implement other projects as mutually agreed. PetroAmerica is, by all guesses, off to a slow start. Nevertheless, it is moving forward in pieces.

The most successful component of the PetroAmerica family is PetroCaribe. According to Rosalía Pleytez, a reporter from Centro America 21, an online news outlet, President Chavez has been following an economic model of petro-indebtedness to extend his political power in the region.

Quoting from President Chavez at the 2008 PetroCaribe Summit at Cienfuegos in Cuba, "That [oil] debt instead of a burden becomes another mechanism of liberation to fight against the asymmetries and impulse the development model of the signatory countries of PetroCaribe." According to Chavez himself, PetroCaribe countries currently owe Venezuela more

195 "Tratado para Constitucion de Empresa Gran-Nacional Energia." http://www.minci. gob.ve/doc/acuerdo_grannacional_energia_a.pdf

than $4.6 billion (a figure experts have validated), making Venezuela by far the largest creditor in the Caribbean. PetroCaribe is a preferential trade agreement between eighteen Caribbean and Central American countries. The terms of the agreement are beneficial to the member countries (or, more specifically, their political leadership). The table represents the repayment amounts and schedules.[196]

Upon further analysis, however, PetroCaribe appears to be a scheme to support the corruption of local leaders as well, providing them with capital to run campaigns and to purchase votes—while indebting their countries to Venezuela. Case in point is Nicaragua. PetroCaribe gasoline sold at the PetroNIC pumps in Nicaragua is no cheaper than the market value. However, PetroNIC only repays one-half of the value up front to Venezuela, with the remaining amount going into sovereign debt. The difference (the remaining half) is funneled into off-budget mechanisms for Ortega and the Sandinistas to support their political activities.

PetroCaribe also carries out development projects among the member-states. According to the Venezuelan government,[197] through 2009 PetroCaribe has spent over $200,000,000 for eighty-four projects in eleven member countries. Most of these projects are in energy and infrastructure, which would further tie member-states to Caracas. PetroCaribe can best be understood as a "gateway" organization to the ALBA. While the ALBA is an ideological alliance, membership in PetroCaribe does not require member countries to buy into "21st Century Socialism" or pursue ALBA membership. Nevertheless, this petro-indebtedness allows the ALBA to exert influence among a larger group of countries by purchasing support in the terms that small energy-dependent nations most desperately need: inexpensive energy. The ALBA plan is to leverage energy and link economics across the Caribbean, which then allows a political/ideological approach, which leads to the potential/ideological relationship and adhesion to the Alliance. Even if full membership is not the result, the ALBA nations have purchased the votes of small countries, votes they can count on during difficult confrontations with the United States and its allies at the OAS or the United Nations.

---

196 PetroCaribe, Energia para la Union. www.petrocaribe.org
197 http://www.vtv.gob.ve/noticias-econ%C3%B3micas/19343

It is important to note that, as the table below shows, much of the planned infrastructure speaks to the ALBA strategy to use energy dependence to fight against isolation brought by their political project, and even to expand their revolutionary footprint across the region. This fact became painfully obvious during the Honduras crisis, when Micheletti's interim government had to deal with an energy crisis caused by a suspension of PetroCaribe oil, atop other issues of instability. Many of these ALBA-funded projects, especially the infrastructure projects involving highly complex operations such as the refineries, are to date only in the planning stage. As mentioned previously, many of the Bolivarians' activities depend on the capacity of the manager in charge, and are not implemented uniformly across the Alliance. For example, the only refinery that has been completed is in Cuba, at Cien Fuegos: a result of Cuba's severe energy needs and its commitment to the project's completion. The storage facilities in El Salvador have been inaugurated, as have storage facilities in Nicaragua, but the promised Nicaraguan refinery remains to be completed (as do those in Ecuador, Panama, Brazil, and others).

Also, while the total amount of oil in the table below seems insignificant for a large consumer like the United States, tiny Caribbean islands require smaller amounts of energy, and are more easily satiated. However, all international organizations still operate by the principle of one country, one vote. The ALBA knows that within the OAS and the UN, if they link the energy demands of small countries to their own supply, they will be able to control these organizations should they ever need to confront the United States or the West.

Finally, as the projects below go, without travel to each individual country and project, it is extremely difficult to ascertain which projects are actually moving forward, and at what speed of implementation. Below is a table[198] that outlines PetroCaribe's scope in member nations.

As the ALBA member-states (such as Ecuador, Bolivia, Venezuela and eventually Cuba) increase their production of and control over their natural resources (oil, gas, silver, coltan, uranium, gold, and so on), they will increasingly also be able to participate, not simply as beneficiaries, but as donors, at Chavez's instruction, in enacting their dollar diplomacy abroad.

---

198 Petro Caribe web site www.petrocaribe.org

This could make the ALBA a formidable cartel. They could also serve as spoilers in the international energy markets, since they don't respect the rules of the game. For example, PDVSA recently announced it would cease releasing production numbers. Without clarity, the energy markets could be plunged into chaos.

Country	Barrels Per Day (bpd) Supplied	Infrastructure Projects	Social Projects
Antigua and Barbuda	4,400		Tourism and sanitation
Belize	4,000		Education, health, sanitation, roads and housing
Cuba	92,000	Cienfuegos refinery expansion from 65,000 bpd to 150,000 bpd, expansion of Hermanos Diaz refinery	Sanitation
Dominica	1,000	Construction of a refinery (10,000 bpd), gasoline and natural gas distribution plant, oil for generation of electricity	Agriculture, sports, education, economic development, health, sanitation, citizen security, food security, tourism, roads
Granada	1,000	Plant for distribution of gasoline and natural gas (41,000 bpd), preparation of tanks (18,000 barrels), support for generation of electricity	Housing and culture
Guatemala	20,000		
Guayana	5,200		Health

Country	Barrels Per Day (bpd) Supplied	Infrastructure Projects	Social Projects
Haiti	14,000	Construction of a refinery (20,000 bpd), electricity generation plants (60 megawatts), gasoline for electricity	Economic, sanitation and housing
Honduras	20,000 (suspended)		
Jamaica	23,500	Expansion of the Kingston refinery to 50 bpd	
Nicaragua	27,000	Construction of a refinery (75,000 bpd), electric generators (120 megawatts)	Humanitarian assistance, sports, ecology, economics, education, health, sanitation, roads and housing
Dominican Republic	30,000		Energy
San Cristobal and Nieves	700	Electricity generation plants (4 megawatts), gasoline and natural gas distribution plant (47,000 bpd), tanks (5,000 barrels)	Housing
San Vicente and the Grenadines	1,000	Plant to distribute gas, natural gas plant, electricity	Culture, sports, education, sanitation, tourism, housing
Surinam	10,000		Culture
Total Barrels Per Day	161,000		

Finally, beyond petro-diplomacy, there is another element of ALBA's strategy to develop energy. This component has received less attention than oil, but could be equally significant. This is the element of electricity production. One of the most problematic issues for the governments of Ecuador and Venezuela has been the electric grid. During 2009 and 2010, Venezuela suffered significant political damage because it was unable to maintain its grid, and the people, accustomed to energy supplies at low cost, began to experience extended blackouts. This was the result of a terrible drought exacerbated by a lack of investment in and maintenance on the grid. With help from Cuba, Venezuela was able to find a low-tech solution to its problem, with the only requirement a resource that was abundant: diesel fuel.[199] Cuba's national energy company, Union Electrica, replicated a project that was successful for them on the island (with the support of Venezuelan hydrocarbons). In the Cuban case, they placed hundreds of Korean- purchased diesel generators around the country. These diesel generators, running twenty-four hours a day, stopped Cuba's 2006 rolling blackouts in several months. During Venezuela's crisis, Cuba's energy minister arrived and assisted in the setup of this simple infrastructure that provides Venezuela with two thousand megawatts of power. Currently, the model is being implemented in Ecuador, where it is set to provide 350 megawatts of power to Ecuador for an undisclosed cost.

ALBA Food Security, Science and Technology, Mining and Industry, and Tourism
On April 23, 2008, in Caracas, the ALBA held its first Extraordinary Summit, where it was agreed to establish a plan to fight food insecurity among ALBA countries. In May of that same year, at a Presidential Summit in Managua, Nicaragua's President Ortega proposed the creation of an ALBA Bank fund for agriculture, energy support for agricultural production through PetroCaribe, a seed bank, and a special emergency fund for food crises. In the first meeting of agriculture ministers of Petro-Food, they set up the Initiative ALBA Food Security. The objectives of this initiative are to (1) develop an ample and sustained cooperation to guarantee food security, (2) develop activities to increase production, and (3) orient these initiatives to support the poorest communities. The initiative itself is organized along the same lines as the ALBA, beginning with the heads of state, followed by the ministers of agriculture, the executive secretariat, and

---

199 "Next Stop of Cuba's Energy Revolution: Ecuador," Cuba Standard, September 11, 2009. http://www.cubastandard.com/2010/11/09/next-stop-of-cubas-energy-revolution-ecuador

the ALBA Grand National projects and companies. The project is financed from the ALBA Bank, wherein PDVSA places in escrow the funding for projects approved by the Council of Ministers of Agriculture of participating states, with the schedule of payouts decided through negotiation.

The following are projects being carried out by Initiative ALBA Food Security[200]:

Country	Project
Honduras	· Seed bank
	· Support for genetic research
Suriname	· Support for fish smoking
Guyana	· Support for cold chain for milk production
Jamaica	· General agricultural support
St. Vincent and Grenadines	· Developing irrigation mechanisms
	· Improving warehousing
Nicaragua	· Production of rice
	· Rehabilitation of agricultural infrastructure
Belize	· Integrated system for livestock and fish production
San Cristobal	· System of distribution for food for the most needy

As with most things ALBA related, finding the reality of the development status of the projects is difficult. Nevertheless, a significant amount of work has been done on using ALBA Food Security to replace traditional providers in ALBA countries with business between member-states. For example, Nicaragua has deepened its commercial relationship with Venezuela, becoming its second most important trading partner with close to two billion dollars in annual exports in 2010[201] (a huge rise over the 2009 numbers featured below. These exports include black beans, livestock and coffee.[202] For its part, Bolivia increased its sales to Venezuela by 110%, for

200 ALBA web site www.alianzabolivariana.org
201 "Venezuela es el Segundo Destino de Exportaciones Nicaragüenses," El Universal 2 de Enero, 2011. http://www.eluniversal.com/2011/01/02/eco_ava_venezuela-es-el-segu_02A4920617.shtml
202 While on a recent trip to Nicaragua myself, friends told me that for the first time they are seeing black beans (not consumed by Nicaraguans, who prefer red beans), and that they often have difficulty in finding their own beans.

a 2010 total of $339 million. Most of the exports are of soy and textiles.[203] Ecuador has also increased exports of foodstuffs to Venezuela, including palm oil, rice and other products.

Ironically, much of the Venezuelan need for foodstuffs comes at the expense of the Venezuelan private sector, where Hugo Chavez has waged a steady campaign of price controls, expropriations and nationalizations, which has left the productive sector of the economy destroyed. In early 2011, Chavez announced that more than fifty percent of the food available in the Venezuelan markets was purchased by the government. An unenviable position and a strange boast. In linking the Venezuelan economy with the other ALBA satellite states, the Venezuelan economy is providing important support for the other ALBA presidents. Therefore, as in most things ALBA, what is a liability for Hugo Chavez domestically is a significant element of his political project.

Branching out slightly from the food security component to industry and science, the ALBA nations are attempting to increase business between each other as a mechanism of strengthening the ALBA as a block. As demonstrated by the official statistics from Banco del Exterior—the Venezuelan import-export bank—the commercial relationship between Venezuela at the center and the other core ALBA countries has increased significantly over the last five or six years.[204]

The next step for ALBA business is to exchange goods and services between other peripheral ALBA countries: not only with the center (Venezuela). There is some indication this is starting to pick up. As of mid-2010, Ecuador and Nicaragua were negotiating a trade agreement within the overarching ALBA framework to increase sales to each other.[205] Bolivia and Ecuador's commerce has remained steady over the past three years, from $30 million in 2008, to $27 million in 2009, and to $28 million in

---

203 "Bolivia aumenta ventas a Venezuela de soya y textiles," Notidiario, 22 de Febrero, 2011. http://www.notidiario.com.ve/index.php?option=com_content&view=article&id=4 297:bolivia-aumenta-ventas-a-venezuela-de-soja-y-textiles&catid=45:economia&Itemid=66
204 Venezuelan Export Bank. www.bancoex.gob.ve
205 "Bolivia aumenta ventas a Venezuela de soya y textiles," Notidiario, 22 de Febrero, 2011. http://www.notidiario.com.ve/index. php?option=com_content&view=article&id=4297:bolivia-aumenta-ventas-a-venezuela-de-soja-y-textiles&catid=45:economia&Itemid=66

2010.[206] However, both countries are members of the Andean Community of Nations, which already offer preferred trade linkages between them. Nicaragua has increased its economic relationship with all ALBA countries: trade with Cuba has increased from $700,000 to $4.6 million; its trade with Bolivia has increased from nothing to $179,000, and with Ecuador it had increased from $18 million to over $100 million in 2008. Cuba's economic activity with other ALBA countries has also increased. With Bolivia, trade went from $360,000 in 2004 to $2.2 million in 2008; and with Ecuador trade went from $6.9 million in 2003 to $17.3 million in 2008.[207] These numbers are still quite small compared to the trade relationship with these countries (with the exception of Cuba) and the United States. Nevertheless, all ALBA nations are demonstrating a real effort to diversify their trade to include more intra-ALBA economic interaction.[208] Nicargua expected to increase in 2011 to $355 million[209].

Total Trade (in thousands of dollars)						
Country	2004	2005	2006	2007	2008	2009
Antigua	1,934	8,083	23,320	322	343	628
Bolivia	209,500	217,729	361,939	378,474	451,128	355,231
Cuba	1,112,152	3,603,437	1,700,294	2,421,945	3,860,314	2,977,790
Dominica	139	783	56	88	620	442
Ecuador	449,767	559,286	653,510	1,649,055	2,331,585	1,810,944
Nicaragua	177,274	204,843	109,236	40,169	346,204	269,426

ALBA Mining and Industry has developed a mining company, which appears to be inactive and essentially a front company for Iranian activity in the region. Iran is an observer-state of ALBA, a status which allows it to piggyback on ALBA mechanisms (such as Grand National companies and the ALBA Bank) to exploit uranium. They have also established import-export companies to attempt to increase trade with ALBA nations.

---

206 Andean Community of Nations. http://estadisticas.comunidadandina.org/eportal/Tema.aspx?codtema=142
207 www.imf.org
208 The difference between these figures and the others is that they would appear to not include govt-to-govt trade.
209 http://www.lajornadanet.com/diario/archivo/2011/julio/8/1.php

ALBA Tourism has developed based on the idea that the ALBA nations will only ever unify if they are familiar with each other's cultures, geography and traditions (this overlaps with ALBA Culture). They also understand that tourism among those in the region is usually the luxury of the rich and middle class. For this reason, and under the unifying project "Route of the Liberator," ALBA Tourism has held various tourism fairs in Caracas.[210] These are meant to promote tourism exchanges between ALBA member countries. This Grand National project is in its nascent phase, but envisions a network of ALBA hotels across member countries, a university degree in tourism, and a network of training institutes, increasing the attractiveness of ALBA countries as tourist destinations, and a macro-plan for social tourism for the poorest citizens. According to Pedro Cahuaya, minister of tourism of Bolivia during the first meeting of ALBA Tourism ministers in Quito in January 2010, "In Bolivia private businesses have monopolized this activity. However, now our governments are focusing on developing a responsible and sustainable community-based tourism."[211]

The transactions are occurring using the new ALBA currency called the SUCRE.

ALBA Finance

During the sixth ALBA Summit in Caracas on January 26, 2008, the ALBA nations of Nicaragua, Bolivia, Cuba, and Venezuela created the ALBA Bank. According to the agreement, "It is indispensable that we design and implement a new regional financial architecture, constituted under the sovereign control of Latin-American and Caribbean countries and oriented to reaffirm the leadership of the region, reduce the external vulnerabilities of the regional economies and transform the productive apparatus, prioritizing the basic needs of our people."[212] The initial funding for the ALBA

---

210 "FitALBA promovera a Venezuela en paquetes multi-destinos," Correo del Orinoco, 9 de Septiembre, 2010. http://www.correodelorinoco.gob.ve/avances/fitalba-promovera-a-venezuela-paquetes-multidestinos/
211 "Ministros del ALBA: Turismo es una Actividad económica primordial," Ministerio de Turismo de Ecuador, 29 de Enero, 2010. http://www.turismo.gob.ec/index.php?option=com_content&view=article&id=1814:ministros-del-alba-turismo-es-una-actividad-econa-primordial&catid=19:noticias-al-d&Itemid=151
212 Bolivarian Alliance web site. http://www.alternativabolivariana.org/modules.php?name=News&file=article&sid=2668#3

Bank was two billion dollars from Venezuela. Within the ALBA ministerial structure, the ALBA Bank falls under the Economic Council, which is chaired by the finance ministers of ALBA member-states that are signatories to the bank agreement.[213]

The ALBA Bank represents the institutionalization of what was previously the ALBA-Caribe Fund, set up by Venezuela to support activities in Caribbean nations. The governments realized that to grow and create institutions that can compete with existing international mechanisms, they needed to have a bank able to provide credibility and legitimacy to the projects. President Chavez has also stated that it is his hope that one day the ALBA Bank will serve to house the ALBA member countries' foreign reserves—right now, estimated at over $48 billion as of July 2011.[214]

The stated purpose of the bank is to (1) finance projects and programs for the stockholders; (2) promote, create and administer the bank's funds (both reimbursable and nonreimbursable); (3) provide resources for technical assistance; and (4) develop and promote practices for fair trade in goods and services. The bank is currently financing the aforementioned Grand National projects of culture, education, health, energy, food, environment and telecommunications. The bank's financial management is as mercurial as that of the respective ALBA governments, however, so finding reliable information has been difficult.[215] The ALBA Bank currently has two offices. The headquarters is located in Sabana Grande, Caracas, while the subsidiary in Cuba is located in Municipio Playa, Havana. Other branches in Bolivia and Nicaragua are set to be opened in short order. The structure of the bank is as shown on page 167.

Following the creation of the ALBA Bank, on October 16, 2009, Venezuela, Bolivia, Nicaragua and Cuba signed an agreement creating a new regional trade currency, SUCRE (*Sistema Unitaria de Compensacion Regional de Pagos*). This new currency is used by the ALBA Bank, and for trade

---

213 Currently these are Jorge Giordanni, Venezuela's Minister of Finance; Luis Alberto Arce, Bolivia's Finance Minister; Ernesto Medina Villaveiran, President of Cuba's Central Bank; and Antenor Rosales Bolanos, President of Nicaragua's Central Bank. The president of the ALBA Bank is Nicolas Maduro, Venezuela's foreign minister.
214 CIA World Factbook. https://www.cia.gov/library/publications/the-world-factbook/rankorder/2188rank.html
215 Multiple requests for assistance to the bank itself went unanswered. I even sent someone to the ALBA Bank headquarters in Caracas; they were turned away at the door.

transactions between member countries. This currency seeks to "break the hegemony of the US Dollar by creating a regional trade currency as another expression of the strengthening of regional cohesion in view to consolidate a regional economic zone."[216] The mechanism for using the SUCRE is quite simple, as explained by the Venezuelan Central Bank's SIP-SUCRE, their system for implementing the trade conversion: each entity seeking to do trade within the framework of the SUCRE (with member countries who accept the SUCRE) deposit funding into a participating bank in their own country and use a "login" provided by the Venezuelan Central Bank. This system receives the funding, transfers it into SUCREs, and dispenses the funding in local currency. The SUCRE is a so-called virtual currency. Currently, the value of the SUCRE is pegged at US $1.25. However, the idea is that when enough transactions are occurring using SUCREs, the currency's value will float upon a basket of member country currencies (such as happened with the euro in the last decade). The SUCRE, affiliated with the ALBA Bank, will gain in power if President Chavez is able to convince other countries to deposit their foreign reserves in the ALBA Bank in SUCREs. It remains to be seen if others will trust a fiscally irresponsible Venezuelan government with their foreign reserves. While the SUCRE is linked to the ALBA Bank, countries can use it without being a member of the bank. Such is the case with Ecuador,[217] which has used the SUCRE for close to $100,000,000 in transactions since its inception. and the goal is to arrive at $400,000,000 by the end of 2011.[218]

The SUCRE is one example of how Chavez is seeking to finance ALBA. Chavez's financing of his number-one foreign policy imperative remains mired in intricate details. The financial incentives, investments, trade agreements and cash flows of funding across the ALBA member nations represent a challenge to any accurate accounting of Venezuelan money expended to date. It would take an army of accountants years to unravel the billions spent by Chavez within the region on his project. However, there

---

216 Tratado Constitutivo del SUCRE, Octubre 16, 2009.
217 SUCRE Web Site. http://www.sucrealba.org/index.php?q=content/ecuador-movi%C3%B3-m%C3%A1s-de-17-millones-en-comercio-trav%C3%A9s-del-sucre
218 "Venezuela: El Sucre sigue siendo un experimento político," El Nacional, 27 de Julio, 2011. http://www.entornointeligente.com/articulo/1143172/VENEZUELA-El-Sucre-sigue-siendo-un-experimento-politico

are several examples that can be used to highlight the sheer volume of money Hugo Chavez is throwing at his ALBA initiative.

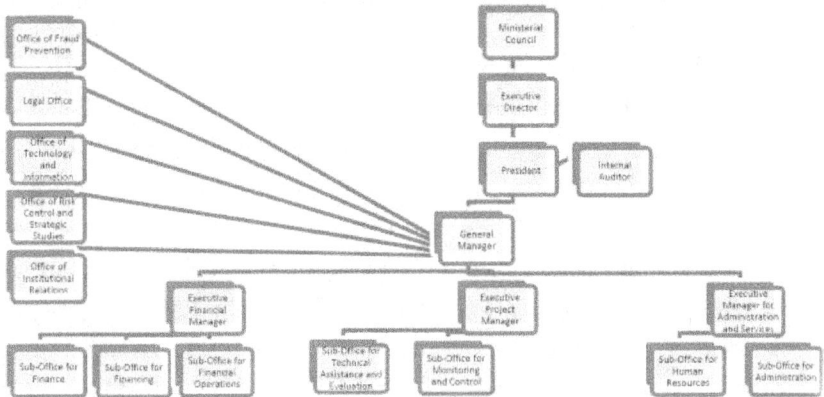

In the first half of 2009, the government of Manuel Zelaya received $100,000,000 within the framework of the ALBA. According to Miguel Angel Mejia, then President of the Supreme Tribunal of Accounts, two million dollars of this funding was taken for emergency donations and the remaining $98 million was passed to the President's palace.[219] According to observers, "Zelaya used to run the government out of suitcases of cash in the palace."[220] The ALBA money remains unaccounted for.

Daniel Ortega's government in Nicaragua receives a special fund for ALBA through the private enterprise ALBANISA, a joint company between Venezuela's PDVSA and a group of former Nicaraguan generals. This fund is funneled through PetroCaribe into PETRONIC, the Nicaraguan state petroleum agency. Fifty percent of the Venezuelan oil's value is repaid immediately to Venezuela; the remainder is repaid over twenty-some years at low interest (it can be paid in kind). According to sources,[221] this billion-dollar cooperation has been replete with accounting irregularities. It has resulted in over $20,000,000 to be unaccounted for and caused an un-auditable situation when finally the Government of Venezuela arrived in Managua in

219 Honduras: Aclaración ante campana de los embustes de el Heraldo y La Prensa sobre uso de los Fondes del ALBA," Aporrea, 23 de Agosto, 2010. http://www.aporrea.org/imprime/n163953.html
220 Author interviews with confidential sources.
221 ALBALEAKS Web Site. www.confidencial.com.ni/albaleaks

August of 2009—with the directors of KPMG Venezuela—to attempt to untangle the murky nature of Nicaragua's ALBA money.

In Costa Rica, parliamentarians of a far-left political party called the Frente Amplio were rumored to have received a briefcase with $2 million to finance the campaign against Costa Rica's free trade agreement with the United States.[222] The author's attempt at a meeting with Frente Amplio leadership failed with their refusal; they have denied receiving any resources from Venezuela. Sources state that Frente Amplio's elected leadership has been close to Ortega and Chavez and there was little doubt of collaboration. Frente Amplio is a member of the Foro de San Paulo and the Social Movements of the ALBA.[223] Through PetroCaribe, the FMLN municipal governments in El Salvador have a series of preferential oil deals through which they receive subsidized gas, which they sell in ALBA gas stations, with the profits funneled to the FMLN political party. There is no public accounting of this funding. The amount is rumored to be $60,000,000 a year.[224]

Announced Public Expenditures for the ALBA from 2005 – 2010 (in $ millions)									
Country Rank	Country	2005	2006	2007	2008	2009	Sept 11 2010	Total	%
1	Cuba	1,879	2,365	6,300	12,512	8,569	2,757	34,382	54.9
2	Bolivia	18	3,112	2,583	1,747	346	453	8,259	13.2
3	Nicaragua	0	0	1,390	1,518	4,519	467	7,894	11.7
4	Ecuador	225	425	969	5,165	208	299	7,291	11.6
5	ALBA	0	0	250	1,840	50	0	2,140	3.4
6	Haiti	0	119	1,376	182	71	110	1,858	2.9
7	Honduras	0	0	0	386	133	0	501	0.8
8	Dominica	0	11	238	8	3	4	264	0.4
	Total	2,122	6,031	13,106	23,340	13,899	4,090	62,589	

222 Rodolfo Ulloa, "Petrocaribe y el ALBA," *El Pregon* 30 de Septiembre, 2008. http://www.elpregon.org/opinion/100-perspectivas/351-petrocaribe-y-el-alba
223 I attempted to get a meeting with Frente Amplio on a trip to Costa Rica but numerous requests were turned down.
224 Author interviews with confidential sources.

According to CIECA,[225] a Venezuelan think tank that monitors announced expenditures (not actual cash transfers), the costs of foreign direct investment (FDI) of Venezuelan money associated with the ALBA over the last five years is approximately $62 billion.

According to the analysis unit of the political party Justice First, based only on public information available through press releases and presidential announcements, Chavez has pledged US $61.4 billion to 38 countries:

#	Country	Amount USD
1	Cuba	$20,462,912,162
2	Argentina	8,567,950,000
3	Nicaragua	7,103,370,000
4	Ecuador	5,657,020,000
5	Brazil	5,251,018,000
6	Bolivia	3,296,585,623
7	PetroCaribe 2009	3,222,000,000
8	Uruguay	1,949,500,000
9	Paraguay	923,000,000
10	Honduras	852,000,000
11	The Caribbean	826,000,000
12	Iran	700,000,000
13	Jamaica	631,150,000
14	Haiti	435,180,000
15	Dominican Republic	349,300,000
16	United States	318,428,265
17	China	300,000,000
18	Guatemala	165,187,740
19	Mali	104,000,000

225 Centro de Investigaciones Economicas, Gasto Publico Anunciado por el Gobierno de Venezuela, 2005–2010.

#	Country	Amount USD
20	Guyana	69,500,000
21	Belarus	68,383,000
22	ALBA	50,000,000
23	Antigua y Barbuda	50,000,000
24	El Salvador	40,500,000
25	England	32,000,000
26	Dominica	32,000,000
27	TeleSUR	10,000,000
28	Grenada	7,500,000
29	San Vicente y Las Granadinas	3,340,000
30	Peru	3,000,000
31	Benin	2,900,000
32	Indonesia	2,000,000
33	Africa	1,160,000
34	Gambia	1,000,000
35	Puerto Rico	250,000
36	Guatemala	187,000
37	OAS	40,000
38	India	30,200
	Total USD	**$61,488,391,990**

The reason for the obscure nature of the financing is the discretionary nature of Venezuelan financial regulations. On August 25, 2005, Venezuelan created the National Fund for Development (FONDEN).[226] This is a government fund affiliated with PDVSA, under the discretionary authority of the executive. According to the law, the price of oil is estimated at a certain value in the national budget. This value determines how much funding

226 FONDEN web site. http://www.fonden.gob.ve/index.php?m=1&t=1

is available for running the government and its social services. Within the course of the year, any value under the projected price per barrel is paid for by debt, while any amount over the estimated oil price is applied to FONDEN for use on Chavez's social projects, missions and other discretionary (off-budget) expenses. To game the system, when Chavez submits his budget to the National Assembly, he places an artificially low oil value to assure the ability to siphon off funding to FONDEN while making up for the shortfall in national expenses by issuing debt (either sovereign debt or debt upon PDVSA, which owes $32 billion as of mid-2011). For 2010, the budget estimate for a barrel of oil was placed at $40,[227] while the real price hovered around $100. FONDEN also receives funding from the Venezuelan Central Bank ($7 billion for 2010[228]). According to Energy Minister (and PDVSA president) Rafael Ramirez, the oil conglomerate had transferred $57 billion to FONDEN through mid-2009.[229] All these numbers are coincidentally close to the $60 billion of both the graphs above. FONDEN also includes internal discretionary spending, which makes it certain that the true amounts could differ widely.

According to Russ Dallen, President of BBO Financial Services and an expert on Venezuelan financial affairs, "FONDEN has received a total of $68.7 billion since it was created in 2005. The fund is like a 'black box' and expenditures are not made public, so we are never sure how the money is spent, but according to an end of the year report from the Venezuela Ministry of Finance, FONDEN had only $4.2 billion remaining at the end of 2010. This means that over $64.5 billion has been spent from what has become Chavez's personal slush fund without any transparency, oversight, or accountability."[230]

Another reason for the mercurial nature of ALBA financing is its use of the ALBA (and ALBA Bank) to finance the Social Movements, some of which are fronts for terrorism, such as the Bolivarian Continental

227 "Ministro de Finanzas Presenta Hoy Presupuesto Nacional 2010," Informe 21, 20 de Octubre, 2009. http://informe21.com/economia-finanzas/ministro-finanzas-presentara-martes-presupuesto-nacional-2010
228 "Venezuela Central Bank transfers 1.5 Billion to FONDEN (Chavez slush fund)," Dow Jones, March 2, 2010. http://www.democraticunderground.com/discuss/duboard. php?az=view_all&address=405x31496
229 "How much money is there in Venezuela's development fund FONDEN," The Devil's Excrement, March 4, 2009. http://devilsexcrement.com/2009/03/04/how-much-money-is-there-in-venezuelas-development-fund-fonden/
230   Author interviews with confidential sources.

Movement (MCB). To use the ALBA Development Bank to provide grants to Social Movements, copying the World Bank and other development banks, but which are actually fronts for terrorism or organized crime, is quite ingenious. If the ALBA Bank were being used as a front to launder drug money and sanctionable Iranian money, that would make it a major subversive element in the hemisphere.

True numbers for the expenditure of the one trillion dollars in oil income earned over the twelve years of the Chavez presidency might remain forever a mystery. Whatever the final amount turns out to be, for a country like Venezuela with an economy of $285 billion and a per-capita income of $12,000, the use of tens of billions of dollars to fund a regional integration project is a significant investment.

ALBA Social Movements

The final piece of the ALBA infrastructure is what Ceresole referred to as the broad-based coalition willing and able to defend the Bolivarian Revolution. These ALBA Social Movements represent many umbrella organizations and individual action-groups willing to take orders from the ALBA. One of these umbrellas is the Foro de Sao Paulo (FSP). The FSP could easily be described—at least now—as the ALBA's political wing. While predating the ALBA, Chavez' global plan has brought the FSP in, is providing it with funding and using it as a platform from which to work.

From July 2–4 of 1990, a group of left-leaning political parties and Social Movements of Latin America met in Sao Paulo, Brazil. The meeting was organized by Fidel Castro and Lula da Silva (who would become president of Brazil), and its purpose was to redefine the role of the extreme "left" in Latin America after the fall of its major supporter—the USSR. The meeting concluded with a document in which those present stated, "We reject all pretenses to take advantage of the crisis in Eastern Europe to give breath to the restoration of capitalism, annul the advances and socialist rights or increase the illusions around the inexistent kindness of liberalism and capitalism (...) the basis of a new concept of unity and continental integration, which includes the reaffirmation of the sovereignty and self-determination of Latin America and our nations, the full recuperation of our cultural and historical identity and the push toward the internationalist solidarity of our peoples."[231] It's easy to see, with words like these, how the Bolivarian project fits neatly into the identity of FSP participants. As of mid-2011, twelve countries in Latin America are governed by parties that belong to FSP—including all six nations.[232] Members include Social Movements, such as the FARC of Colombia, the FNRP of Honduras, many civil-society organizations and others.

The FSP holds an annual conference and provides intellectual support to its member governments. It also seeks to influence the internal affairs of other countries, through their electoral processes, in favor of FSP objectives. It has been a generally successful and influential group, and it has had no stronger supporter than Hugo Chavez. Venezuelan funding has reportedly financed the far left in Peru, Bolivia, Ecuador, Argentina, Chile, Mexico, Costa Rica, Honduras, Brazil, Nicaragua, El Salvador, Uruguay, and a number of Caribbean nations. Chavez has provided weapons to the Tupamaros in Uruguay, has helped organize the Sin-Tierras in Brazil and has provided material support to the FARC. Within the FSP, Chavez has found the foot soldiers he needs to defend his Bolivarian project against internal and external enemies.

Another important group is the Bolivarian Congress of the Nations[233] and the Bolivarian Continental Movement (MCB). These would appear to be two sides of the same coin. The BCN has denied any affiliation with the MCB. The Bolivarian Congress of the Nations is an organization presided by the Argentine Fernando Bossi, one of the ALBA's preeminent thinkers. This congress consists of ten national peasant associations from Bolivia, Brazil, Guatemala, Mexico, Nicaragua and Peru. Eleven national indigenous organizations are also represented from Bolivia, Brazil, Chile, Colombia, Ecuador, Nicaragua and Venezuela. Also associated with the congress are eighteen national workers' unions from Argentina, Brazil, Colombia, Cuba, Mexico, Panama, Peru, Uruguay and Venezuela. They bring together forty-seven political parties, from Argentina, Bolivia, Brazil, Chile, Colombia, Costa Rica, Cuba, Dominica, Ecuador, El Salvador, Guatemala, Honduras, Mexico, Paraguay, Peru, Puerto Rico, Uruguay and Venezuela. These parties

---

231 Foro de Sao Paulo. http://forodesaopaulo.org/?p=98
232 Bolivia, Brazil, Cuba, Dominica, Dominican Republic, Ecuador, El Salvador, Nicaragua, Paraguay, Peru, Uruguay, Venezuela.
233 Congreso Bolivariano www.congresobolivariano.org

include the communist parties from across the region, as well as former terrorist organizations like Tupamaros, FSLN, and so on. Finally, there are six groups, referred to as territorial organizations, from Argentina, Chile, Panama, Puerto Rico, Uruguay and Venezuela. The congress is an organization, "where the popular, democratic and patriotic forces of our America can discuss and agree upon joint actions and activities that promote integration and unity." Their stated purpose is to "build the great South American Nation," Ceresole's Patria Grande, Simon Bolivar's Congress of Panama. This is achieved through community mobilization and as they say, joint action to attempt to install friendly governments.

An example of the activities of the Congress can be found in Peru. The coordinator for the Bolivarian Congress of the Nations in Peru is a man named Roger Taboada. Taboada attended the first Bolivarian Congress in Caracas in 2003. According to a Peruvian intelligence report, there has been "significant Venezuelan infiltration of Peru" since 2006.[234] This report identifies Fernando Bossi and the Bolivarian Congress of the Nations as the social wing, the CCB (Bolivarian Continental Coordinator, now MCB) as the militant/terrorist wing, the ALBA as the diplomatic wing and TeleSUR's communication infrastructure as the informational wing. In 2007, fifteen Peruvian mayors were invited to Caracas to receive training and support to form a Bolivarian alliance of mayors. Through the ALBA infrastructure, the Social Movements have also infiltrated more than eighty ALBA Friendship Houses across Peru. Through the ALBA social missions, Peruvians have benefited from Venezuelan largesse. According to the intelligence report, Ollanta Humala's Peru Wins Party was on this list. This party is also a member of the FSP. Allegedly, the Bolivarian Congress of the Nations representatives met with the 2006 presidential candidate on five different occasions. That year, Humala lost.

However, Chavez, renowned for his patience, stepped up the infiltration. It worked. According to reports, President Chavez continued to support candidate Humala, including the funding of $12 million for his presidential campaign. Important campaign support came also from the Popular Party of Brazil, President "Lula" da Silva's party and member/

---

234 "Inteligencia alerto sobre penetración bolivariana en el Peru desde 2006," El Comercio, 8 de Julio, 2009. http://elcomercio.pe/politica/311706/noticia-inteligencia-alerto-sobre-penetracion-bolivariana-peru-desde-2006

founder of the San Paulo Forum. Instrumental in this were Brazilian experts Luis Favre and Joao Santana. On June 5, 2011 this same Humala won the Peruvian presidency.[235] Chavez was able to add another piece of the puzzle to his desire to build the "Patria Grande."

Yet another important organization within the ALBA Social Movements is the Bolivarian Continental Coordinator (MCB). This organization (discussed more in depth in the terrorism chapter) is a loose grouping of far-left social movements and organizations. Unlike the Bolivarian Congress of the Nations, the membership of this organization is not public. According to information from the MCB itself, membership might include more than one hundred organizations (and perhaps others unlisted) from all the countries of Latin America. In 2009, from their offices in Caracas, the CCB took the organizational step to form the Bolivarian Continental Movement (MCB). The reason for this change was to move to a more coherent and cohesive continental organization. There is reason to believe that the MCB and the Bolivarian Congress of the Nations are two sides of the same coin, the BCN being public and political and the MCB being the subversive terrorist front. According to documents from the computer of former FARC commander Raul Reyes after he was killed in the raid on Angostura Camp in Ecuador in 2009, the FARC funded a network of hundreds of civil-society groups throughout the continent. The MCB is one of the mechanisms to do this. According to the aforementioned Peruvian intelligence report, there are eleven Peruvian organizations tied to this movement: PCP-Patria Roja, MNI, PSR, PCP, MRTA, CGTP, SUTEP, Grupo Amauta, Integracion Estudiantil, Movimiento 4 de Junio, Movimiento 9 de Junio, Colectivo Todas las Voces. Some of these are openly terrorist organizations.

Through declarations and activities, the MCB provides political and ideological support for President Chavez and the ALBA through the Social Movements. They identify themselves as part of the project to create a "Patria Grande," and coordinate their activities with the ALBA. According to Narciso Isa Conde, President of the MCB and revolutionary from the Dominican Republic:

235 "How Hugo Chavez's Petro-Dollars made it to Peru," Peru 21, June 4, 2011. http://interamericansecuritywatch.com/how-hugo-chavez%e2%80%99s-petro-dolars-made-it-to-peru/

The ALBA is a political, cultural and economic alliance between states and governments that are revolutionary and progressive, and open to social movements. The ALBA assertively created its Council of Social Movements with the same ranking (within the hierarchy) as the council of governors. That demonstrates an integration project that goes beyond simply the state or commerce. That is very positive and the MCB should give support and seek participation in the Council of Social Movements and in extra-governmental projects supported by the ALBA. While more support and participation the people give to the ALBA, much better will that formidable integration mechanism be.[236]

There are also chapters of the MCB in other, (non-ALBA) countries reportedly receiving economic support from Venezuela. The participation of the MCB in the ALBA Social Movements shines a light on the nefarious intentions of the ALBA's Social Movements, since the MCB is an important front organization for the FARC, which will be outlined more in the coming chapter on terrorism.

In Cochabamba, Bolivia from October 15–17, 2009, the ALBA Social Movements held their first meeting. This 2009 gathering was the result of the Fifth ALBA Summit in 2007, where member states had agreed to organize the ALBA Social Movements. At their 2009 meeting, the ALBA Social Movements stated:

The Social Movements, the expression of the originary indigenous organizations, afro-descendants, peasants, union organizations, youth, laborers, teachers, workers, the landless, the coca growers, the neighborhood organizations, professional progressives and others that fight not only for their salaries, but for respect for the mother earth, from before, and that have always been the real architects of the revolutions and the profound transformations. Let us not forget that the Social Movements have played a central role in the last years in the perspective of democratization and profound decolonization of our countries, for a substantive change and genuine transformation in the economic and the super-structures...[237]

---

236 Since publication of an article with this content, the site is no longer active. http://www.pcv-venezuela.org/index.php?option=com_content&task=view&id=6039&Itemid=101

237 Manifiesto General de la Primera Cumbre de Consejos de Movimientos Sociales del

The ALBA Social Movements are central to the ALBA's arsenal to extend itself through the region. At times, this is successful—as in Nicaragua, Bolivia, Ecuador and Peru. Sometimes the governments don't change—such as Costa Rica, but the rulers know Chavez and his army of marchers can paralyze cities and make the region ungovernable, and think twice before they pick a fight. Sometimes governments change but don't immediately join the ALBA or embark as quickly upon the radical package of reforms, such as in Paraguay and El Salvador. There, Social Movements continue to be active in pressuring the governments to finally join the Bolivarians.

Chavez formally recognizes that, in Latin America, the days of using armed revolutionaries are over. They are no longer able to carry out the activities of the past—and the world no longer accepts violence as acceptable to advance a political agenda. Yet Chavez has learned that he has something more important at his disposal: an army of activists, bloggers, journalists, union members, taxi drivers and public-bus drivers, youth, indigenous groups, environmentalists, anarchists, communists and socialists, who will shut down cities and subvert institutions in the name of social justice.

In addition, he has learned the world accepts the activity of that which is perceived as organized civil society, and has learned from the best of the FSP experts how to talk about their activities: They don't want to change regimes, they want to advance social justice. They don't want to destroy capitalism, they want to advance workers' rights. They don't want to eliminate private property, they want to support collective property. Through the freedom to do discretionary spending, Chavez has successfully established an army of quite literally millions that promotes his new order, and that will come to his defense at any time. He has additionally learned that fielding this army is relatively cheap. Weapons are expensive; the costs of producing the propaganda and other instruments necessary to energize a mass of activists is marginal.

Finally, as he learned in Bolivia, Ecuador, Nicaragua, Argentina and Venezuela (and almost in Mexico, and for a time Honduras), ousting governments is easy when institutions are weak and organized and motivated hordes on the presidential palace steps send them easily into exile.

ALBA-TCP, Cochabamba, Bolivia, 15 al 17 de Octubre de 2009.

CHAPTER 10

How Does the ALBA Behave?
A Venezuela Story

Parallel to other considerations, it is wise to look at several anecdotes in Venezuela (as the leading imperial nation guiding ALBA along its path). The results of this scrutiny will highlight the real situation on the ground. Again, for those studying the ALBA countries, we know that as goes Venezuela, so goes the ALBA.

In fact, these activities discussed in this chapter have led the world to be concerned about Chavez' (and by extension, the ALBA's) democratic credentials.

As in most places, the devil is very much in the details. Chavez has dismantled Venezuelan democracy incrementally and gradually. The benefit of 21st Century Socialism is that, through the sophisticated manipulation of the levers of power within what appears on the surface to be democracy, democracy has been dismantled with hardly a world from democrats—and even applause from the traditional left. Following are examples of activity that has garnered Chavez criticism from those willing to pay attention.

Political Prisoners: Each story of the political prisoners in Venezuela is heart breaking, since they affect the lives of individuals and families who dared to stand up against Chavez. In 2009, the State Department recognized thirty-two political prisoners in Venezuelan jails.[238] One of these political prisoners was General Francisco Uson. Uson, a retired general, was

---

238 State Department 2009 Human Rights Report. http://www.state.gov/g/drl/rls/hrrpt/2009/wha/136130.htm, http://www.venezuelaawareness.com/informevaf/report2009.htm

sentenced to five years of jail after a military tribunal (even though as retired military he was due a civil trial). His crime: giving—as a civilian—his professional opinion that two soldiers who died in a fire after being jailed for voting against Chavez in the 2004 referendum were in fact killed by a flamethrower.

Also, there was Eduardo Lapi, former opposition governor of Yaracuy State, held for nine months pending trial for corruption. He was not given the right to bail, as the constitution guaranteed, and his trial suffered multiple delays. He was able to escape and is currently living in exile. Capriles Radonski, Governor of Miranda State, was held for four months in the Political Police (DISIP—now SEBIN) jails, for allegedly masterminding an assault on the Cuban embassy during the April 2002 coup (even despite videotaped evidence of the Cuban ambassador thanking him for his work staving off damage to the embassy).

There have also been several police officers used as scapegoats to blame the April 11, 2002 violence on the opposition. Judge Maria Lourdes Afiuni released a banker on bail after he had been held for more than two years (the maximum legal limit) without a trial. Chavez ordered her detention, and she is under house arrest awaiting trial for doing her job.

Political Persecution: There are currently more than three thousand people on Venezuelan government lists, being processed for various political crimes.[239] These include members of the civil society organization SUMATE, the organizers of the 2004 recall referendum, who are on trial for treason for accepting NED (National Endowment for Democracy) funding for a civic education campaign. The four hundred people who signed the Carmona Decree (a document supporting the interim government of Pedro Carmona after the 2002 coup) are also on trial for treason. In the run-up to the 2008 municipal elections, over four hundred people were declared ineligible to run by the Comptroller General's Office, even though the constitution says only those found guilty of a crime by a judge are unable to participate. The Venezuelan government uses the tax services to harass opposition.

Political Discrimination: After the August 2004 recall referendum, Chavez instructed a National Assembly Deputy to review the signatures of people

---

239 Press Release of the Democratic United Table in Venezuela. http://www.unidadvenezuela.org/tag/perseguidos-politicos/

who signed a petition calling for a recall vote (3.4 million signatures). These signatures, ID numbers, birthdates, addresses and other information were put into a database called the "Lista Maisanta" (the Maisanta List, named after a revolutionary hero), which was then distributed across the country.[240] This list was used by the Venezuelan government, at Chavez' instruction, to discriminate politically against anyone who had tried to have him removed from office. Since the Venezuelan government is being transformed under the current government into a super-state, as dictated by Chavez' 21st Century Socialism, and is the largest employer, runs housing loan programs, public hospitals, and a myriad of other social services, many people found themselves excluded from the system.

Education Reform: Chavez' many attempts to rewrite history in his image have received significant opposition from the population, who see education as their children's only chance for advancement. The substitution of Che Guevara poems for math and science leaves Venezuelan children far behind others in the world. This was exemplified by a "Morality and Lights" campaign (named after a speech by Simon Bolivar). In this, Chavez' brother Adan worked for two years to produce the new national curriculum. After the end result was a twenty-page pamphlet, Adan was fired and sent into political exile in his home state of Barinas.

Expropriations: The Government of Venezuela has seized over 2.5 million hectares of private property across Venezuela. This has caused the country's productive capacity to collapse, requiring the government to import more foodstuffs from Brazil and other countries. Mr. Chavez has also seized private businesses as he attempts to create socialism. Over the years he has nationalized 623 companies large and small—from great steel-processing plants and oil refineries to mom-and-pop grocery stores in the capital, accused of hoarding chicken or soap.[241] In Caracas, more than sixty buildings have been taken over by Chavistas with no compensation to the rightful owners. These expropriations are politically motivated; they are not a serious land-redistribution program by the Venezuelan government. The redistributions are meant to reward cronies and punish political opposition.

---

240 You can download the Maisanta List from here should you desire. http://www.filecrop.com/LISTA-MAISANTA.html
241 "Chavez ha expropiado y mal administrado," La Prensa 4 de Febrero, 2011. http://www.laprensa.com.ni/2011/02/04/politica/51076

Chavez gives lip service to land reform, but since Venezuela is ninety-five percent urbanized, with huge tracks of fertile land unused, this has simply become a mechanism to take productive farms from upper or middle-class enemies and distribute the properties to his cronies (or his family, who allegedly now own seventeen huge farms). Decades of inadequate investment, overdependence on importation, and now price caps on food, have made domestic agriculture untenable. While a grocery owner can try to recoup their losses on basic goods by charging $25 for a box of imported cereal, there is little a producer of eggs or milk can do to cover their losses when the price is fixed.

Violence: Violent crime is increasing to uncontrollable levels. What were five thousand murders per year when Chavez took office has become between sixteen and nineteen thousand in 2009.[242] The Venezuelan government position on crime, outlined by the former Minister of the Interior Pedro Carreno during one of the countless hours of propaganda on national television, is that "We are not going to send the National Guard and the police on every street corner in the barrios. We are not about repression just because these people are darker-skinned and poorer, and understand when people need to steal to feed their families. I know much greater thieves than these, and they live in the Country Club and in the East."

Hearing this, the violent criminals understand that the Venezuelan government will not go after them. Caracas is now the single most-violent city on the planet, with 130 murders per one hundred thousand. The country has between fifty-two and fifty-four murders per one hundred thousand. Addressing this, a subsequent minister of the interior said, "These murders generally happen between rival drug gangs and don't, therefore, affect the general security situation in Caracas." Official government murder statistics were classified as state secrets in 2005. Even should they be released, the government considers any murder committed with six or more bullets to be settling of scores and doesn't officially categorize them as murder. This has led the criminals to become more and more violent to avoid prosecution.

The violence extends to the prisons, where between four and five hundred inmates are killed and thousands injured each year.

---

242 INE Estudio de Victimizacion.

Judicial Manipulation: One of Chavez's first acts was to increase the number of judges on the Supreme Tribunal of Justice from sixteen to twenty-four, assuring control of the courts. Judges are terrified to issue rulings that could attract the ire of President Chavez. During a study of judicial independence carried out by the nongovernmental organization Consorcio Justicia, of one thousand judges approached only seven were even willing to answer a simple questionnaire.[243] When the Supreme Tribunal of Justice was made aware of the survey, they opened an investigation into this local NGO. Currently, due to the fear of making the wrong decision and getting fired, there are over six million open cases in Venezuelan courts.

Electoral Manipulation: As discussed previously, elections are used by Chavez and the ALBA to justify dismantling democratic institutions. This makes it essential to keep winning elections. Chavez uses manipulation of the electoral process to assure his victories. This includes (but is not limited to):[244] (1) stacking the electoral registry (allegedly with one million ghost voters); (2) use of state resources through FONDEN for partisan campaigns; (3) having courts declare popular opposition politicians ineligible to run; (4) voter intimidation; (5) gerrymandering; (6) a system called the *"morochas"* (twins) which manipulates the Handt method of proportional representation by allowing the creation of ghost parties—but only for the pro-Chavez side, and thereby securing a larger percentage of seats proportionally than votes cast. Since Chavez refuses to allow an audit of the electoral registry, and uses state resources as petty cash, truth about the extent of electoral manipulation may never be known.

Financial Fraud: Chavez is using the Venezuelan oil industry and its earnings as his private political bank account. In 2006 CITGO de-listed from the New York Stock Exchange, purchasing back their shares[245]. CITGO is a US-registered petroleum company, which is the wholly owned subsidiary of Petroleo de Venezuela (PDV America), Venezuelan state oil company PDVSA's international holding. PDVSA also has not released profit numbers for years, and its current level of company debt is at $32 billion. This is due to the fact that PDVSA passes money to FONDEN, bypassing the

---

243 Author interviews with confidential sources.

244 Author interviews with confidential sources, research and personal experience.

245 SEC Delisting Notice http://www.sec.gov/rules/delist/1-14380_012006.pdf

Central Bank which is the legal pass-through for all money entering the country (not to mention government accounts). Chavez uses this public money to fund partisan electoral events, marchers and protesters, transport voters, and for other partisan activities.

Corruption: As demonstrated by Transparency International indicators, Venezuela has become one of the most corrupt countries in the world. Venezuela's ranking has collapsed since Chavez came to power. Chavez is managing a kleptocracy that rivals Mobutu's Zaire, and hands out money to the military to purchase their loyalty; he hands out money to local leaders through the Consejos Comunales (and communes).[246] The so-called "*boliburguesia*" (Bolivarian Bourgeois), members of the Chavez government who are now rich, are buying apartments for cash in upscale neighborhoods, and taking expensive vacations. Meanwhile, the infrastructure of the country crumbles. Hospitals are ripped apart. The roads grow increasingly potholed. Blackouts are on the rise. And the poor get poorer, inflation increases, and discontent grows. The economy itself is collapsing, with Foreign Direct Investment almost vanishing and making Venezuela the only country economy in the continent contracting following the 2007 economic crisis.

Attacks on the Media: During Chavez' tenure attacks on the free media have increased exponentially. Chavez's verbal attacks were intense against opposition outlets. He has called Globovision, an opposition all-news station, a "terrorist network," "stinking cesspool," and so on, and threatening them with closure if they don't "*cojer minimo*" (chill out). There are roughly seventy to eighty attacks on journalists each year. Some of these are physical. Frequently, reporters of Globovision are pushed around or beaten while covering pro-Chavez events. Attacks on Globovision installations have become commonplace, usually involving spray-paint and the like. In 2007, a local newspaper's photojournalist was shot and killed while trying to cover a march. A famous editor of an online news-journal/blog had his car bombed. Anonymous strangers threatened his children. There

---

246 I have personally witnessed this, for example, during a trip into Venezuela's interior. I stopped at a bakery for a coffee and overheard a conversation for a local Consejo Comunal. The president of the council had received a transfer, and was working with other council leaders to decide how much to give out. He was writing each member a check for Bs. 5,000,000, which at the time was roughly $2,500.

are also judicial threats, such as the charging of Gustavo Azocar (a reporter in Tachira State) for defamation after he criticized local National Assembly Deputy Iris Valera. There was the fining of famous comedian Laureano Marquez for $15,000 (and $400,000 against the newspaper where he published, *Tal Cual*), for publishing a letter to Chavez's daughter—this, after Chavez said he was changing the National Coat of Arms because his daughter had asked him why the horse was running right instead of left.

Of course the most famous attack was the closure of RCTV television station. The most popular station in Venezuela, Chavez said he was closing it because they supported the coup of 2002. If this was indeed the case, then this would be grounds for a trial against the production manager, not closure of the station. However, no case was brought against RCTV for anything in any court of the land. They were simply shut down and their equipment seized.

Harassment of Civil Society: The right to assembly is sacrosanct in the Venezuelan constitution. However, in all soft dictatorships such as Venezuela, civil society has become a powerful force of opposition and democracy. Movements peopled by organized citizens demanding their rights be respected have replaced the coups of the sixties and seventies. The creation of this new sector in democracies has empowered citizens who want to do something to protect their values. Organized civil society has become partners in democracy promotion throughout the world. For such a small group of individuals they carry significant power. Chavez understood this, and his tripartite Chavez-Military-People triangle saw no place for organized civil society that was not loyal to him. Therefore, he has tried hard to shut down civil society, using legal means and intimidation. SUMATE leadership was accused and put on trial for treason.

Human rights defenders were particularly hard hit. A human rights defender protecting the rights of the displaced was gunned down in southern Zulia. Another, working on the right to education, was shot in Anzoátegui. A human rights leader in Portuguesa State was accused of running a car-smuggling ring. Many of the human rights defenders have received death threats. Of particular concern to Chavez was the funding of NGOs, specifically by the United States (NED and USAID). Chavez believes if he can strangle off the NGOs' funding sources, he can destroy them. He first tried judicial threats. Next, state television channel VTV has a segment that attacks different NGOs on a constant basis. For example, VTV obtained the list of NED grantees in Venezuela and read them one by one on the air, threatening and insulting them. The station obtains materials, programs or books used by NGOs to ridicule and threaten them. It seeks to link them with the US embassy at every opportunity. The National Assembly held hearings into the alleged US infiltration of Venezuela using civil society. Rather than being cowed, Venezuelan NGOs work harder.

Most recently, the National Assembly passed the Self-Determination Law in the waning hours of the lame duck supermajority in December of 2010. This law forbids any individual or group involved in "political activity (as defined by the Venezuelan government)" to have any support or contact with foreigners. The Chavez government considers human rights and citizen participation political activity. It has become impossible to even register an NGO.

International Meddling and Blunders: As mentioned previously, Chavez's ALBA is expansionist in nature. As I mentioned in the second chapter, Chavez' goal is to rebuild the empire of Gran Colombia that was lost by Simon Bolivar when he was betrayed by Generals Paez and Santander during the Third Republic. However, Chavez's expansionism is tempered by fear. While he wishes to build a Latin-American confederation, Chavez realizes that an invasion of another country would be a war that his corrupt and politicized military could not win. It could also, in his mind, spark retaliation by the United States, his nemesis and his most feared adversary. For this reason he uses instead the ALBA Social Movements—both legal and terrorist—as a front for infiltration.

CHAPTER 11

Nicaragua, Bolivia & Ecuador's 21st Century Socialism

Perhaps the most succinct description of the ALBA's 21st Century Socialism came from a document filtered from the Sandinista Party (FSLN) at an internal planning meeting.

In 2009 in Nicaragua, a document surfaced entitled "Revolutionary Brotherhood—21st Century Socialism."[247] This document is purported to have been authored by the FSLN Secretariat following a meeting with Venezuela's President Hugo Chavez. The document explains point by point how the FSLN intended to build their "Second Sandinista Revolution" based on Chavez's model of 21st Century Socialism.

Specifically, the document lays out the fundamental building blocks used to construct 21st Century Socialism. These tenets include extending presidential mandates, changing governing constitutions, co-opting the branches of government under the party's revolutionary tutelage, fomenting social conflict between different strata of society, limiting basic rights such as property, speech and assembly, and using government resources for partisan political purposes. The document, in its entirety, reads as follows.

Frente Sandinista de Liberacion Nacional
Project
21st Century Socialism, "Revolutionary Brotherhood"

The President of the Government of Bolivarian Unity of Venezuela, Hugo Chavez Frias, proposed to Companion President Daniel Ortega

247 Hermandad Revolucionaria." http://www.scribd.com/doc/39192834/Hermandad-Revolucionaria-Socialismo-Siglo-21

Saavedra the project of 21st Century Socialism "Revolutionary Brotherhood." This is a Latin-American program for the sustainability of 21st Century Socialism: Nicaraguan Chapter. This program, the Nicaraguan Revolutionaries, true sons of Sandino, have denominated the "Second Sandinista Revolution." From Bolivar to Sandino, we have proudly approved this and presented it at a private meeting with Commander Hugo Chavez, in Managua. This meeting was held in the secretariat of the FSLN, in the month of January of 2009.

On that occasion we were addressed by a very enthusiastic and optimistic Commander Chavez, who explained to his companion Daniel Ortega that similar projects were already being implemented in the rest of the countries befriended by the ALBA, albeit with their own characteristics. Among those are Honduras, Ecuador, Bolivia, El Salvador, Nicaragua and Venezuela. Sponsored politically and economically by Venezuela. He insisted that the financing would be assumed entirely by the brother nation of Venezuela with a participation of 1,000 million dollars a year per country.

The ALBA countries that are promoting the project are: Ecuador, Bolivia, Honduras, Nicaragua, Cuba and Venezuela. Other candidates will be incorporated, specifically: Dominican Republic and El Salvador.

Among the guiding principles of the Project Revolutionary Brotherhood, is the indispensable need to maintain control of the governments of the aforementioned countries and extend it for fifteen years, at a minimum, with the continuation of the power of the revolutionary leaders Manuel Zelaya, Daniel Ortega, Evo Morales, Rafael Correa, Raul Castro and Hugo Chavez. In Nicaragua and Honduras, where to date the revolutionary succession of the current presidents is not secured, there should start an immediate and uninterrupted campaign beginning with the next Sandinista Congress to take place in October of 2009. In the case of Honduras we will work for the reelection of Zelaya in November 2009.

Nicaragua Chapter
"Second Sandinista Revolution"

A group of valuable Sandinista cadres, coordinated by the companion Rosario Murillo, have adjusted this revolutionary initiative of the people to the concrete realities of the free Nicaragua of Sandino. Now we have a tool, a plan which at the same time is a guide to action. We have agreed that we will make it known to our members in the next Sandinista Congress. We are sure that the same will be enriched and we will all implement in according to our Sandinista mystique in a deliberate fashion.

The new strategic lines of action are defined as the recuperation of the revolutionary rights that have been lost.

To implement them we require a new Political Constitution. In which shall be reformed all the powers of the state, seizing the quotas of power from the liberals; that way we will forever end the blackmail and our adversaries won't be able to recuperate power within the next fifteen years.

It is important to gain followers in the Armed Forces who support the Sandinistas and make them understand that in this way they are assuring and protecting the interests of the people and their investments and interests between revolutionary Sandinista brothers.

These reforms will guarantee the necessary transformations in the political, economic, social, cultural and even religious areas. Reaching both the city and the field, principally in possession of education, health, popular housing, agriculture and other key emblematic programs, like the Citizen's Power, and the resurgence of the cooperatives and the reconversion of the police and the Army.

Principle Areas of Focus

1) Conduct within the mark of 21st Century Socialism and the Bolivarian Alliance for the peoples of our America, ALBA, the popular conflict against the oligarchs and imperialism. Minimize the figures of the United States and Europe, emphasizing Venezuelan solidarity and the leadership of Commander Hugo Chavez.

2) Establish the Citizen Power as the central figure of leadership and revolutionary organization, which will substitute the historic "National Board" of the old FSLN. Restructure the party with new leadership where Commander Daniel Ortega and the Citizen Power will be the symbol par excellence of the Second Sandinista Revolution.

3) Transform the institutions of the state into inexpugnable bastions of Sandinistas; carry this out as secretly as possible, including the Armed Forces, Police and Army linking themselves directly with the party and the organizations of the Citizen Power. Quickly there has to be felt again among the people the "Armed Forces of the Citizen Power." For this, implement revolutionary outreach nationally with joint participation between members, military and police together with the people.

4) Break the link that exists between members of the Armed Forces with the "right" and teach them new revolutionary concepts, with support to and from our Venezuelan and Cuban brothers.

5) Deepen the weakness and division of the political opposition, taking advantage of their weaknesses, and by the means and methods necessary monopolize the National Assembly, the Supreme Court of Justice and the Supreme Electoral Council.

6) Promote a tactical alliance with businesses, concentrating our effort in giving political "alms" which provide them certain minimum spaces in which they can be allies and not enemies of FSLN. Concentrating on characteristics of personal leaders to gain their support of our system.

7) Recuperate the Sandinista Citizenship, which in the neoliberal governments has left defeated, lost, demoralized, demobilized or deserted, making them protagonists of their new Sandinista Revolution and beneficiaries of the partisan governmental policies.

8) Recuperate at all cost the spaces lost in the arena of the media, investing human and economic resources until we totally dominate this arena, which is strategic for our fight. Revert the tendencies against Sandinismo, taking the media war to the heart of the Nicaraguan society.

Actions to guarantee the Popular Revolutionary Power

Assure that we do not hand over power until at least three consecutive terms of Sandinismo. That is to say after fifteen years of revolutionary government.

Obtain the constitutional reforms that change the political panorama based upon essential supports:

1. Hegemonize and control the powers of the state and the institutions considered key:
    A. Control the National Assembly
    B. Control the Supreme Court of Justice
    C. Control the Supreme Electoral Council
    D. Obtain support from the police and the army
    E. Not challenge the private sector

2. Recuperate the revolutionary rights lost, upon which are dependent the popular support and vote:
    A. Political
    B. Economic
    C. Social
    D. Educational/Cultural
    E. Religious

3. Approve laws which totally modify the national policies and which reject the model of savage capitalism:
    A. Economic
    B. Health
    C. Education
    D. Governance
    E. Agrarian
    F. Social

4. Recuperate the Sandinista Citizenship:

We must guarantee the consolidation of 2 million Sandinista Party members before the next elections in 2011. This support will be sufficient to guarantee victory.

Activities to carry out

- Restructuring and organizing the party communally with the CPC down to the local level

- Updating our statistics
- Printing ID cards
- Activate the organic life of the party, everybody in the field, nobody should stay at home
- Prize and stimulate our affiliates with jobs in government, such as municipalities
- Carry out constant political and popular activities
- Maintain active the Electoral Commandos to be able to utilize them as support for any circumstance.

5. Strengthen our position against the official Catholic Church. Highlighting the figure of Cardinal Miguel Obando y Bravo, as a symbol of our alliance with the Church that supports the Government of Reconciliation, Peace and National Unity. At this moment it is essential the support of members of the National Convergence and some sectors of the opposition but currently allies: Nicaraguan Resistance, Evangelical Pastors, people who are not motivated and notable figures, among others.

6. Highlight the achievements of the emblematic programs of the administration of Daniel Ortega, such as Hunger "zero," houses for the people, roads for the people, zero usury, the productive bonus, literacy, etc.

7. Creation of the block "Sandino Vive"; made up of loyal companions, to confront and oppose whatever armed group which is supported by the right, especially by Monsenor Abelardo Mata

8. Impede the unity of the so-called "Democratic Forces"; negotiate and torpedo whenever possible with the liberal leaders to keep the image of the pact alive, which can be a cornerstone to deepen its contradictions and divisions.

9. Keep compartmentalized and secret our plans within the partisan and governmental discipline

10. In the case of an external intervention from the United States.

If it becomes necessary we can convoke and establish the participation of "Patriotic Citizens" to defend our sovereignty, pulling in members of the ALBA.

Managua, Nicaragua
Secretariat Frente Sandinista de Liberacion Nacional (FSLN)
(End of document.)

In order to extend his control over Nicaragua, President Ortega has been gaming the system. Generally speaking, ALBA countries attempt to change political constitutions to strengthen the executive power. In Nicaragua, especially in Ortega's first (and only constitutional) term, this is difficult. Instead, Ortega decided to manipulate the judiciary to extend his control.[248] He re-nominated several Sandinista judges, whose terms had expired, allowing them to remain on the bench. Ortega then filed a case in the same Supreme Court against the state, arguing that the term limits set in the 1995 constitutional reforms violated his rights. On October 20, 2009, the court (with the same judges still illegally in place) ruled in his favor, thereby effectively eliminating term limits. This has set the groundwork for Ortega's own reelection in 2011. In 2008, Ortega staged[249] a fraudulent municipal election, using traditional tricks such as ballot stuffing to steal upwards of twenty municipalities including the mayor of the capital, Managua. This fraud cemented his control over a majority of Nicaraguans. Simultaneously, the Ortega government has closed twenty television and radio stations, and has continued to threaten independent newspapers like *La Prensa* and *El Nuevo Diario*. According to the Nicaraguan parliamentarian Wilfred Navarro, President Ortega has violated the Nicaraguan constitution sixty-seven times.[250]

Through a trinity of national security laws[251] passed in December of 2010 by the FSLN-controlled parliament, Ortega has increased his control over a once professional and nonpartisan security apparatus that serves to

---

248 "Golpe de Estado de Daniel Ortega al poder Judicial," La Gaceta, 14 de Agosto, 2010. http://www.intereconomia.com/noticias-gaceta/internacional/golpe-estado-daniel-ortega-al-poder-judicial-nicaragua

249 Carlos Salinas Maldonado, "El fraude electoral divide a Nicaragua," El Pais,14 de Noviembre, 2008. http://www.elpais.com/articulo/internacional/fraude/electoral/divide/Nicaragua/elpepuint/20081114elpepiint_1/Tes

250 Maria Jose Uriarte, "Ortega viola 67 veces constitución," La Prensa, 10 de Septiembre 2010. http://www.laprensa.com.ni/2010/09/10/politica/37336

251 "Diputados aprueban leyes de defensa y seguridad nacional," La Jornada, 14 de Diciembre 2010. http://www.lajornadanet.com/diario/archivo/2010/diciembre/14/2.html

continue to build his Revolutionary Brotherhood. The military is an important piece of 21st Century Socialism, as outlined by Ceresole. Ortega has understood this and has therefore consistently tried to undermine the independence guarded so cautiously by the Nicaraguan military. These laws are his first, tentative attempt to arrive at a point where, as in Venezuela and Bolivia, the military is willing to salute and defend "Fatherland, Socialism or Death."

The ALBA has played a central role in helping Ortega consolidate power. The main mechanism the ALBA has used to support Ortega is financial support. Shortly after joining the ALBA, Daniel Ortega registered a private company, ALBA de Nicaragua S.A. (ALBANISA). This company is forty-nine-percent owned by PetroNIC, Nicaragua's oil company and PDVSA. The President of ALBANISA is Asdrubal Chavez,[252] a vice president of PDVSA, on the board of directors of CITGO and cousin of President Hugo Chavez. Francisco Lopez, President of PetroNIC is the vice-president of ALBANISA (and also treasurer of the FSLN). One of ALBANISA's principal actors is Rafael Ortega Murillo, the eldest son of President Ortega and his powerful wife, Rosario Murillo.

ALBANISA is financed through the PetroCaribe oil agreement. Through this agreement, PetroNIC receives gas that it sells for market value through its affiliates in the country. Of the value of the gas, fifty percent of the amount is paid up front, with twenty-five percent transferred to the ALBA fund, for use in social projects across the ALBA. The remaining twenty-five percent is passed to ALBA-Caruna which is a micro-finance organization that acts as the ALBA's bank in Nicaragua.[253] The funding for ALBANISA is transferred from ALBA-Caruna. Rosario Murrillo is the coordinator for the ALBA in Nicaragua. The ALBANISA company has spread out like an octopus into the Nicaraguan economy, spawning many other "ALBANITAS," small daughter companies. These include ALBA Transport, ALBA Security, ALBA Equipment, ALBA Ports, ALBA Power Generation, ALBA Warehouses, ALBA Agriculture and ALBA Tourism.

---

252 "ALBANISA, ALBA y Soberania Nacional," Palabras de Rosario Murillo. http://www.presidencia.gob.ni/index.php?option=com_content&view=article&id=190:albanisa-alba-soberania-y-dignidad&catid=58:febrero-2009&Itemid=54
253 Luis Galeano, "Albanisa es un Pulpo," El Nuevo Diario, 28 de Septiembre 2009. http://www.elnuevodiario.com.ni/nacionales/58180

These businesses have allowed President Ortega to purchase hotels such as the Seminole in Managua, farms and ranches, and even TV Channel 8 (which was formerly the primary opposition channel). According to the "2009 Annual International Cooperation Report" published by the Nicaraguan Central Bank, international cooperation with Venezuela in 2009 was the primary source of FDI, reaching $443 million. According to this report, during the same period Venezuelan petroleum assistance was $236 million. From this amount, $117 million was a grant and $119 million was a loan to ALBA-Caruna.

Parallel to the petroleum assistance, the ALBA has also provided Nicaragua with fifty thousand tons of Venezuelan fertilizer.[254] Fifty percent of the value of this fertilizer is paid to Venezuela, twenty-five percent is deposited into ALBA-Caruna, and it is sold for twenty-five percent less on the market. There are no controls on the use of these funds.[255] According to information leaked recently from inside the Ortega Administration, ALBA Caruna currently has $500 million in liquid assets in the banks. ALBA assistance has totaled well over one billion dollars since Ortega took power.

This funding has allowed President Ortega to activate social programs sponsored by the Citizens Power—of which Rosario Murillo is the head. Citizens Power is a para-state organized at the grass roots, responding directly to the president's wife as part of the leader-people link (outlined by Ceresole). These citizens' power committees meet, decide on their needs, and submit requirements through the mayor's office to the center. These needs are met by staff of ALBANISA, who carry out the initiatives. These projects are programs such as "Zero Hunger" which involves providing cows and chickens to local populations. According to a Dutch study[256] of this program, real malnutrition was brought down by four percent. However, the study also acknowledged that the FSLN participated in the selection of beneficiaries and that the program was populist political posturing, not development. Nevertheless, it has had a huge impact in

---

254 "Venezuela entrega 13,200 toneladas de fertilizante para productores de granos en Nicaragua," El Nacional, 14 de Septiembre 2010. http://www.el-nacional.com/www/site/p_contenido.php?q=nodo/154891/Econom%EDa/Venezuela-entrega-13.200-toneladas-de-fertilizante-para-productores-de-granos-en-Nicaragua
255 Author interviews with confidential sources.
256 Paul Kester, "Zero Hunger: Development or just Raindrops," February 2009. http://www.envio.org.ni/articulo/4141

the minds of the poor. Other projects have been the "6 Sheets of Zinc" which supports rural areas with roofing; a bonus of $25 for all 125,000 public servants (in a recent announcement in the run-up to the 2011 elections, Ortega increased this to $32 for 155,000 people); public transport subsidizing for the city of Managua; and others. Recent polls indicate that the brotherhood plan is working. The first principal area of focus from the document states the desire to replace the United States with Chavez/ Venezuela as the most recognized friend of Nicaragua. According to a poll carried out in September 2010 by M&R Consulting, a full 50.1 percent of respondents see Venezuela as Nicaragua's greatest friend; in the same poll only 18.5 percent see the United States as such.

As stated in the "Revolutionary Brotherhood" document (and following much more closely Heinz Dieterich and Norberto Ceresole), Daniel Ortega has refused to engage in a pitched battle with the private sector. Perhaps having learned from his experience in the 1980s, he has instead offered the private sector a deal; if they do not oppose him politically (or finance the opposition), they will be protected and included in business deals.[257] With the amount of ALBA money flowing through the country, and having experienced Ortega's wrath in the 1980s, most businessmen have capitulated. This does not bode well for the Nicaraguan opposition.

In November of 2011, President Ortega won re-election in an electoral event which was widely regarded as fraudulent. Ortega was able to not only control the Presidency but was also, according to the independent national observer Etica y Transperencia, to swing between 8 and 12 parliamentary seats; effectively handing the FSLN control of congress. President Ortega's plan is to perpetuate himself in power while using his ALBA money to assure an absolute majority in the National Assembly, at which point he will be able to change the constitution at will and continue to advance his authoritarian plan.

Nevertheless, these plans may have suffered a setback due to a scandal associated with the Nicaraguan management of ALBA funding. On March 5, 2011, Carlos Fernando Chamorro, a well-known journalist and son of former president Violetta Chamorro, released a new website called ALBAleaks that contains internal financial documents obtained from

---

257 Author interviews with confidential sources.

the ALBANISA and all its ALBANITAS.[258] These documents outline in detail the transactions over the last three years of ALBANISA, totaling over one billion dollars. Two accountants who reviewed the Excel spreadsheets concluded that ALBANISA is un-auditable. The rift happened when PetroNIC and ALBANISA refused to account to PDVSA for the funding. This caused PDVSA auditors—accompanied by the president of KPMG (an international accounting firm) in Venezuela—to arrive in Managua. In a meeting dripping with irony due in part to the venue, the Venezuelan auditors met with their Nicaraguan counterparts in the lobby of Daniel Ortega's Seminole Hotel. The purpose was to discuss the accounts, and the activity that has led Daniel Ortega to become arguably the richest man in Nicaragua. As of publication, the conflict is ongoing, and has led to the temporary cessation of oil exports from Venezuela to Nicaragua and a rift between Nicaragua and Venezuelan revolutionaries.

Bolivia

Perhaps the closest relationship within the ALBA is the relationship between Evo Morales' Bolivia and Hugo Chavez' Venezuela. Morales was elected President of Bolivia on December 19, 2005, after years of instability, in part a result of Morales' Venezuela-funded agitation. Waving coca branches in the air, he headed to the polls hoping to become the first Bolivian president of indigenous descent. While billing himself internationally as an indigenous leader, Morales is actually a mestizo (of mixed European and American Indian origin), of Aymara origin, with no indigenous leadership responsibilities. His political base is instead the coca growers association (called *cocaleros*), of which he was (and remains) president. Morales played a key role in the instability leading to the overthrow of former President Carlos Mesa. During this time, and fanned by his many trips to Caracas, rumors swirled that coca union leader Morales was receiving funding and support from Venezuela's Hugo Chavez.

Bolivia joined the ALBA on April 29, 2006. Immediately, Morales began to implement the ALBA package of 21st Century Socialism. On July 2, 2006, voters agreed to a Constituent Assembly to rewrite the constitution,

---

258 ALBALEAKS web site. http://www.confidencial.com.ni/albaleaks

and voted on the 255 delegates.[259] In the first setback to the Morales regime, his Movement Towards Socialism (MAS) Party failed to secure an absolute majority of the delegates—which was needed to approve the constitution before it went to the people for a national referendum. Morales's MAS is Bolivia's primary political movement . According to Rene Antonio Mayorga, Bolivian political scientist:

Since its beginnings as a conglomerate of cocalero syndicates forged by direct action, the MAS has been essentially an authoritarian and antidemocratic movement, where internal debate, acceptance of dissent and the clash of ideas are foreign concepts. As a governing party the MAS has become an organization controlled by a small group of people who exercise power in the name of indigenous social movements and whose members, like [vice president Alvaro] Garcia Linera or [minister of the presidency] Juan Ramón Quintana were never members of the MAS and who joined the party during the electoral process.[260]

Simultaneously, voters in four of Bolivia's nine states—called colloquially "the crescent"—voted for greater autonomy from the central government. This would lead to violence in the future. Not to be stymied by a vote, and in true Bolivarian fashion, Morales's MAS illegally altered the number of votes needed to pass the constitution (from an absolute majority to a simple majority). This move provoked instability in the regions, especially the crescent areas. Strikes, work stoppages, parliamentary walkouts and violence followed in the next months as the MAS-dominated Constituent Assembly continued to push for its new constitution. Instability continued through 2007 as Morales nationalized the gas sector (managed by PetroBras: the Brazilian Energy Conglomerate), fought with the United States over counter-narcotics issues, began budding relationships with Iran and Gaddafi's Libya while deepening its ties with Venezuela. He expelled the US DEA, increased the amount of land legally available for coca production and expelled the US ambassador.

Domestically, in an act of defiance, unable to dislodge the new constitution from the Constituent Assembly due to the opposition delegates, on

---

259 Timelines Web Site. http://timelines.ws/countries/BOLIVIA.HTML
260 René Antonio Mayorga, "Sociedad Civil y Estado Bajo Un Populismo Plebiscitario y Autoritario," La "Nueva Izquierda en América Latina: Derechos Humanos, Participación Política y Sociedad Civil, edited by Cynthia J. Arnson et alia, The Woodrow Wilson International Center for Scholars, (January 2009): P111.

December 9, 2007 the MAS delegates sequestered themselves in a military base, excluding the opposition parliamentarians from entry, announcing that they had abstained from voting and passed the new constitution. On February 28, 2008, the MAS-controlled assembly approved the new constitution. In mid-2008, Morales survived a recall referendum aimed at shoring up support; however, the referendum lost by wide margins as the crescent region voted for greater autonomy. On January 25, 2009 the Bolivian people voted in the referendum on the polemic constitution, which passed easily. This constitution will allow Morales to govern until 2014. It allows for reelection, and Morales has asserted that he is eligible to be reelected because that was his first election under a different constitution. The new constitution provides greater rights for indigenous citizens and for the environment, and changes the name of the country to the Plurinational State of Bolivia (an attempt to recognize the indigenous "nations" within the country). This new constitution has set in place the "leader-people" link so important to 21st Century Socialism through "protagonist democracy" and "indigenous governance" language. It also sets in place Evo Morales as the maximum indigenous leader—the chief of chiefs—through which he can exercise his caudillo control.

Throughout this process, Venezuela and the ALBA have been exceptionally supportive. One important target of Morales' revolution has been the military. Initially, the Bolivian military rejected Evo Morales' political project, more specifically the intromission of Hugo Chavez and his security services in the internal issues of the country. During the worst instability in 2008, when it looked like President Morales would go the way of other Bolivian presidents and be forced from power or the country would be divided in two, Chavez stated, "In the supposed case that the oligarchic forces of Bolivia were to do damage to that brother country—that has the name of Bolivar—Venezuela will not stand by with its arms crossed."[261] This led to the Bolivian military, through General Luis Trigo, then-commander of the army, to state, "The Bolivian Armed Forces will not permit foreign military to set foot in Bolivia."[262] Morales realized he had a problem

261 (Video), Chavez Amenaza con Intervenir a Bolivia, 9 de Mayo, 2008. http://www.marthacolmenares.com/2008/05/09/chavez-amenaza-con-intervenir-bolivia-video/
262 "Fuerzas Armadas de Bolivia Rechazan la intromisión de Chavez," Noticias 24, 12 de Septiembre, 2008. http://www.noticias24.com/actualidad/noticia/17520/

with the military, and began slowly replacing independent military officers with those loyal to him: an element of the ALBA strategy. As Doug Farah has stated:

Perhaps most worrisome on an international level is Morales' increasing reliance on autocratic, nondemocratic states for financial, military and intelligence support. The two most prominent are Venezuela and Iran, in addition to Cuba and Nicaragua. Of particular note is Venezuela's Hugo Chavez, who each year directly pays tens of millions of dollars to the senior leaders of Bolivia's military and whose government is building a series of new military outposts, while providing intelligence training and equipment. At least another $110 million a year goes to directly pay for presidential program "Bolivia Changes, Evo Fulfills His Promises" (*Bolivia Cambia, Evo Cumple*). None of the money passes through the normal budgetary process, but rather flows directly to the presidency with no outside accountability or oversight.[263]

Through this support, and the Venezuelan military advisors who have become so close to Morales they have direct and private access to the president,[264] Morales has gained full control over the military. As of March 2010 the Bolivian military, parroting the Venezuelans, have begun to use the term "Fatherland, Socialism or Death."[265] The ALBA's military training school for asymmetric warfare is based in Santa Cruz.

Morales's next move, part of his protagonist model, was influence over the selection of judges. As this book goes to print, these judges have been initially approved by the MAS-dominated Congress before being voted by the people. The MAS in congress is pushing for stipulations that each of the candidates for judge must be part of a union, and must have participated in the famous Social Movements. The government, through the Electoral Council (controlled by Morales), has stated that any candidating by individual candidates would be unfair, and so the EC itself will be responsible

fuerzas-armadas-de-bolivia-rechazan-intromisiones-de-hugo-chavez/

263 Douglas Farah, "Into The Abyss: Bolivia under Evo Morales and the MAS," International Assessment and Strategy Center.

264 "Wikileaks: Venezuela Sending Money to Top Bolivian Officials," Latin American Herald Tribune. http://laht.com/article.asp?ArticleId=380789&CategoryId=10717

265 "Morales impone a militares lema Patria, Socialismo o Muerte," Reuters, 12 de Marzo, 2010. http://www.eluniverso.com/2010/03/12/1/1361/morales-impone-militares-bolivianos-lema-patria-muerte.html

for divulging information about the candidates. The MAS's selection of judges has been fraught with allegations of influence peddling, nepotism, corruption and abuse of power.[266] Election of these judges is scheduled for October 2011.

The ALBA has supported Bolivia in other areas as well. During the height of the conflict with the "crescent," the Venezuelan embassy in La Paz handed out checks to municipal governments—funds that did not pass through the Bolivian parliament or other official mechanisms. Venezuelan military participated in the protection of the constituent assembly in Sucre state: and are even reported to have fired upon the Bolivian opposition who attempted to storm that military base.[267] Significant support was also received for "Evo Cumple," a populist program allowing Evo petty cash for village projects managed by his constituents at the base.[268] Bolivia has also benefited from the "Yes I Can" Cuban literacy program. Overall, the second-greatest recipient of funding from the ALBA has been Bolivia. As in Venezuela, most of the money is in the form of handouts with little to no accountability, which increases the possibility of corruption but improves Evo Morales' standing in the communities.

Finally, within the ALBA, Evo Morales has been working to define a special "niche" role for Bolivia. This appears to be self-driven, yet comes with a certain support from ALBA countries. Using indigenous symbols, especially in the Inca figure of the "*pachamama*" (mother earth), Morales is attempting to place Bolivia at the center of an alternative climate change and environmental protection movement. During the Copenhagen summits in 2009, Bolivia and the ALBA congealed international opposition to the backroom agreements orchestrated by President Obama and a select group of other countries. This success emboldened Bolivia. On April 19, 2010 in Cochabamba, Morales hosted the First World Conference of the People on Climate Change and the Rights of Mother Earth.[269] Civil-society organizations from more than one hundred countries participated,

---

266 Author interviews with confidential sources.
267 Author interviews with confidential sources.
268 "Bolivia: Manejo de Dinero de Evo Cumple es Secreto," La Razon, 26 de Agosto, 2007. http://www.offnews.info/verArticulo.php?contenidoID=9192
269 World People's Conference on Climate Change and the Rights of Mother Earth web site. http://pwccc.wordpress.com/

as did leaders from the ALBA countries. During this conference, Morales called for reparations against countries suffering from climate change, proposed the creation of a climate court, and proposed establishing the idea of planetary rights to parallel the human rights discussion. Naturally, this Bolivia-led initiative, while not gaining significant international traction yet, has placed President Morales as a beloved figure by international climate change activists. He has been proposed for the Nobel Peace Prize.

Ecuador

Ecuador arrived the latest, and the most timidly, to the Bolivarian Alliance. Like Bolivia, Ecuador had suffered for the last decade with serious instability. In 1997, President Abdala Bucaram was removed from office by the country's congress for mental instability. Since his ouster, Ecuador experienced six presidents in rapid succession. On November 26, 2006, the Ecuadoran people elected Rafael Correa as their seventh president in almost as many years. Correa, an American-educated PhD in Economics from the University of Illinois, seemed to many the best solution to end Ecuador's un-governability. As with Chavez several years before, people were looking for a change that might lead to increased political stability. As with Chavez, political longevity of the elected official has brought more stability at the top, but Correa's now apparent 21st Century Socialist convictions has led to an increase in authoritarian behavior and concerns for foreign investors.

Correa and Chavez have been friends for many years. When Correa was finance minister under then-President Palacio, he negotiated a loan from Venezuela. Fallout from that forced him out of the Palacio government, only to reappear the following year as a presidential candidate. He had already developed a rapport with Chavez, and famously spent a night at Chavez' parents' house in Barinas in late 2005.[270]

On January 15, 2007, Correa assumed the Ecuadorian presidency. Just as in Bolivia, rumors of Chavez's funding of Correa were rampant. According to the US embassy, current foreign minister Ricardo Patino was allegedly responsible for shuttling between Quito and Caracas to pick

---

270 Nikolas Kozloff, "The Rise of Rafael Correa," Counterpunch, November 27, 2006. http://www.globalexchange.org/countries/americas/ecuador/4369.html

up funding for Correa's campaign. The funds are said to have come from Chavez and the FARC.[271]

What happened next is the now familiar process of setting up, as Oscar Alvarez describes them, the dictatorships of the 21st century. The series of events in rapid and short order have allowed Correa to accumulate power in the executive. This power grab was done more quickly than in Venezuela, and more successfully and without as many hiccups as Bolivia.[272] On inauguration day, Correa signed a decree calling for a Constituent Assembly to rewrite the nation's constitution. On January 30th, Correa's supporters assaulted the congress building with sticks, demanding a Constituent Assembly. On February 13, the congress capitulated to the protesters and agreed to hold a referendum on whether a Constituent Assembly should be held. On March 7, the electoral court fired fifty-seven parliamentarians who were still in opposition to the constitutional referendum. On March 20, under cover of night, a group of pro-Correa parliamentarians was sworn in. On March 28, the electoral court fired a judge who ruled in favor of the ousted parliamentarians. On April 4, the country's constitutional court issued a ruling backing up the ouster of the members of parliament. On April 15, in a national referendum, the Constituent Assembly was approved. One week after the assembly was approved, the parliamentarians were returned to their seats by order of the high court. However, Correa immediately sent in the police to physically prevent the return of the parliamentarians to hold their elected seats, while the pro-Correa congressmen who remained voted to dismiss the country's high court.

On September 20, 2007, the country went again to the polls to elect members of the Constituent Assembly; Correa obtained a simple majority. On September 28, 2008, a new constitution was approved in yet another election. This new constitution allows Correa to govern with two additional mandates through 2017, allows him to disband parliament and call snap elections, and sets mechanisms in place for popular, protagonist democracy that we have already seen in Venezuela and Bolivia. On October 29, an interim supreme court took over that institution.

---

271 Wikileaks.
272 Timelines Web Site. http://timelines.ws/countries/ECUADOR.HTML

In December of 2008, Ecuador defaulted on its foreign debt—setting in place a debt crisis that, due to Ecuador's dollarization, did not become a monetary crisis. On April 26, 2009, Ecuadorians participated in their fifth national election in two years—wherein Correa again won a simple majority, but enough to avoid a runoff. The remainder of the following year was occupied by Correa's attempts to close independent television stations (he closed three), consolidate his authority, and increase spending on social programs. On September 30, 2010, another crisis emerged with an uprising of the national police, who were upset about a new public service bill. Correa waded into the kerfuffle and managed to find himself sequestered for twelve hours, under mysterious circumstances, in the police hospital. While on the phone with President Chavez, he called it a coup attempt. Chavez responded with political support, and the OAS Secretary General parroted Chavez' words. After a brief and highly suspicious firefight, Correa was "freed," and subsequently used the incident to restructure the police with officers loyal to him. The opposition cried foul, declaring that it was a "self-coup," intended for Correa to identify dissenters in the military.

As mentioned in the Nicaraguan "Revolutionary Brotherhood" instruction guidelines, creating a conflict buoys popular opinion. In the aftermath of the police dustup, Correa's popularity went up. He has also fired over thirty generals from the police and installed new leadership loyal to him.

On May 7, 2011, Ecuadorians again went to the polls, where they approved ten questions proposed by President Correa. One of these disbanded the supreme court, to be replaced by a ruling *junta* of three, one appointed by Correa, one appointed by the Social Movements (controlled by Correa), and one appointed by the Congress (controlled by Correa). President Correa has succeeded in usurping control of the judiciary. Other limitations in the questions were to freedom of speech and private property. The takeover of Ecuadorian democratic institutions is almost complete.

Most recently, President Correa won a case in the Ecuadorian courts, suing four members (three owners and one editor) of the opposition newspaper *El Universo* for defamation of character for an article in which they claimed the president had authorized the use of lethal force in their attempts to free him from the police hospital where he was located during the police uprising of September 2010. They were sentenced to prison time, and to pay millions in damages.

Just as happened in Venezuela and Bolivia with the energy sector nationalizations, in mid-2008, Ecuador unilaterally renegotiated the petroleum exploration contracts with the large foreign energy companies and expelled Occidental Petroleum from the country. Simultaneously, Venezuela supported Ecuador's return to OPEC. Venezuela has also been refining Ecuadoran oil while assisting in the construction of a new refinery (a project that has brought conflict due to PDVSA's inability to even start the construction process). Again, in Bolivia and Venezuela, this increased government revenue from the oil sectors: in Ecuador's case, by thirty-seven percent in 2010.[273] Conversely, this also created significant investor nervousness and is expected to lead to production issues—as happened in Venezuela and Bolivia—since the best technical knowledge for management is through the transnational energy companies. Venezuela so far has been forced to quietly invite the transnationals back in; in Bolivia the now-government run gas industry is experiencing a leveling off of gas production and revenue.

While Ecuador has been extraordinarily politically active internally, Correa has been quite careful with overt meddling by the ALBA. Correa was the most recent addition to the 21st Century Socialist club, and only joined the ALBA in June of 2009 after power was consolidated internally. The lion's share of the ALBA support has been to the energy sector—whereby Chavez is attempting to increase the ALBA countries' control over extractive industry on the continent. Perhaps understanding the challenges presented by a too-overt relationship with Ecuador, and perhaps at the behest of Correa himself, President Chavez has been content to provide behind-the-scenes support while Correa consolidates power. This is not to say Chavez has been unsupportive. Ecuador ranks fourth in the ALBA commitments—but arrived late to the table, at a moment when Venezuela itself was experiencing difficult economic times. Also, Ecuador has significant resources of its own. As demonstrated by the police dustup, Chavez continues to be the person who helps his satellite countries during difficult moments. Ecuador has also participated in social projects supported by the Cuban government: energy

273 Felipe Bedoya, "Threats to Latin American Gas Subsidies Spark Protests," Revenue Watch Institute, March 15, 2011. http://www.revenuewatch.org/news/news-article/international/threats-latin-america-gas-subsidies-spark-protests

initiatives such as the generator project, which has returned electricity to parts of Venezuela, Cuba and Nicaragua; the tourism program; the medical training program; and the literacy program. There are reportedly thirteen thousand Cubans and eighteen thousand Venezuelans assisting Correa in setting up the ALBA model.[274] Ecuador received support from both the Cuban "Yes I Can" literacy program, and the Mission Miracle health program and others.

Correa has yet to join the ALBA Bank, having stated in a recent summit of ALBA economic ministers that the trajectory of the Bank was unclear. It is envisioned that Ecuador will join the ALBA Bank at the next summit of ALBA nations in late 2011. Despite this fact, Ecuador has energetically embraced the bank's currency, the SUCRE. Most recently, Ecuadorian officials have been energetically promoting the use of the SUCRE as the money of choice of UNASUR (the Union of South American Nations), a political construct meant as a replacement for the OAS.

Ecuador, like Bolivia, has attempted to find a niche for itself within the ALBA. It appears that this will come in the academic and technical arenas. Rafael Correa considers himself an intellectual. In May 2005, when he was a member of the Latin-American parliament, Correa literally wrote the book on the ALBA, a compilation of essays and speeches titled, Building the ALBA—Our North is the South. Correa, the one who envisioned the idea of Monroeism vs. Bolivarianism and an academic by nature, is better accepted within the traditional Latin-American left due to his credentials. Chavez is seen as a military man, Ortega as a throwback to a different time, and Morales (with limited formal education) has a much more indigenous leadership role. Correa lends legitimacy to the intellectual credentials of Bolivarianism.

It is no surprise, given this reality, that Ecuador is at the forefront of what the "Third World Approaches to International Law" (TWAIL) movement calls, "emancipatory international law."

In short, the Bolivarian Revolution provides the structural (state) and popular (people) support needed to shift discussion away from the dominant Eurocentric international legal regime toward a dynamic pluralist alternative.[275]

---

274 Author interviews with confidential sources.
275 Third World Quarterly, Vol. 31, No. 3, (2010): PP 347–363.

Ecuador is becoming the center of what TWAIL outlines. In April of 2010, after a year of analysis and legal maneuvering, President Correa issued an executive order that interrupted international property rights (IPR) for drug companies on drugs to treat what are considered sensitive diseases in Ecuador. This agreement allows third parties to apply for the rights to produce drugs patented by others. The first case involved HIV/AIDS drugs produced by an American drug company called Kaletra.[276] Through this process, Ecuador is leading the other ALBA countries to follow in the interruption of IPR for their own purposes. This is for international law what asymmetry is for laws of war, and what direct democracy is for civil and political rights. These are attempts to alter the existing internationally accepted framework. Part of the ALBA "new world order," this new framework seeks to rewrite the rules and playbook of international arbitration, conflict resolution, and the fundamental nucleus of human rights. It is a bold initiative—a daring plan that, as demonstrated by the TWAIL analysis above, continues to receive significant support.

While not yet discussed outside several declarations by President Chavez, there exists the rumor that an upcoming ALBA initiative will be an ALBA court, which will allow the redress of ALBA government grievances across the ALBA. This would naturally place in peril transnational companies operating in one or more ALBA countries.

Cuba

As Chavez has said on various occasions, there is now virtually no differentiation between Cuba and Venezuela. "We are one country," Chavez and Fidel have often said. How much of this is true is a subject for debate. Nevertheless, it is a given that all the ALBA activity outlined in this book is supported, facilitated, and even in some cases instigated by the Cuban government. This government has been sponsoring terrorism for years, including relationships with Gaddafi's Libya, FARC, ETA, and others. Cuban agents assist Chavez, Morales, Correa and Ortega in spying on the opposition. Cuban strategists plan for the co-opting and takeover of democratic institutions. And Cuban doctors and sports workers are the backbone of

---

276 "Paises del ALBA adoptaran medidas para interrumpir licencias de medicamentos en manos de monopolios," Aporrea, 9 de Septiembre, 2010. http://www.aporrea.org/tecno/n165202.html

the ALBA social projects across the region. One cannot minimize Cuba's role in the construction of the ALBA.

However, and this might be a more controversial claim, the idea of the ALBA is one of President Chavez himself. This has brought Chavez into quiet conflict with Raul Castro. Raul sees himself as the inheritor of the revolution from his brother Fidel. Raul seems offended by the Venezuelans' indiscipline and inability to make their revolution work. He is also jealous that Chavez receives so much attention, and that he has the incredible economic fortune of the oil production. And there is resentment in having to depend on Venezuela for eight billion dollars a year for the survival of their revolution.

Be this as it may, 21st Century Socialism belongs to Hugo Chavez. Although the Cubans provide support, the new mechanisms for co-opting democracy are being learned and pushed by the Bolivarians, not the Cubans. One should not minimize the importance of the Cubans in Chavez's ambitions; without Chavez, the Castros revolution would collapse: For the Cubans, the advance of the ALBA is essential. As Chavez's cancer advances, it has become even more evident of the "one state" nature of the Venezuelan and Cuban relationship. The Cuban government is very concerned that should Chavez succumb to his illness, the continuity of revolution in Venezuela is not guaranteed. They have stepped up their work to assure control over political stability of their most important international partner.

Caribbean Countries

An intuitive reader will also notice three Caribbean countries who are ALBA members that do not appear in this book. St. Vincent and the Grenadines, Antigua and Barbuda, and Dominica, are also ALBA members. They participate in the congresses, and they support ALBA declarations. They vote with the ALBA when asked. Why not? As the prime minister of Barbuda said on that country's admission into the ALBA, "Venezuela provides more support to the region than the United States." These small countries enjoy Venezuela's largesse. This costs them nothing, and brings them no negative consequences to date. They do not, however, participate in the most nefarious activities of the ALBA. This might change, in terms of drug trafficking especially, but for now they want to enjoy Venezuela's money without crossing the United States, at least overtly.

As is clearly reflected in this chapter, the ALBA countries are following very closely the plan of 21st Century Socialism designed in Havana/Caracas. This plan has its own progress and idiosyncrasies depending upon the political realities within member countries. Nevertheless, the process of destroying institutions, cementing individual power, co-opting the military, abridging civil and political rights and moving towards more authoritarian models of government is quite obvious.

CHAPTER 12

The ALBA, Iran & Terrorism

The expansion of cooperation with Iran is a holy task for Venezuela and will be pursued with seriousness, (…) Independent countries like Iran and Venezuela have suitable potentials and if they use these potentials, then it will considerably increase our power against imperialism, (…) Our ties with Iran are solid and brotherly and Venezuela will stand beside the great nation of Iran under any circumstances.

— President Hugo Chavez, October 19, 2010, quoted after meeting with Ahmadinejad in Tehran

The relationship between Iran, Syria and the Bolivarian Alliance has been one of the hallmarks of the ALBA's foreign policy. Both Iran and Syria have observer status within the ALBA. The first step in cementing Iran's relationship with the ALBA has been diplomatically and economically. According to American Enterprise Institute, "In December 2009, International Monetary Fund (IMF) data analyzed by the Latin Business Chronicle confirmed that Iran–Latin-American trade soared 209% in 2008, totaling $2.9 billion. While Brazil remains Iran's main Latin-American trading partner and exporter, Ecuador has replaced Peru as the main importer of Iranian products. Iran's trade with Ecuador skyrocketed between 2007 and 2008 from $6 million to $168 million."[277] For example, in December 2008, Tehran hosted the first Iran-ALBA joint congress for the expansion of economic and industrial cooperation. As of publication, Iran's trade

---

277 American Enterprise Institute Iran Tracker. http://www.irantracker.org/foreign-relations/ecuador-iran-foreign-relations

with the region is about two to three percent of its economy. The two have stated their intention to increase it to fifteen percent. At the congress, Venezuela, Cuba, Ecuador, Nicaragua, Bolivia and Dominica displayed their products at the Tehran Permanent Fairgrounds in a trade fair connected to the seminar, which at the same time boasted the participation of eighty-one companies from the abovementioned countries.

Chavez has become Mahmud Ahmadinejad's most fervent supporter and promoter. He has aggressively inserted Iran into Latin-American issues with a singular zeal. At Chavez' behest, Ahmadinejad traveled to Bolivia with Chavez in 2007 on a Venezuelan Air Force jet, where Chavez introduced him to President Evo Morales. On that trip, Iran promised a one-billion-dollar development fund for Bolivia. Following this visit, Morales moved Bolivia's only embassy in the Muslim world from Cairo to Tehran. In 2009, in solidarity with Ahmadinejad, Bolivia severed ties with Israel. Again in 2009, Ahmadinejad visited La Paz and promised a $250 million loan. In 2010, Evo Morales visited Tehran and awarded the concession of a lithium reserve to an Iranian company run by the Revolutionary Guard.[278] This lithium deposit, in Potosi, is suspiciously close to Bolivia's uranium deposits. The company set to extract the lithium is the same as is set to extract gold in Venezuela. This Iranian company IMPASCO, however, has no experience with either lithium or gold, only uranium.[279]

There have been other interesting developments in the relationship between Iran and the ALBA. In 2009, Iran provided funding for a television channel in Chapare, Bolivia, which would be managed by the Social Movements (mentioned in previous chapters). This television station provides Shiite Islamic programming to the largest cocaine-producing region in Bolivia.[280] Iran has also financed several clinics in Bolivia, including one in El Alto, which caused a stir when television displayed Bolivian nurses forced to wear the traditional hijab.[281]

278 "Bolivia elige a Iran para explotar litio," La Razon, 28 de Octubre, 2010. http://www.la-razon.com/version.php?ArticleId=120281&EditionId=2328
279 Roger Noriega, "Chavez's Secret Nuclear Program," Foreign Policy, October 5, 2010. http://www.aei.org/article/102623
280 Author interviews with confidential sources.
281 Emilio Martinez, "Relaciones Peligrosas," Bolivia 2010.

In 2007, Chavez traveled to Rafael Correa's inauguration with Ahmadinejad in tow, and Iran and Ecuador agreed to establish embassies that same year. In 2008, President Correa stated that Ecuador was "not going to stop getting closer to Iran because (the United States) has it on a blacklist." In 2007, trade officers were established in Quito and Tehran. In 2009, Ahmadinejad promised to increase cooperation to Ecuador by $200,000,000. In March 2009, Iran agreed to finance two new power plants in Ecuador. In September of that same year, Iran granted a $40 million loan for Ecuadorian exporters. Iran has also considered depositing $145 million into Ecuador's Central Bank. According to the US Treasury Department, this move by Iran is "in response to international sanctions and the refusal of many responsible banks to do business with Iranian banks."[282] The US Treasury Department has said that Iran has begun using less prominent institutions, such as the Export Development Bank of Iran, to handle many of its financial transactions to circumvent UN banking sanctions. As recently as late 2010, Ecuador and Iran have set up a joint mining company to exploit minerals.[283]

During Easter 2011, Iran's foreign minister signed a new set of agreements with Correa, one of which included the expansion of mining and investment cooperation.

Iran's relationship has deepened with Nicaragua as well. This is not a surprise, given that the two countries had a cozy relationship in the 1980s during President Daniel Ortega's first period of rule. This has also been a source of friction for the Iran-Nicaragua relationship—which has remained hampered by Iran's refusal to forgive $164 million in debt owed by Nicaragua, dating from the 1980s.[284] Nevertheless, in January 2007 Ahmadinejad traveled to Managua for Ortega's inauguration. Iran has funded several development and aid projects since 2007, including providing over $230 million for a hydroelectric dam (February 2008) and $2 million for a new hospital. In June 2007 President Ortega visited Tehran, where he gave a speech at

282 American Enterprise Institute Iran Tracker. http://www.irantracker.org/foreign-relations/ecuador-iran-foreign-relations
283 Jose Cardenas, "Iran's Man in Ecuador," Foreign Policy, February 15, 2011. http://shadow.foreignpolicy.com/posts/2011/02/15/irans_man_in_ecuador
284 "Iran cobra deuda a Nicaragua," El Nuevo Diario, 6 de Octubre, 2009. http://www.elnuevodiario.com.ni/politica/58812

the Islamic University stating that, "the Nicaraguan and Iranian Revolutions are twins," and emphasizing the need to "create a new world order and replace capitalism and imperialism."[285] In September 2007, Iran and Venezuela pledged $350 million to build a seaport for Nicaragua at Monkey Point—one of several sea infrastructure projects Iran is planning around the world. In February 2009, Iran announced it would commit an additional $200 million to fund joint energy and agriculture projects in Nicaragua.

The deepest relationship between Iran and the ALBA, naturally, is with Venezuela. The promotion of Iran's increasing regional footprint seems to be a pet project of the Venezuelan president, and one of his most important foreign policy imperatives. Chavez has consistently supported Iran's nuclear ambitions as well. Venezuela, Cuba and Malaysia were the only countries to vote against the IAEA resolution, rebuking Iran for building a second uranium enrichment plant in secret. In October 2009, Chavez announced that Iran was helping Venezuela mine for uranium, and announced joint nuclear cooperation for a peaceful nuclear program in Venezuela. He even joked with Ahmadinejad, "How's the uranium for the bomb working out?" Venezuela has been rumored to be shipping uranium to Iran; rumors which are as of yet unconfirmed. Iran has also made extensive economic investments in Venezuela. The government of Iran purchased the Venezuelan Banco International de Desarrollo (BID). This bank, whose board of directors consist of only Iranians, mostly with Iranian Government credentials, serves as a pass-through to launder Iranian money and avoid UN sanctions.[286]

In October 2009, Venezuelan First Secretary for Energy Affairs in Venezuela's Tehran embassy, Louis Mayta, stated, "Iran and Venezuela are establishing an oil company named Beniroug which allows us to make investments and activities [sic] in other countries, including Cuba, Sudan, China and Bolivia."[287] Spain helped mediate some of the difficulties in Beniroug's registration process and will host the company's headquarters.

---

285 Emilio Martinez, "Relaciones Peligrosas," Bolivia 2010.
286 "Un Extrano Banco Irani que Opera en Venezuela," Noticias 24, 23 de Marzo, 2008. http://economia.noticias24.com/noticia/191/un-extrano-banco-irani-que-opera-en-venezuela/
287 American Enterprise Institute Iran Tracker. http://www.irantracker.org/foreign-relations/bolivia-iran-foreign-relations#_ftn15#_ftn15

Beniroug also plans to build a refinery in Syria with the capacity of 140,000 barrels of oil per day. To date, Venezuela and Iran have signed more than two hundred trade and cooperation treaties. In January 2010, following an agreement signed in March of the previous year, Venezuela announced that it has removed visa requirements for Iranian nationals wishing to visit, making it the third Latin-American country to do so along with Nicaragua and Ecuador. Former US National Intelligence Director Dennis Blair has, for two years in a row, highlighted the challenge of Venezuela's Iran connections: "Chavez' growing ties to Iran, coupled with Venezuela's lax financial laws and border controls and widespread corruption have created a permissive environment for Hezbollah to exploit." An unclassified Pentagon report to the US Congress has outlined the presence of Quds force in Venezuela.[288] There is a great deal of speculation on the reason for the financial agreements. It would appear that most of the agreements remain inoperative – while millions or billions are pledged there is very little activity which takes place in the implementation of these agreements. This leads experts to surmise that they are merely mechanisms by which Iran can launder sanctionable money and increase economic activity away from the prying eyes of UN, EU and US investigators.

There is also a direct flight between Caracas, Tehran and Damascus, which does not pass through customs and doesn't release passenger or cargo manifests. Regarding these flights, on April 5, 2011, General Douglas Fraser, head of the US Southern Command, was quoted as saying, "My concern, as I look at it, is the fact that there are flights between Iran and Venezuela on a weekly basis, and visas are not required for entrance into Venezuela or Bolivia or Nicaragua (...) So we don't have a lot of visibility in who's visiting and who isn't, and that's really where I see the concerns."[289] Air-Terror, as the airline is called colloquially, is always full. Passengers traveling on these flights do not go through immigration, and cargo does not go through customs.

---

288 "Iran's Quds Force in Venezuela, Latin America: Pentagon," AFP, April 22, 2010. http://hello.news352.lu/edito-36553-iran-s-quds-force-in-venezuela-latin-america-pentagon.html
289 "US General Voices Concern over Iran Venezuela ties," AFP April 5, 2011. http://www.google.com/hostednews/afp/article/ALeqM5gMdmJ9NnlROhzcDjs457Jwn0gBEg?docId=CNG.692381365d745fc505df40c97673c9ec.861

The link between Iran and the ALBA has been well established and is now a matter of common record. Nevertheless, perhaps a more important discussion is to answer the question, "Why?" These countries are not natural trading partners—in fact, with all of them (except Nicaragua) petroleum or natural gas-producing countries, they should be competitors. Despite this, they have been deepening their economic, diplomatic and military relationships with an unprecedented velocity.

For the ALBA countries, they see their political project as "one chapter of a global revolution";[290] and as Carlos the Jackal said in his autobiography, "Et la revolution aujourd'hui est, avant, tout, islamique" (translation: "And the revolution today is, before anything else, Islamic").[291] As Chavez, Morales, Correa, Ortega, Fidel, and Ahmadinejad never tire of saying, their goal is to create a new world order. To do this, they must bring the current world order, led by the United States and Western Europe, to its knees. In Iran, the Bolivarians see the only revolutionary country that has successfully stood against the west for generations, even defeating it on occasions. The affinity the Bolivarians have with Iran is revolutionary, not religious. It is ideological, not economic. It is—above all—subversive. As previously discussed, the Bolivarians see asymmetric warfare as their only way to guard against what they are certain will be an eventual attack by the United States. They watched this type of warfare carried out by Muslims in Iraq and Afghanistan and understood its power. For this reason, they have joined forces to attempt to upset the applecart, creating a propitious atmosphere in the world conducive to the creation of their new world order.

This relationship has brought the ALBA countries—with Venezuela at the lead—into the murky world of international terrorism. It is now common knowledge that Venezuela and the ALBA sponsor terrorist organizations. At a House Foreign Affairs Committee hearing on Venezuela on March 10, 2011, Arturo Valenzuela, former Assistant Secretary of State for Western Hemisphere Affairs, admitted that Venezuela was a state sponsor of terrorism.[292] The ALBA's closest terrorist ties are with five groups: the

---

290 Fernando Bossi, "10 Puntos para Entender el ALBA," Cuadernos de Emancipacion, #35, ISSN 0328-0179.
291 Ilich Sanchez Ramirez, "Islam Revolutionaire," (2003): P 23.
292 Press Release, Congressman Connie Mack. http://www.internationalrelations.house.gov/press_display.asp?id=1493

FARC, MRTA, ELN, ETA and Hezbollah. While other groups piggyback on these relationships, these are by far the deepest associations with the ALBA. There are several reasons the ALBA would take such a perilous risk. First, President Chavez has been supporting terrorists for a long time, namely the Revolutionary Armed Forces of Colombia (FARC). Colombia, to remind, is the crown jewel of Simon Bolivar's two-century-old political project—and Bogota was the capital of the Gran Colombia during its short-lived existence. President Chavez is eager to bring Colombia into his Bolivarian confederation. Doing so would, in his mind, culminate a historic project and make the recreation of Simon Bolivar's vision irreversible. Nevertheless, Chavez has realized he will be unable to do this through the manipulation of the vote. The high polling numbers of former President Alvaro Uribe, and of current President Juan Manuel Santos—coupled with the lack of any traction whatsoever for his Bolivarianism—has led him to believe the only way to assure Colombia's addition into the fold will be by a military takeover by the FARC.

For this reason, he has provided significant material and logistical support to the FARC. He has allowed FARC bases to be set up on Venezuelan territory—something Rafael Correa, President of Ecuador has also allowed in Ecuador. As outlined by information acquired through the computers of Raul Reyes, Chavez promised to provide $300,000,000 to the FARC (something it is unclear if actually materialized).[293] In this same raid, Colombian military found Iranian field manuals and thirty kilos of low-grade uranium[294] buried in the ground. According to a CNN documentary titled, Los Guardianes de Chavez (Chavez' Guardians), there are up to seventeen FARC bases inside Venezuela. The FARC also supported the candidacies of Nicaragua's Daniel Ortega, and even more enthusiastically Ecuador's Rafael Correa, according to the US State Department and the IISS.[295] Six high level officials of Chavez' government: Henry Rangel Silva, General in Chief; Hugo Carvajal, Chavez' military intelligence director; Freddy Bernal,

---

293 Douglas Farah, "Ecuador at Risk: Drugs, Thugs and the Citizens Revolution," International Assessment and Strategy Center, January 24, 2010.
294 David J. Myers, "Iran and Venezuela: Capacity to Influence" CSIS. April, 2009.
295 "Las FARC aportaron a la campana de Correa," El Diario, 12 de Abril, 2011. http://www.eldiario.com.ec/noticias-manabi-ecuador/188088-las-farc-aportaron-a-campana-de-correa/

former Mayor of Caracas and current National Assembly Deputy for the PSUV; General Cliver Alcala, head of the Venezuelan Armed Forces 4th Division; Ramon Isidro Madriz Moreno, member of SEBIN (Venezuela's political police); Amilcar Figueroa, Venezuelan representative on the Latin American Parliament; are all on the OFAC (US Treasury Department's Office of Foreign Asset Control list)[296] for material support to the FARC. Another former interior minister for Venezuela, Ramon Rodriguez Chacin, is also on OFAC.

Some of the most important support to the FARC comes through the ALBA's Social Movements, where the Bolivarian Continental Movement (MCB) is an active member. The Bolivarian Continental Movement, with hundreds of civil-society groups as members and with chapters in dozens of Latin-American countries, is effectively a front organization for the FARC. Forgetting the proFARC propaganda on their website,[297] such as repeated calls for the FARC to be given the status of a belligerent force (something Chavez and Correa have pushed for) and invitations to workshops titled, "From the Sword of Simon Bolivar to the FARC-EP," there are many more important connections.

Narciso Isa Conde, the President of the MCB, admitted in a letter to the OAS that he was a close friend of Raul Reyes and visited him in his camps in Colombia, "many times." He also admitted that the FARC participated actively in the MCB.[298] In his book, Raul Reyes: The Foreign Minister of the Mountains, journalist Jose Gregorio Perez asserts that Reyes—killed in Ecuador in 2008 in a Colombian bombing raid—was effectively the FARC's international spokesperson. With the arrest of Rodrigo Granda, the FARC's foreign minister (protected by the Chavez Administration) in Caracas, Reyes had assumed a higher profile. Perez outlines how the FARC came to more closely depend upon foreign support: most importantly from Cuba, Ecuador and Venezuela.[299] This was mainly the result

---

296 Treasury Department OFAC lists. http://www.treasury.gov/about/organizational-structure/offices/Pages/Office-of-Foreign-Assets-Control.aspx

297 For those interested in visiting, be aware that his website transmits a computer virus.

298 Site no longer available. http://www.pcv-venezuela.org/index.php/internacional/7037-pronunciamiento-de-narciso-isa-conde-ante-la-acusacion-del-gobierno-de-uribe-en-la-oea

299 Raul Reyes, El canciller de la montana. Bogota: Grupo Ediorial Norma, 2008. 277p. - (1a. ed). ISBN 978-958-45-1535-3.

of Ivan Marquez, who in an email obtained from Raul Reyes' computer, outlined that the FARC would use the MCB as an excuse to open an office in Caracas. The office was opened, managed by Rodrigo Granda (before his abduction by Colombian forces). In another email, Marquez assured Reyes that the plan had the support of Freddy Bernal, then mayor of the municipality of Caracas and member of the PSUV, Chavez' political party. Bernal and Chavez remain close. Marquez bragged that the office would be "a space for engagement between leaders, promoters and organizers of the Latin-American left, including insurgent groups, to combat neoliberalism and forge an interaction of the ideological principles of Marxism-Bolivarianism."[300] The offices were set up in the Tacagua building of Parque Central, which is a nest of Cuban agents and Bolivarian ideologues. Marquez announced that they were ready for the first Bolivarian Continental Congress—to take place in Caracas that year. According to Marquez, at the margin of the political meetings, two Australian arms dealers were in the Tacagua offices, meeting with Bolivarian Congress participants to negotiate weapons deals.

The Second Bolivarian Continental Congress took place in Quito, Ecuador, and participants included more than seventy-five leaders from around the region, such as Walter Wendelin, and Inaki Gil de San Vicente. Walter Wendelin is the head of ASKAPENA, the Basque terrorist group ETA's political branch and BATASUNA's Latin-American program.[301] The meeting was inaugurated by a video uplink from Raul Reyes[302]. According to Colombian intelligence, Wendelin and Gil de San Vicente entertained secret meetings with the FARC during the congress (allegedly with Marquez himself). Ivan Marquez was also on the list of invitees.[303] Following this meeting, five Mexican participants went into the jungle to the camp of

300 "Chavez, las FARC y la Coordinadora Continental Bolivariana," CNA 7 de Septiembre, 2010. http://impactocna.com/2010/09/07/chavez-las-farc-y-la-coordinadora-continental-bolivariana/
301 "Wendelin, el 'embajador' de BATASUNA en America Latina," Ideal, 28 de Septiembre, 2009. http://www.ideal.es/granada/rc/20100928/espana/walter-wendelin-embajador-batasuna-201009280902.html
302 "Raul Reyes Saluda Segundo Congreso Continental Bolivariano," http://www.youtube.com/watch?v=X2kySlbqbbU
303 Jaime Lopez, "El entorno de ETA se infiltra en el movimiento bolivariano de Hugo Chavez," El Mundo, 8 de Mayo, 2008. http://www.elmundo.es/elmundo/2008/06/07/espana/1212867060.html

Raul Reyes, where they became "collateral damage" during the Colombian military bombing of Reyes's camp in which Reyes was killed.[304]

The MCB has its political wing the Bolivarian Congress of the Nations, led by Fernando Bossi. They have their own congresses, suspiciously close in time to the others. The Bolivarian Congress of the Nations has denied any association with MCB.

Wendelin went from Quito back to Argentina, where he was living and working for the University of the Madres de Plaza Mayo (MPM) allegedly at the behest of Hebe Bonafini (president of the MPM, and member of Bossi's Bolivarian Congress of the Nations), an important ally of Hugo Chavez. Wendelin was arrested, ironically at the behest of the Spanish ambassador upon attempted entry into Venezuela in 2010. Venezuela and Spain had been involved in a difficult spat due to Venezuela's unwillingness to extradite Arturo Cubillas—another ETA member—wanted for training ETA on a base in Venezuela. Wendelin then flew to France (his onward ticket's destination) and was detained by Spanish police upon reentry into Spain, on a warrant for material support to ETA.

Upon his return to Peru from the second Bolivarian Congress, Roque Gonzales la Rosa (who did time in a Peruvian prison for association with the MRTA) was arrested by the Peruvian police. He, along with fifteen other members of the Peru chapter of the MCB, were charged by the Peruvian government for connection to the FARC. During his hearing, he admitted receiving money from Caracas to travel to the congress. In his seized notebook, Gonzales la Rosa also had the numbers of the Venezuelan embassy in Quito and its First Secretary.[305] This is not the only connection to the MRTA. Felipe Quispe, Bolivian indigenous leader and head of the MRTA–Bolivia branch was named Honorary President of the CCB.[306] Quispe's foot soldiers during their terrorist years included Alvaro Garcia Linera, Peru's vice-president under Evo Morales. Garcia Linera and Quispe are reported

---

304 "Dominican Leftist Leader has links to the FARC," Dominican Today, March 18, 2008. http://www.dominicantoday.com/dr/local/2008/3/18/27363/Dominican-leftist-leader-has-links-to-the-FARC-El-Dia-says

305 "Jefe de coordinadora bolivariana en Peru admite respaldo financiero de Venezuela," La Republica, 16 de Marzo, 2008. http://www.larepublica.pe/archive/all/larepublica/20080316/1/node/22454/total/01

306 "Felipe Quispe fue presidente honorario de la Coordinadora," Radio Caracol, 21 de Julio, 2008. http://www.caracol.com.co/nota.aspx?id=635893

to maintain friendly ties privately, while feuding publicly. The MRTA international movement is currently presided over by a Venezuelan Tupamaro who we will meet in the next section.

Since 2008, the MCB reportedly has a chapter in the United States, in New York. Parallel to the MCB is a group called the Bolivarian Congress of the Nations (BCN). This organization is run by Fernando Bossi. According to analysis by Peruvian intelligence, this is the political wing of the MCB. The Bolivarian Congress of the Nations has also held meetings, most of them in Caracas. Particularly significant were participants such as Juan Barahona, close to Manuel Zelaya of Honduras. Jorge Schafik Handal, candidate for the presidency of El Salvador (who died after a heart attack brought upon by a visit to Evo Morales' 14,000-feet-above-sea-level capital city) was also in attendance at some meetings. Assisting the Morales government was Osvaldo Peredo, a member of the leadership of Morales' MAS political party. Ruben Garcia, member of Uruguay's Tupamaros (an organization to which the US Government accused Chavez of sending weapons) was present. Alexis Ponce from Ecuador, president of the Latin American Association for Human Rights (ALDHU)—, and many others. The most notable guests were Puerto Rico's own Rafael Cancel Miranda, famous for having infiltrated the US Capitol Building and shooting five Congress members in 1954. Miranda served time at Alcatraz Prison.

On March 11, 2004—after witnessing the train bombings in Madrid—investigative reporter Antonio Salas (a pen name) became Muhammad Ali Tovar Abdallah Abu Aiman, AKA, "El Palestino." Salas had just released a book about his story wherein he had infiltrated the European skinhead movement, and was looking for his next project when, in an international terrorist attack, he found it. Salas invented "El Palestino," a Venezuelan of Palestinian descent whose supposed wife was killed in an Israeli raid in Gaza. This cover story was plausible; there are many such stories in Venezuela. While hanging around the central mosque in Caracas, he became friends with Vladimir Ramirez, brother of Ilich Ramirez—more commonly known as Carlos the Jackal. Through the Jackal, Salas as "El Palestino" was ushered into the world of international Islamic terrorism and its unlikely Venezuelan connection.[307]

---

307 Antonio Salas, "El Palestino," Temas de Hoy, Agosto, 2010. ISBN: 978-84-8460-859-2.

Antonio Salas (again, a pen name) became the right-hand man of his mentor the Jackal—Carlos' man on the outside. In charge of managing his website, writing and responding to emails and making contacts, Salas was drawn into a dark world few have the opportunity to witness. What he saw shocked the world.

Salas claims to have received his terrorist training in a camp around the city of Caracas—he says that there are six. In those camps (presumably the same ones managed by Arturo Cubillas, the ETA leader in Venezuela Salas also got to know), he learned to fire weapons and plan and carry out terrorist activities, and came into contact with important ETA and FARC leaders. He describes a shadowy world where Carlos the Jackal—good friend of Hugo Chavez —still leads an important terrorist outfit from his French prison. Through his relationship with Carlos, Salas met other terrorists working in the ALBA countries. Among those was Teodoro Darnott. Darnott, a self-styled leader of Hezbollah-Latin America, who had spent the better part of the last decade attempting to convert the Wayuu, an indigenous group on Venezuela's western border with Colombia, to Islam. He rose to brief notoriety after placing two pipe bombs in front of the US embassy in Caracas in 2006 and papering the area with Islamic leaflets.[308] The bombs never exploded and Darnott, who has no real connection with Hezbollah in Venezuela (run out of Margarita Island, not Maracaibo's Wayuu community) has since been sent to the SEBIN (Venezuela's political police jail) which is located in an old, dome-shaped shopping mall constructed in the 1960s.

While connecting with some characters as ridiculous as Darnott, Salas also encountered important Venezuelans such as Chino Carias, head of the Venezuelan organization Tupamaros. The group controls the barrio 23 de Enero. This is the neighborhood where Chavez hid after his failed coup attempt in 1992, where he lived for years after his release from jail in 1994, and where he still votes. During the eighties Carias was involved in fighting in the Central American wars, where he met important figures such as Daniel Ortega, Eden Pastora, and even Comandante Marcos. He returned to Venezuela to make contact with the military.

308 Clinton W. Taylor, "Hezbollah in Latin America," The American Spectator, November 30, 2006. http://spectator.org/archives/2006/11/30/hezbollah-in-latin-america

"In the year [19]85 we contacted a few Venezuelan military, who had woken up in the face of so much misery, so much repression, torture, assassination, disappearances.... And these military informed us that there was an internal rebellion in the Armed Forces, and that they created the movement Bolivarian Revolutionary Movement-200 (MBR-200, based on the 200th anniversary of the birth of Simon Bolivar), and that they needed an alliance between the military and us, civilians who were up in arms. We started to plan the civic-military insurgency of 1992. I was contacted by the lieutenant Lucho, the lieutenant El Gato, who God must have in his arms because he died in combat in 1992."[309] The MBR-200 was the Venezuelan revolutionary group within the armed forces founded by Hugo Chavez and thirteen other soldiers in 1983 under the famous tree, the Saman de Guere in Maracay where they promised to overthrow the Venezuelan government. Carias is the leader of the Venezuelan Tupamaros and president over the MRTA international, which was mentioned previously in relation to Felipe Quispe and the CCB.

Perhaps the most bizarre side-story that arises from Salas' contacts is the case of the Bolivian-Hungarian terrorist Eduardo Rozsa Flores. Rozsa had converted to Islam in 2003 and became the head of Hezbollah in Hungary. Rozsa was an old friend of Carlos the Jackal, from their joint operations in Europe. He had also fought during the Croatian war on the side of the Croats and received honorary citizenship. On April 16, 2009, he was gunned down by Bolivian antiterrorist police in his hotel room in the city of Santa Cruz, Bolivia.[310] Bolivian authorities accused him of an attempt to assassinate President Evo Morales. The altercation occurred at the height of the separatist discussions of the "half moon," and has been used by the Morales government as their most important political case against the opposition. Yet recently, in January 2011, the situation became far murkier. Following the shootout, District Attorney Marcelo Soza presented Ignacio Villa Vargas "El Viejo" as the prime witness in the case against a group of thirty-nine of Santa Cruz's most powerful citizens alleged to

---

309 Marwan Paz, "Chino Carias, El Ultimo Guerrillero," Al Seher Blog, 24 de Noviembre, 2006. http://alseher.blogspot.com/2006/11/chino-carias-el-ultimo-guerrillero.html
310 "Eduardo Rozsa Flores and Aprad Magyarosi are the two Hungarians killed in Bolivia," Hungarian Ambiance, April 17, 2009. http://www.hungarianambiance.com/2009/04/eduardo-rozsa-flores-and-arpad.html

have financed Rozsa. The situation became explosive when "El Viejo" was filmed allegedly receiving $31,500 and told, "This is your last payout, now go to Argentina."[311] The man allegedly making the payment was Edison Ali Espinoza, who was the right-hand man of Alfredo Rada, former Bolivian Minister of the Government under Evo Morales. As soon as the video emerged, El Viejo went from being the star witness to being indicted in the Rozsa case. He has claimed he was tortured by Bolivian government agents. The US Government itself has said, in classified cables, that Rozsa was hired by Bolivian Intelligence Director Coronel Jorge Santiesteban and Captain Walter Andrade to fake a "setup" to defame the Bolivian opposition to Morales based in the eastern part of the country[312]. The Bolivian government has continued with the case, although given the ham-handed mismanagement of the conspiracy, it might find it difficult to proceed in charging the thirty-nine Santa Cruz citizens.

As demonstrated by Salas, the MCB and other sources, the contact with the FARC on the one hand and the relationship with Iran on the other has turned Venezuela into a hotbed of foreign terrorist activity. Caracas has become, today, what Damascus was in the 1980s: a mecca and safe haven for terrorists to meet, plan and conspire, all under the protective safety net of the Bolivarian government. The reason for this is the military doctrine of asymmetric warfare—terrorism as official military doctrine. Those best experienced in the peripheral war are terrorist organizations: organizations Carlos the Jackal has been keen to introduce to his friend Chavez. These organizations, in exchange for safe haven, participate in the training of Venezuelan irregular "militias." These militias are increasingly important for Chavez as he turns to asymmetry to avoid the trappings of institutional democracy. The current Venezuelan Vice-President, Elias Jaua, is a sympathizer of ETA, the Basque terrorist organization. The Spanish government has demanded the extradition of Basque terrorist Arturo Cubillas for his participation in training ETA fighters in Venezuela. Cubillas, a nationalized Venezuelan citizen, has an important job as director of security for the

---

311 "Video de soborno a 'El Viejo' hace tambalear credibilidad en caso Rozsa," La Patria, 16 de Enero, 2011. http://www.lapatriaenlinea.com/?nota=55354

312 Cooper, Patrick, "Wikileaks claims Irishman gunned down in Bolivia was set up." January 2, 2011 http://www.irishcentral.com/news/Wikileaks-claims-Irishman-gunned-down-in-Bolivia-was-set-up-112769104.html

National Institute of Land, where Jaua was president before assuming his current role. The Venezuelan government continues to protect Cubillas, who maintains his current job.[313]

ETA in Ecuador came to light during the polemic when Dax Toscano, a journalist, writer and professor coordinated the visit of Inaki Gil de San Vicente – a suspected ETA member –when he arrived in Ecuador to deliver a course at the Central Ecuador University. This was at the same time when he and Walter Wendelin were in the country for the 2nd Bolivarian Congress (Wendelin is head of ASKAPENA, ETA's Latin-America wing). Toscano's house was even under observation by Ecuadorian police following the second Bolivarian Congress of the Nations.[314]

According to the US Government, starting in 2004, Venezuela began to fund and train (with the help of the Cuban government and the FARC) Ecuadorian radicals, in an attempt to plunge that country into chaos and set up a more friendly government[315] (part of ALBA's political strategy).

The group Hezbollah has been active in Venezuela for many years, from its center on Margarita Island.[316] In 2008, the United States designated two Venezuelans as specially designated global terrorists: Ghazi Nasr al Din and Fawzi Kan'an. In 2006, Nasr al Din, currently Director of Political Aspects at the Venezuelan embassy in Syria, brought Hezbollah representatives to the Lebanese parliament to Venezuela, to solicit donations for the terrorist group and announce the opening of a Hezbollah-sponsored community center and office in Venezuela.[317]

---

313 "ETA Suspect Arturo Cubillas fails to appear in Spanish Court," El Universal, December 14, 2010. http://english.eluniversal.com/2010/12/14/en_pol_esp_eta-suspect-arturo-c_14A4853251.shtml

314 Jaime Lopez, "El entorno de ETA se infiltra en el Movimiento Bolivariano de Hugo Chavez," El Mundo, 8 de Mayo, 2008. http://www.elmundo.es/elmundo/2008/06/07/espana/1212867060.html

315 "EEUU sospecho que Venezuela impulso terrorismo en Ecuador," El Universal, 24 de Abril, 2011. http://politica.eluniversal.com/2011/04/24/eeuu-sospecho-que-venezuela-impulso-terrorismo-en-ecuador.shtml

316 "Hezbollah: Financing Terror Through Criminal Enterprise," Testimony of Dr. Matthew Levitt, Senior Fellow and Director of Terrorism Studies, The Washington Institute for Near East Policy. May 25, 2005. Committee on Homeland Security and Governmental Affairs, United States.

317 "US Treasury Designates Two Venezuelan Men as Hezbollah Supporters," ADL, June 24, 2008. http://www.adl.org/main_Terrorism/venezuela_hezbollah_supporters.htm

For Iran, being able to use the relative legitimacy of Venezuela to hide money subject to sanctions and support their interests is important. According to the Pentagon, the Quds force in Venezuela is helping train the militias and preparing to be able to hit US interests in the event of an attack on Iran's nuclear facilities. Equally important, it appears that Iran is using Venezuela as a pass-through to ship weapons to Hezbollah. In 2009, the Israeli navy seized Iranian rockets heading from Venezuela to Lebanon—rockets meant for Hezbollah. The relationship with the ALBA countries allows wide swaths of areas for Iranian agents to operate without the scrutiny of global intelligence organizations. Iran is also using Venezuela as a place to carry out weapons manufacturing. The Iranians have established industries in Venezuela that are widely seen as front companies for illegal activities. For example, the tractor factory in Bolivar state has not produced a single tractor. More concerning, in 2009 the Turkish military seized a shipment labeled as tractor parts from Iran to Venezuela. Upon inspection, the contents were revealed as weapons components.[318]

An important element of the relationship between the ALBA and Iran is for uranium exploration. Both Bolivia and Venezuela have important uranium deposits, as it would appear Ecuador does; Venezuela's deposits could be up to 50,000 tons. According to a secret Israeli report leaked to the Associated Press from May 2009, both Bolivia and Venezuela have been supplying Iran with uranium.[319] In October of 2010, Hugo Chavez made an announcement, followed shortly by an announcement from Evo Morales, that their countries would be developing joint, peaceful nuclear programs. According to the information provided, they both signed agreements for nuclear assistance with the Russian government. Iran has a gold mining concession, run by an Iranian government company expert in mining uranium. Their concession in Venezuela is close to the Iranian tractor factory that produces no tractors and to which access is denied. In Bolivia, the same company has a concession in Potosi for lithium mining close to Bolivia's uranium deposits. Due to the proximity of the Iranian investments to uranium deposits, the presence of Iranian companies experienced only

318 "Turkey holds suspicious Iran Venezuela shipment," AP, January 6, 2009. http://www.ynetnews.com/articles/0,7340,L-3651706,00.html
319 "Israel says Iran gets Uranium from Venezuela and Bolivia," AP, May 25, 2009. http://www.nytimes.com/2009/05/26/world/middleeast/26israel.html

in nuclear energy, and rapid shift in announcements between Iranian and Russian nuclear cooperation (both countries announced they would cooperate with Iran and quickly changed their story to Russia), all clues point to assistance from Iran on uranium and nuclear activity. Whether this is to assist Venezuela, or is Venezuelan cover for an Iranian program, is open to question.[320] Finally, Iran also obtains important support from the ALBA in Iran's international affairs—including opposition to UN sanctions and vocal opposition in the IAEA. At a moment when an isolated Iran is looking for friends, places to hide money, to place agents, and to position itself as the main revolutionary opposition to the United States, the ALBA is a godsend.

---

320 In my research this year, I have spoken off-the-record with many people in Venezuela and abroad who have outlined the Iran-uranium link. I have no doubt that Chavez is assisting Iran with their nuclear program. There is, nevertheless, no smoking gun yet. To the naysayers, I ask: why wouldn't he? What good reason would Chavez have for not assisting Iran in what is obviously an important initiative for Iran—important enough to risk war with the west? How better to upset the apple cart than have a bomb?

CHAPTER 13

The ALBA as a Narco-Organization

There is an important overlap between a terrorist state that supports Iran, Hezbollah and the FARC and a narco-state where drug running becomes an important economic activity at the highest levels of government. The relationship with the FARC and the avenues to support money laundering for Hezbollah and other terrorist organizations has created fertile ground for drug runners to use the national territories of the ALBA countries as places to produce, refine, stockpile and ship cocaine (and other drugs produced in the Andes). Military and civilian leaders in the ALBA governments have taken advantage of these avenues to personally enrich themselves and provide much needed off the books liquidity to their ongoing attempts to destabilize other governments in the region as well as the United States and Western Europe.

The scope of the problem is unprecedented. To demonstrate the scale of the problem, below are the figures of estimated cocaine production in the Andean region.[321]

Potential Manufacture of Cocaine in Metric Tons						
	2003	2004	2005	2006	2007	2008
Bolivia	79	98	80	94	104	113
Colombia	550	680	680	660	630	450
Peru	230	270	260	280	290	302
Totals	859	1,048	1,020	1,034	1,024	865

321 UNODC 2009 Report, Section 2.3, Cocaine Use and Production.

It is exceedingly difficult to determine the full amount of the cocaine that is produced. We know what is seized, even if purity differs. According to the United Nations Office of Drugs and Crime, purity was reported at roughly fifty-one percent in 2008. During this same period, it is estimated that approximately forty-two percent of global cocaine was seized—leaving a supply of 501 metric tons.[322] Estimating the value of the cocaine market is also quite difficult. Since there are many intermediaries, money lost in transit, the resale of seized cocaine, and other issues, estimating the total money changing hands is complicated. The United Nations Office of Drugs and Crime (UNODC) uses the retail street value at point of consumption. According to UNODC, in 2008, consumption accounted for 480 metric tons (with twenty metric tons of shrinkage). The total street value of this product in 2008 was $88 billion. A staggering figure, one larger than the Gross Domestic Products of 123 countries. Below is a chart from the 2009 UNODC drug report on the value of cocaine.[323]

Global Cocaine Consumption 2008					
	Amount Consumed MT	Average Retail Price (US$ per gram)	Average Purity at Retail Level	Purity Adjusted Prices	Value (in Billion $USD)
North America	196	108	56%	192	38
EU/EFTA	124	101	37%	273	34
South America, Central America, Caribbean	95	11	66%	17	2
Africa	26	22	34%	65	2
Asia	14	142	73%	195	3
East and South-East Europe	13	125	48%	260	3
Oceania	11	291	53%	549	6
Total	480				$88

On top of simple production, drug transit and trafficking have become major problems for the Andean region. According to the United Nations

322 UNODC, 2009 report, 1.3 "The Global Cocaine Market."
323 UNODC, 2009 report, 1.3 "The Global Cocaine Market."

Office of Drugs and Crime, "One of the core activities of organized criminal groups, drug trafficking, has major security implications.... In some regions, the huge profits generated through this activity even rival some countries' GDPs, thus threatening State authority, economic development and the rule of law[324] (...) Organized crime contributes to State weakness, impedes economic growth, fuels many civil wars, regularly undermines United Nations peace-building efforts and provides financing mechanisms to terrorist groups."[325]

As is the case for hosting terrorists, Venezuela has become one of the most important drug-transit countries in the world. UNODC states, "According to the new Maritime Analysis Operation Centre (MAOC-N), more than half of all intercepted shipments in the Atlantic (sixty-seven incidents between 2006 and 2008) started their journey in the Bolivarian Republic of Venezuela. In addition, many undocumented air flights leave the country, and all the clandestine air shipments of cocaine detected in West Africa appear to have originated in the Bolivarian Republic of Venezuela. The country also appears to be the source of cocaine flown to clandestine airstrips in Honduras, with devastating effects there. At the same time, the Bolivarian Republic of Venezuela seems to be experiencing a remarkable upturn in criminal violence. This trend is difficult to track because the Venezuelan government stopped publishing official crime statistics after 2003, but some institutions continue to monitor the issue."[326]

Official statistics from the US Drug Enforcement Administration suggest that up to three hundred metric tons of cocaine pass through Venezuela each year, or forty percent of the global cocaine produced. In July of 2009, Senator Richard Lugar of Indiana, ranking Republican member of the Senate Foreign Relations Committee, commissioned a report from the General Accounting Office, titled "US Counternarcotics Cooperation with Venezuela Has Declined."[327] This GAO study uncovered important information about Venezuela's drug ties. It states in the introduction, "Venezuela has extended

---

324 High-level Panel on Threats, Challenges and Change, A more secure world: Our shared responsibility. United Nations, (2004). P53.
325 Report of the Secretary-General, In larger freedom: towards development, security and human rights for all. United Nations General Assembly, Fifty-ninth session (A/59/2005), 21 March 2005, P27.
326 UNODC 2009 Report, "Trafficking and Instability," section 3.0.
327 GAO Report. http://www.gao.gov/new.items/d09806.pdf

a lifeline to Colombian illegal armed groups by providing significant support and safe haven along the border. As a result, these groups, which traffic in illicit drugs, remain viable threats to Colombian security. A high level of corruption within the Venezuelan government, military, and other law enforcement and security forces contributes to the permissive environment, according to US officials." According to the GAO, "Venezuelan government officials have provided material support, primarily to FARC, which has helped to sustain the Colombian insurgency and threaten security gains achieved in Colombia,"[328] further stating that, "Evidence in the Reyes files (the aforementioned computer seized after the bombing of the FARC camp in Ecuador) not only confirmed their suspicions but indicated that FARC relationships with Venezuelan government officials were well established and had been in place longer than suspected," and stating that, "Venezuelan officials also facilitated arms sales for FARC, including the purchase of Russian and Chinese rifles, grenade launchers, machine guns, and missiles."

The report goes on to state that Venezuela has provided a safe haven for FARC and other rebels to operate. According to an article in *Financial Times* by Robert Morgenthau, Manhattan's District Attorney, Venezuelan drug money could be being used to finance Hamas and Hezbollah militants, and to buy equipment for Iran: "We've developed an expertise in tracing the international movement of funds for criminal purposes and we are applying that to looking at what may be going on in Venezuela,"[329] Morgenthau wrote.

An increasingly important connection is the drugs headed from Venezuela to Africa. According to UNODC, one hundred percent of drug flights between South America and Africa (to transit drugs into Europe) emanate from Venezuela. The US State Department, in its annual drug report, refers to a Boeing 727 that was found abandoned in the Mali desert. According to the US Government, this plane had been loaded with cocaine and sent from Venezuela to that African nation. Drug kingpin Walid Makled (below) asserted that he had begun to use cargo planes to ferry the drug to West Africa, where he had complicity from people in the governments of certain West African nations.

---

328 GAO Report. http://www.gao.gov/new.items/d09806.pdf P16.
329 "Israel ties two nations to Iran's Uranium," *Financial Times*. http://www.ft.com/cms/s/0/4848e022-9cd1-11de-ab58-00144feabdc0.html#ixzz1JKI1XZ7E

None of this is surprising. In 2005, President Chavez accused the US Drug Enforcement Administration (DEA) of spying, and severed all co-operation. The vetted units were dismantled, joint investigation and inter-diction ceased, and the Venezuelan foreign ministry began to deny visas to DEA agents. Since that moment, Venezuela has been listed on the US State Department's list of countries uncooperative in the drug fight—and has been decertified every year since.[330] In 2008, three high-level Venezuelan government officials were placed on the Treasury Departments Office of Foreign Asset Control (OFAC) lists for links to drug networks and the FARC. Those listed were former Interior Minister Ramon Rodriguez Chacin, Military Intelligence Director Hugo Carvajal and General Henry Rangel Silva. In 2011 four additional people were added; Freddy Bernal, former Mayor of the Municipality of Libertador (greater Caracas) and currently National Assemblyman for Hugo Chávez's United Socialist Party (PSUV); General Cliver Alcala, head of the Army's 4th Division; Ramón Isidro Madriz Moreno, who is a part of the Bolivarian Intelligence Service, Venezuela's political police; and Amilcar Figueroa, who represents Venezuela at the Latin-American Parliament.

More startling accusations about Venezuelan government involvement in the drug trade have come from another OFAC-designated drug king-pin. On August 19, 2010, Walid Makled Garcia, a Venezuelan national of Syrian origin, was arrested in the Colombian border town of Cucuta by Colombian intelligence agents supported by the DEA.

Makled, either forty-one, forty-three or forty-seven years of age de-pending on which report one is reading, was born to a family of poor Syrian immigrants in the small town of Tinaco, in Cojedes State in Venezuela's interior. Shortly after his birth, his family moved to the city of Valencia, capital of Carabobo State.[331] In the 1990s, when Makled was in his early twenties, he became involved in small-time crime; he sold stolen merchan-dise and robbed cars and trucks on the highway. His criminal band was composed of his brothers, Adel, Alex Jose, Al Chiar Abdala, Basel and

330 Certification is a process by which the US State Department, by law, is required to assess each country in the world based upon their cooperation with the US in the fight against drugs. There are usually four countries that are de-certified each year.
331 "Walid Makled en Tiempo Real," Tal Cual Digital 9 de Noviembre, 2010. http://www.talcualdigital.com/especiales/Viewer.aspx?id=43665

Ander. During this time, they had some run-ins with the law and made friends with some of the more unscrupulous local military officials: among them was Luis Felipe Acosta Carles. Acosta Carles had been one of the military men who, in 1983, swore an oath with President Chavez under the Saman de Guere. Under this tree in Maracay, where The Liberator Simon Bolivar was said to have rested, Hugo Chavez and a small group of other military men created the Bolivarian Revolutionary Movement-200 (MBR-200), and swore to overthrow the existing Venezuelan state, which they saw as beholden to the rich. In doing so, the Makled brothers had linked themselves to one of the inner circle.

The Makleds' rapid rise came in 2002, when a national strike threatened to topple President Hugo Chavez. The Makleds decided to take sides and supported President Chavez through those difficult months. Finally, the national strike ended in a whimper, with a weakened Chavez clinging desperately to power. Much to the Makleds' satisfaction, a hero of the strike had been General Luis Felipe Acosta Carles, who had delivered "the burp that saved the republic."[332]

The Makleds sealed their place within Chavismo when, according to Makled's own words, he gave two million dollars to General Acosta Carles to support Chavez during the attempted recall referendum in 2004. Chavez won, and Acosta Carles—who ran for governor shortly afterward—also won. In gratitude, Governor Carles awarded Makled the administration of Puerto Cabello, the most important port in the country. From there, the Makleds ran drugs through the port, supplying weapons to the FARC in exchange for cocaine, which they then trafficked through Central America and to West Africa. Walid Makled, head of the "mafia of the port," (as it was commonly known) became one of the most important drug traffickers in the world. He purchased the Venezuelan airline Aeropostal, a newspaper in Carabobo, ranches and other properties. He also held a monopoly on the fertilizer industry in Venezuela, the same industry used to prop up Ortega, and whose products can be used to process drugs and explosives. According to Makled, at the height of his power, his net worth was over $1.4 billion. In 2008, perhaps confident of their power, Makled's younger brother Abdala ran for mayor of Valencia.

---

332 After drinking a soda taken from a private warehouse he had militarily raided with the media in tow, he issued a burp into the microphones and declared that the army would begin to seize private food stockpiled, for distribution to the poor.

Makled, Venezuela's Pablo Escobar, had reached the pinnacle of wealth and power. It was short-lived. In the summer of 2008, President Chavez broke with General Luis Felipe Acosta Carles. Saying, "The regional governor's office was too big for him," Chavez accused Acosta Carles of setting up a network of extortion rings and of trafficking in drugs. In circles as closed as Chavez' are, it is sometimes hard to pinpoint the exact cause of the rupture of relationships. Perhaps Acosta Carles had gotten too greedy. Perhaps he had crossed other, more powerful people inside Chavez' inner circle. Whatever the case, general and former Governor Acosta Carles was out.

This spelled doom for the Makleds. On November 13, 2008, Venezuelan intelligence raided one of Makled's fincas and found four hundred kilos of cocaine. Basel and Alex Makled were arrested and jailed (where they remain today), and Walid chose to go into hiding: keeping his drug network intact.

On August 19, 2010 Walid Makled was arrested in Cucuta, Colombia, on a warrant from a New York federal court for trafficking ten tons of drugs a month into the United States and Europe. In May of 2009 he had been designated a drug kingpin by the US Government, and was referred to by the White House as the third most-important drug trafficker in the world.

Since his arrest, Makled has made extremely controversial claims, especially about the involvement in the drug trade of high-level officials in Hugo Chavez' government. He claims to have paid the brother of Interior Minister Tarek Al-Aissami $100,000. He has named Military Intelligence Chief Hugo Carvajal and General-in-Chief Rangel Silva as major drug players. OFAC listed Carvajal and Silva a full year before it listed Makled. He claims to have paper (and video) proof of all this, which he was able to smuggle out of Venezuela into safekeeping.

While he was arrested on US drug-trafficking charges, Chavez demanded his extradition to Venezuela on the charge of murder. "Over there is a bandit who is a Venezuelan drug trafficker and I am waiting, Nicolas [Maduro, Venezuela's foreign minister], that the government of Colombia—like President Santos told me via telephone—he told me they were going to send him here," said Chavez during a televised program, "and now he's[Makled] saying that he paid I don't know how many millions to a general and another ... so all the more reason, Nicolas, we have to ask our brothers in Colombia that they send him back here."

In a 2011 television interview with Univision, Makled continued to make important assertions. He claimed to have kept forty Venezuelan generals on the payroll, and a larger number of junior officers. He claims to have paid five million dollars a month to the military. He also says he kept five Venezuelan National Assembly Deputies on the payroll "for whenever I need them." He also says he was responsible for running six airplane-loads of cocaine from southern Venezuela into Honduras—which coincides with Manuel Zelaya's time in office as well as the UNODC reports designating Venezuela as the source of Honduran cocaine. When Makled began to make these revelations, Chavez promoted General Rangel Silva to General in Chief of the armed forces, a new position. There can be no other reason for this than Chavez guaranteeing to the narco-military elements their pre-eminence in the armed forces. Rangel Silva reciprocated by famously stating, "If the opposition wins [the upcoming presidential elections] they will not take power."[333] Makled also confirmed that he purchased seized cocaine from National Guardsmen in Venezuela for resale.

Here, there is an important point to notice. Experts in drug issues say that it is important, especially in countries suspected of having high levels of corruption and government involvement in the drug trade, to rely less on the amount of seized drugs and instead on the public destruction of the drugs. Normally, with DEA support, countries will burn seized drugs. In ALBA countries, drugs seized has usually less to do with drug interdiction than it does with rival gangs fighting each other over turf or transit zones. Makled has confirmed this in Venezuela on several occasions.

Bolivia

The ALBA relationship with drug production and trafficking does not stop in Venezuela. As stated before, the strategy to support the FARC through permissive operating environments and raise additional off-budget money is part of the ALBA's dark underbelly. Bolivia is increasingly involved in this world. As stated previously, Evo Morales did not need to be convinced of the importance of cocaine production. While he trumpets himself as an indigenous leader for international recognition, his power base is in fact the

333 "Henry Rangel Silva, accused drug kingpin, Hugo Chavez's pick for General in Chief," Huffington Post, 11 of December, 2010. http://www.huffingtonpost.com/2010/11/12/henry-rangel-silva_n_782974.html

"cocalero" coca growers' union: one of the most powerful unions in the country. He does not even speak Aymara, the language of his ethnicity; he is a mestizo. According to Doug Farah (award-winning journalist and investigative reporter), "The Morales government has also allowed formal and informal ties to the Revolutionary Armed Forces of Colombia."[334] Bolivian law permits the cultivation of twelve thousand hectares of coca leaves, allegedly for cultural practices by the majority indigenous peoples. Under President Morales, hectares under cultivation have increased to 30,500, with an estimated production of 113 metric tons of cocaine.

Under increasing pressure from the US Drug Enforcement Agency to bring Bolivian coca harvests to within legal limits (and thereby stem cocaine production), the Morales Administration expelled the DEA from the country in 2008. Bolivia has since been decertified in the fight against drugs.

According to the Colombian–Mexican drug dealer Jose Eduardo Valencia Arbelaez, currently imprisoned for seventeen years in the United States for dealing drugs, he visited Bolivia early in 2009 to attempt to establish an alternate drug route from that country to West Africa (which serves as a transit zone to Europe). He even purchased a used Gulfstream airplane for that purpose.[335]

The operation of Bolivian government officials in the drug trade has also been confirmed. In its own Walid Makled moment, Bolivian General Rene Sanabria was arrested in February 2011 in Panama on a US warrant for smuggling drugs into Africa.[336] In 2007 and 2008, Sanabria was Bolivia's Drug Czar. Following Sanabria's arrest, Bolivian authorities arrested Colonel Milton Sanchez Pantoja, Major Edwin Raul Ona Moncada and Captain Franz Hernando Siles Rios. Felipe Caceres, Bolivia's deputy minister for social defense, admitted there were fifteen other officials identified in Sanabria's drug gang. In response to the embarrassing arrest, and

---

334 Douglas Farah, "Into the Abyss: Bolivia Under Evo Morales and the MAS," International Assessment and Strategy Center, (2010): P2.

335 "Cartel quiso traficar droga a Bolivia a Africa en viajes naves," FM Bolivia, 16 de Noviembre 2010. http://www.fmbolivia.com.bo/noticia40454-cartel-quiso-traficar-droga-de-bolivia-a-frica-en-viejas-naves.html

336 "Former head of Bolivia's drugs police is sent to U.S. to face cocaine trafficking charges," Daily Mail, February 28, 2011. http://www.dailymail.co.uk/news/article-1361384/Bolivias-drugs-police-head-Rene-Sanabria-face-cocaine-trafficking-charge-US.html#ixzz1JbdftFcM

engaging in damage control, Bolivia's vice president, Alvaro Garcia Linera, admitted[337] to a "powerful and dangerous" drug cartel operating in the country, and put the amount of illicit monies at $700 million, and that they are linked to the Zetas.

Ecuador

Ecuador is a newcomer to the ALBA club, yet it has quickly become involved in the world of narco-terrorism. One of the first acts Rafael Correa promised as president was the closure of the US drug-surveillance base operating out of Manta, Ecuador. In 2009, Correa followed through on his promise and closed the base, thereby severely limiting the US DEA's ability to run drug interdiction efforts in Ecuador. At the same time and at the local level, Ecuador has been engaged in a consistent effort to curtail drug cooperation through vetted units and joint interdiction efforts.[338] They have also been actively replacing military officers with connections to or received training from the United States with more revolutionary leaders. Since the police dustup of September 2010, the national police force, a professional and apolitical organization, has increasingly been surrendering its responsibilities for internal order to the military (which have had more connections to the FARC).

The FARC presence in Ecuador has been longstanding. With such a long and porous border and without adequate national resources to police internally, the FARC has used Ecuador as a center for money laundering and escape from the Colombian army for many years. Yet it would seem that now, the FARC has one of their own as president. Evidence of Correa's links to the FARC is strong. An Ecuadorian government commission stated in 2009 that Ecuador was on the verge of becoming a narco-state.[339] According to the US State Department, Correa's current foreign minister, Ricardo Patino, allegedly received funding from Venezuela and the FARC for Correa's campaign.[340] On his deathbed, the FARC's

---

337 "Bolivia admite presencia de peligroso cartel narco mexicano en el país," EFE, 15th of July, 2010. http://www.emol.com/noticias/internacional/2010/07/15/425067/bolivia-admite-presencia-de-peligroso-cartel-narco-mexicano-en-el-pais.html
338 Author interviews with confidential sources.
339 Francisco Huerta Montalvo, et al, "Informe Comisión de Transparencia y Verdad: Caso Angostura," Dec. 10, 2009.
340 "Ecuador President's campaign to be investigated for FARC funding," Colombia

second-in-command "Mono Jojoy" read a statement where he admitted to funding the Correa campaign.[341]

Ecuador's Makled, or perhaps Sanabria, is in the family Ostaiza Amay. They were detained by the Ecuadorian antinarcotics police on an Interpol warrant in October 2007 in a massive drug case which has been dubbed the "Hurricane of the Border". This family, which included Edison and Miguel who are currently in an Ecuadorian prison and Jefferson, who escaped justice, admitted to operating a cartel in seven provinces of Ecuador.[342] They claimed that they had a relationship with Jose Ignacio Chauvin, formerly with the Ministry of Internal and External Security; as well as an ex-lawyer of a human rights organization operating on the border, Diego Benitez Osejo and the Colombian Roosevelt Borda Linares (alias El Paisa), a presumed member of the Cali cartel. Chauvin was a long-time friend of Raul Reyes, who was killed during the Colombian bombing of Angostura. On the 19th of May, 2010 Chauvin was found innocent in the case of Hurricane on the Border[343], in the case in which 8 out of 16 defendants sentenced to jail time. The Ostaiza Amays were caught with close to four tons of cocaine ready for processing. Diego Benitez was ordered released on bail by an Ecuadoran court in September of 2011. President Correa has accused his opposition and the press of using the Hurricane on the Border case to defame his government – and says those implicated will return to government when they are absolved of any crime[344].

Ecuador has increasingly been moving from a hotbed of money laundering to an increasing role in cocaine processing as well as a secondary role in transport (behind Venezuela). The Ostaizas have accused high level

Reports, 15 of April, 2011. http://colombiareports.com/colombia-news/news/15633-ecuador-presidents-campaign-to-be-investigated-for-farc-funding.html

341 "FARC admit financing campaign of Rafael Correa," Colombia Reports, July 17, 2009. http://colombiareports.com/colombia-news/news/5050-farc-admit-financing-presidential-campaign-of-rafael-correa.html

342 "Red narco en que se implica a los Ostaiza operaba en 7 provincias," El Universo, 15 de Febrero, 2009. http://www.eluniverso.com/2009/02/15/1/1355/DACC3203118B467997CD94B94476F1E8.html

343 "Jose Chauvin quedo absuelto en caso de Narcotrafico" Mayo 19, 2010 http://www.ecuavisa.com/noticias-nacionales/23981.html

344 Utlima Hora, "Larrea volverá al equipo de gobierno ecuatoriano cuando se esclarezca el caso Ostaiza" 19 de Marzo, 2009 http://www.hoy.com.ec/noticias-ecuador/larrea-volvera-al-equipo-de-gobierno-ecuatoriano-cuando-se-esclarezca-caso-ostaiza-338382.html

ministers in the Correa government of being involved in their crime ring.[345] The Correa government itself was accused of receiving $1,690,000 from the Ostaiza Amays. In a recording presented at the trial of the Ostaiza Amays in April of 2010, their father, Ariolfo Ostaiza, for his part, submitted a recording of stating, "There's another sector, led by (Foreign Minister) Patino, that say clearly that the Ostaiza brothers are tired of the blackmail (…) to the government (using the Ostaizas as bait) for positions and business.…" Ariolfo Ostaiza is accusing others of attempting to use the declarations of his son to create a case against the government.[346]

This messy case continues to play out in the courts. Nevertheless, what is becoming clear is that the Ostaiza Amay brothers operated with impunity as the interlocutors of the FARC to segments of Correa's government before they fell afoul of the law.

Similarly, there has been evidence of other Ecuadorian government officials interacting with the FARC. In 2005, Gustavo Itarralde, currently in charge of the Office of Money Laundering and head of the Ecuadorian Communist Party, admitted a relationship with the FARC.[347] The February 2008 Bolivarian Continental Congress (MCB) meeting took place at the GoE Casa de la Cultura (culture house, similar to the Kennedy Center in Washington). Nubia Calderon—known as the FARC's foreign minister in Ecuador and who was immediately reported as having been killed in the Colombian bombing of the FARC camp in Angostura—was in fact granted political exile in Nicaragua shortly after the bombing. It came out that she had a second job in the Ecuadorian congress, and that the Ecuadorian police knew she had not been killed in Angostura but delayed the news, allowing her time to escape.[348]

---

345 "Larrea niega cita con los Ostaiza," April 22, 2010. http://www.hoy.com.ec/noticias-ecuador/etapa-decisiva-en-huracan-403924.html

346 "Se cumple audiencia en caso Huracan de la Frontera," Expreso 21 de Abril, 2010. http://ediciones.expreso.ec/ediciones/2010/04/21/nacional/judicial/se-cumple-audiencia-en-caso-huracan-de-la-frontera//

347 "Partido comunista del Ecuador admite ser nexo entre Gutierrez y las FARC," Ecuador Inmediato, 20 de Enero, 2005. http://www.ecuadorinmediato.com/Noticias/news_user_view/partido_comunista_del_ecuador_admite_ser_nexo_entre_gutierrez_y_las_farc--7920

348 "Ecuador: podrá Nubia Calderon aclarar finalmente el caso de Franklin Aisalla," Ecuador Inmediato, 18 de Agosto, 2008. http://www.ecuadorinmediato.com/index.php?module=Noticias&func=news_user_view&id=85460&umt=Ecuador:%20

Another important actor is alleged to be some groups that supposedly work in human rights on the border – which are alleged to have involvement with the 48th Front of the FARC[349]. This work amazingly even involves support to the US Government-funded Plan Ecuador—the sister program to Plan Colombia. In a lawsuit submitted against Chauvin (above), there were alleged illegalities in facilitating identification cards (ID cards) to rural populations along the Colombian border with the assistance of these groups.[350] There could easily have been FARC among the beneficiaries of Ecuadorian ID cards during that operation. Chauvin denies any relationship with the FARC, although he has admitted talking to Raul Reyes in the atmosphere of humanitarian exchanges for kidnapped people.

These are only a handful of the links the Correa government is alleged to have with the drug-trafficking organizations. Yet they serve as a glance into the murky underworld of Correa's government, and how the ALBA works. As Doug Farah says, "There are indications from the FARC documents that the Colombian group donated heavily to Correa's campaign. It is also clear that he developed a close relationship with the FARC in the first fifteen months of his presidency. This included meetings between Correa's personal envoys and cabinet ministers that touched on changing military and police commanders in the border zone where the FARC was most active, to help the FARC."[351]

Nicaragua

Daniel Ortega has so far managed to avoid a Makled, Sanabria or Ostaiza Amay moment for his administration, which limits the exposure of the drug trade in that country in the international press. Nevertheless, independent journalists in that country have, at great risk to themselves, been

%BFpodr%E1%20Nubia%20Calder%F3n%20aclarar%20finalmente%20el%20caso%20de%20Franklin%20Aisalla?

349 Mena, Paul, "Dos miembros del ALDHU son identificados como ex guerrilleros en General Farfan," 8 Febrero, 2009 http://www.eluniverso.com/2009/02/08/1/1355/516A AC7063B94CF2809376FF3B592B51.html

350 "La carnetizacion de la ALDHU genera escándalo," Hoy, 14 de Septiembre, 2009. http://www.hoy.com.ec/noticias-ecuador/la-carnetizaci%E2%80%A6nero-escandalola-carnetizacion-de-la-aldhu-genero-escandalo-367727.html

351 Douglas Farah, "What the FARC Papers Show Us about Latin American Terrorism," NEFA Foundation, April 1, 2008. www.nefafoundation.org/miscellaneous/FeaturedDocs/nefafarc0408.pdf

investigating and reporting on the Nicaragua drug situation. One of these, Roberto Escobedo, has outlined what he calls "ALBA-Drugs SA," a cozy arrangement between the military in Nicaragua and Venezuela to reassemble Nicaragua's role in the drug trade.[352] According to Escobedo, high-level officials in Nicaragua's navy have been enlisted in reestablishing the links with the FARC and drug traffickers that existed during President Daniel Ortega's first administration in the 1980s. These include currently retired military officials responsible for the construction and management of the new mega-port project at Bilwi (on the Caribbean coast), financed by the ALBA. They also include legendary figures like those of Eden Pastora. Pastora, a prominent Sandinista guerilla leader before be broke with the FSLN, became a Contra, and has since returned to the party and is currently managing a project "dredging" the San Juan River on the border with Costa Rica. According to the Costa Ricans[353] the dredging project constitutes an invasion and seizure of Costa Rican land. Escobedo states that in 2001, Pastora was accused of managing a clandestine airfield in the area for the running of drugs, until it was shut down by then-president Arnoldo Aleman.[354] This dredging project, financed by the ALBA as well, is said to be an attempt to reestablish Nicaragua as a drug route. Nicaragua has become increasingly important in the drug-transit industry since President Manuel "Mel" Zelaya was removed from power. According to Walid Makled, he flew six flights a day into Honduras, the planes filled with cocaine, while "Mel" was president. Currently in Nicaragua, in the Autonomous Region of the North Atlantic (RAAN), President Ortega has used ALBA money to purchase significant land. It is unclear what Ortega plans to do with this land; however, the rumors are of a joint military establishment between the Venezuelan and the Nicaraguan armed forces. According to Escobedo, this establishment could be set up to provide clandestine airfields for the use of drug traffickers.

---

352 Roberto Escobedo Caicedo, "ALBA Drogas, S.A." Nicaragua Hoy, 19 de Diciembre, 2009. http://www.nicaraguahoy.info/dir_cgi/topics.cgi?op=print_topic;cat=Opinion;id=58080

353 Author interviews with confidential sources.

354 Roberto Escobedo Caicedo, "Que Persigue Ortega con la pantomima de dragar al San Juan?" Nicaragua Hoy, 6 de Noviembre, 2010. http://www.nicaraguahoy.info/dir_cgi/topics.cgi?op=print_topic;cat=Opinion;id=60136

President Ortega has had contact for many years with the FARC and drug traffickers. That contact has allegedly picked up again. According to the US Government, both the FARC as well as Venezuela provided economic support to Ortega's election campaign, and Nicaragua's former Director of State Security, Lenin Cerna, was the FARC's man in Managua; he worked to provide funding to judges who released drug traffickers. Specifically named are the judges Rafael Solis and Roger Camillo.[355] On one occasion, Camillo developed a scheme to provide $609,000 to lower-court judges and FSLN candidates. According to a press report from La Prensa, a six-person FARC delegation attended the anniversary of the 1979 Sandinista Revolution, despite having received an advisory from Interpol on their outstanding arrest warrants.[356] After the Angostura attack in Ecuador following the second Bolivarian Congress, Ortega offered asylum to FARC rebels Doris Torres Bohorquez, Martha Perez Gutierrez, and Mexican national Lucia Morett.

Honduras

While Honduras is no longer a member of the ALBA, it is important to mention that officials from Zelaya's government also had contacts with the FARC and drug dealers. Documents from Raul Reyes' computer stated that pro-Zelaya Party for Democratic Unity was on the FARC's list of international collaborators.[357] Throughout Zelaya's presidency, airplane-loads of cocaine continued to fly into Honduras in places such as Olancho, La Ceiba, as well as the Mosquito Coast. Perhaps more importantly, after being ousted, Zelaya confirmed he was planning to close down the US military base Palmerola, known as "Soto Cano,"[358] ostensibly to convert it into an international airport. Soto Cano houses the primary radar facilities—run by US Southern Command—that identify drug flights over Honduran airspace. Zelaya knew this. Similar to the closure of Manta in Ecuador,

---

355 "State Department Cable accuses Ortega of Receiving Drug Money," Insight, December 7, 2010. http://www.insightcrime.org/insight-latest-news/item/316-state-department-cable-accuses-ortega-of-receiving-drug-money

356 Douglas Farah, "Ortega steps into the breach with the FARC," July 23, 2008. http://www.douglasfarah.com/article/376/ortega-steps-into-the-breach-with-the-farc.com

357 Mary O'Grady, "The FARC's Honduran Friends," *Wall Street Journal*, August 10, 2009. http://online.wsj.com/article/SB10001424052970204251404574340570960456550.html

358 "Palmerola debe convertirse en un aeropuerto civil, afirmo Zelaya," Alternativa Latinoamericana, 16 de Febrero, 2011. http://alternativalatinoamericana.blogspot.com/2011/02/palmerola-debe-convertirse-en-un.html

limitation of the United States' ability to combat the illegal drug trade is part of the ALBA's political, economic and ideological program.

On May 10, 2011, the London-based think tank International Institute of Strategic Studies launched, "The FARC Files: Venezuela, Ecuador and the Secret Archive of Raul Reyes." This publication was the result of a two-year study by the Institute of the computers of Raul Reyes, the FARC leader killed in Angostura. The Colombian government, under orders from President Uribe, had given the IISS unprecedented full access to the computer.[359] The results were stunning.

The IISS effectively concluded that, during the presidency of Hugo Chavez, the relationship between the Venezuelan Government and the FARC became very fluid. Venezuelan ministers solicited FARC support in political assassinations against opposition figures (it is unclear if they ever were carried out); FARC used Venezuelan territory to train and organize; FARC enjoyed safe-haven status with the Venezuelan government which gave them cover; Chavez worked with FARC as part of his political revolutionary continental project; and the FARC has unprecedented access to President Chavez. This included promises of $300 million as well as operational support.[360]

With Ecuador, the relationship was more nascent and less fluid. While the relationship between President Rafael Correa and the FARC was very close, and the FARC assisted in financing Correa's presidential campaign – something of which President Correa was probably aware despite his public denial – Ecuador itself (at least up until 2008) was not a FARC state, as was Venezuela.[361]

The report, and the corresponding 800 pages of emails released, demonstrate a fascinating political role for the FARC in the continent. Seizing upon Chavez's advice and the FSP's support, they have been wildly successful as a political organization. The emails even demonstrate the disappointment of the FARC commanders when Ollanta Humala was not elected President of Peru in 2006. Undoubtedly the FARC is now pleased.

---

359 "The FARC Files: Venezuela, Ecuador and the Secret Archive of Raul Reyes," International Institute for Strategic Studies, May 10, 2011.
360 Nigel Inkster, "The FARC Files Launch Remarks," May 10, 2011.
361 Nigel Inkster, "The FARC Files Launch Remarks," May 10, 2011.

As with terrorism, entire tomes can (and should) be written regarding the increasing infiltration of drug networks into Bolivarian Alliance countries. We are only beginning to see the dark underbelly of the drug trade's impact in these countries, and much more needs to be explored.

As can be seen in the drug cases of Makled, Sanabria and the Ostaiza Amays, as is witnessed by the messy judicial manipulation, the planting of evidence for the creation of political prisoners, and the constant subversion of their own systems which often goes awry, the Bolivarian process is messy. The governments of the Bolivarian Alliance (with the exception of Cuba) are not totalitarian regimes, they are authoritarian regimes. This means they chose to operate within corrupted and manipulated institutions to preserve a veneer of legitimacy, in the attempt to hoodwink those either unwilling or unable to see and understand or keep up with their Machiavellian efforts at social control. We in the west see elections and we infer democracy, making an immediate value judgment before considering the full range of actions by the Bolivarians.

This is what the ALBA is counting on. And for them, it works well. President Hugo Chavez, despite being in power for thirteen years and governing virtually by decree, retains a certain amount of international democratic credibility. This credibility is much more so for other countries that are less blatant about the abuse and that, let us be honest, do not receive much attention anyway, such as Bolivia and Ecuador. Yet, there is a downside to all these countries' choice of dictatorial models. It means that, occasionally, things slip out of their control. Sometimes they are betrayed from inside, such as is the case for the drug dealers mentioned above. Sometimes a judge chooses to disobey and rule based on their conscience, such as was the case with Judge Afiuni. Occasionally, even their herculean attempts to rig elections cannot make up for wildly unpopular initiatives. For those who prefer to use these as examples of freedom, I would argue that they are instead the occasional but inevitable lapses in the Bolivarian authoritarian scheme. The Bolivarians should not be rewarded for these by international positive opinion; those who love freedom should not cease to take advantage of these rare occurrences to point out the corruption and abuse of power that mar the Bolivarian model.

Finally, as this book goes to print there are important changes happening within the Bolivarian project. The most important is the diagnosis of President Hugo Chavez with cancer. At the time of writing, it is unclear the gravity of President Chavez's disease and whether he will survive. Should President Chavez succumb to the disease, it would put significant stress on the Bolivarian model. It is unclear whether anybody else has the charisma and intelligence to continue to lead Venezuela down the ALBA path. This could mean several important changes. First, it could mean that the opposition could win the upcoming elections. This would take the beating heart out of the ALBA – and would remove the significant funding that Venezuela provides to this project. It would also close the space that Hezbollah, Iran, the FARC and other criminal organizations have come to count on in the hemisphere. Should the opposition be unable to assume power, it is also unclear who would assume control over the GoV and the Bolivarian project. It could be that, if Chavez is no longer at the head of the project, that it will collapse. With only six years of longevity, it is arguably too soon for the ALBA to survive without the personal direction of President Chavez. Needless to say, whatever happens, there are important developments in the region which will affect the outcome and future of tens of millions of people. Only time will tell what the future will hold.

AUTHOR'S NOTE

The Consent of the Governed

The hallmark of western democratic governance is the principle that the individuals within society surrender the right to use force, the right to sit in judgment and the authority to use coercive methods based upon an act of willful consent; this is called the consent of the governed.

This consent is not static; it changes, morphs, as the governments that sit above society become more or less representative of the people they are chosen to lead. It is for this reason that transparency, accountability and good faith are important in the acts of governing. When governments use populist pandering and authoritarian maneuvering to secure electoral victories that allow them to radically socially engineer their societies, they lose the consent of an increasingly large portion of their societies. And in this process they break the social contract they signed with their citizens: to govern for the wellbeing of the majority with the careful protection of the minorities, within the rule of law and abiding by their constitutions.

The ALBA has violated these fundamental rules. In their attempts to build authoritarian states that guarantee the permanence of the ruling elite and the ruling elite's ability to build their partisan, illegal and dangerous political project, they have dismantled the democratic institutions that have been so carefully crafted and painstakingly protected. This has been done with the complicity of the Organization of American States and the west. This book has served to highlight the political project of the Bolivarian Alliance of the Americas, as well as its philosophical foundations and its desired end state. Research for this project was long and arduous, and involved travel to a half dozen countries of the region and interviews with hundreds of people, as well as the review of hundreds of documents, articles and studies.

The constitution of Venezuela clearly states that the purpose of that magna carta is to "establish a democratic society (...) which consolidates the values of liberty, independence, peace, solidarity, the common good, territorial integrity, peaceful coexistence and the empire of the law.[362]" It is

362 Constitucion de la Republica Bolivariana de Venezuela de 1999 http://pdba.george-town.edu/constitutions/venezuela/ven1999.html

for those who come after to decide whether the political project of Hugo Chavez and his ALBA live up to those lofty ideals.

I fought with myself quite a bit while researching and writing this book, about how far I should go in attempting to demonstrate some of the abuses and dangers represented by the ALBA countries. I was repeatedly urged by people I greatly respect—to be intellectually honest with my research and demonstrate some of the benefits brought by the ALBA to the world. Yet as I thought about these requests, I realized these are the same people who consistently refuse to condemn Fidel Castro as he is perched in luxury atop his island gulag. They refuse to condemn Hugo Chavez as he wraps the frayed fabric of a society ever tighter around his widening shoulders. And, they are the people who say Morales should be able to get away with blatant abuses of power represented by illegitimate constitutions written by excluding opposition from deliberations. Yet I watch the political prisoners rot in Venezuelan jails and I see mass political discrimination across the continent. I watch violence, drug trafficking and criminality wrack the foundations of these societies and the morgues fill up with the brutalized bodies of people who had no power to control their fate and their future. I chat online with my friends who have had their farms seized, or with human-rights colleagues on trial for treason. And for those of us who have friends exiled from the ALBA because of political beliefs—we listen to stories of secret cemeteries wherein the buried bodies of the ALBA's foes lie. As we hear stories about tortures and drug battles between gangs controlled by government ministers seeking to seize the lucrative trade to West Africa, as loved ones are forced to repeat the empty epithets of the revolution to find work, as the tales become more sordid, of beautiful Miami penthouse apartments for revolutionary leaders, of whiskey and parties, of intrigue and sex and drugs, I am slapped with a stunning reality.

The reality is, more than the revolutionary leaders simple desire to enjoy the power their pilfering provides, they crave the legitimacy of their model. While the lights burn late into the night within the revolution's most sacred watering holes, these leaders' best defense comes from the uninformed. And it is a dastardly scheme. While the brutality continues without end, those of us attempting to shine a light on the bloodbath are told by the apologists for 21st Century Socialism that we must discuss the merits of their project. They press us into semantic discussions on words of democracy, or of freedom. They force us to carry out surveys ad infinitum, using, of course, their official statistics collected by revolutionary bureaucrats to demonstrate the benefit in the lives of the poor. Denying within their own countries the freedom that allows them to pontificate in ours, we are cajoled by the overwhelming weight of their propaganda.

Then it came to me, this is what the Bolivarians are counting on. The ALBA and their minions abroad wish us to argue about maternal mortality rates, about global acute malnutrition and income inequality until we are all exhausted. Meanwhile, they deepen their power and control over their abused societies. If they ensure that the discussion remains on supposed social well-being instead of fundamental freedoms, they can keep their paid foot soldiers working in manipulation of the global discussion. But our principles are not and cannot be for sale. We must not allow ourselves to be caught in their twisted logic, and thereby legitimize a plan that has as its end dictatorship and suffering. Theirs is not the path toward freedom—as the data above present more clearly than I ever could. And this is not the path toward well-being—as is argued, if unwillingly, by even the United Nation's own figures. And I must reiterate now, once again, the fundamental tenets that have always brought about improved well-being in countries that have decided to work in honesty and principled discipline within the agreed-upon bounds of a free society.

We do not owe dictatorship the benefit of the doubt. And for my friends who think that tearing a hole in representative democracy for the stated intention of improving well-being, of allowing the 21st Century Socialists of the world to dismantle the basic freedoms set forth in the International Covenant on Civil and Political Rights, in hopes that in doing so they will more quickly reduce hunger or illiteracy, I remind you of the truths we all continue to hold self-evident. The exclusion of representative democracy will never increase well-being. The curtailing of individual freedoms will always bring misery.

This book, therefore, is not about an analysis of the different economic models, a debate between 21st Century Socialism and capitalism—as most apologists of revolution so desperately wish. I have no desire to mock the tried and true ideals of liberal democracy. In doing such, I would be no worse than the dictators themselves as I compare, on a level playing field, the benefits of good versus evil. I instead want to present with clarity of mind what I believe is an actual, current danger growing like a cancer in the hemisphere.

I want to thank you for accompanying me through this tedious process. I have tried in the previous lines, and in my year's study, work and research, to understand what the Bolivarian Alliance of the Americas (ALBA) is doing in the hemisphere, to unravel their plan, to tease out their intentions, and to shine a light into the dark corners of their Bolivarian Revolution. During my research and interviews I met many men and women of good faith, people who love their countries and want to build a better tomorrow for their children. They see in the ideals of solidarity, of complementarity, and of compassion a greater, less predatory nation where they will be able to at long last cast aside the chains of poverty and bondage and live up to their full potential.

That, my friends, is what makes this so sad. As I hope you have had the courage to see, the Bolivarians of bad faith use the work of the poor in their countries to install a system that seeks not their benefit, but their control. They use the right language to befuddle the weak of mind across the world, and they use powerful propaganda and mechanisms of internal control to sell their project. They use their loud voices screaming the right words at the tops of their lungs to hide a more devious, more dastardly scheme. It is for this reason that the Bolivarian Alliance's result will be only more slavery, more suffering, and more death. As it expands its lecherous grasp across a continent, the United States and the lovers of freedom sit back and watch with indifference. Worse than that, those of a particular political ideology in fact applaud as the institutions they so freely enjoy in their own countries are rived asunder for the personal, populist project of a group of powerful men.

Now that you know the truth, I welcome you to share it with others. Don't shy away from a controversial challenge, but embrace the debate with enthusiasm and a sense of privilege and honor. We who promote freedom and democracy are a lucky few, lucky to be in the place at the time when we can make a difference. Yet, we are few because a decreasing number are able to clearly identify, articulate and defend the truths we all hold as self-evident; that man was created to enjoy his own life, his own liberty and his own happiness. So to honor that vision, we must always stay true and boldly reject the dictators' visions of "fatherland, socialism or death."

Acronyms

ALBA – Bolivarian Alliance of the Americas
ALBANISA – ALBA of Nicaragua S.A.
ALBA-TCP – People's Trade Agreement
ANTV – National Assembly Television of Venezuela
AP – Associated Press
ASKAPENA – Basque ETA's Political Wing of for Latin Ameirca
RAAN – Autonomous Region of the North Atlantic
BID – Banco International de Desarrollo
BATASUNA – Political wing of ETA terrorist organization
Battle of Boyaca
BCN – Bolivarian Congress of the Nations
MCB – Bolivarian Continental Movement
CAN – Community of Andean Nations
CARICOM – Economic Community of the Caribbean
CCB (now MCB) – Bolivarian Continental Movement
CELAC – Community of Latin American and Caribbean States
CIECA – C nter for Economic Investigations
CGTP – General Confederation of Peruvian Workers
CITGO – Venezuelan Petroleum Company in the USA
DEA – US Drug Enforcement Administration
DISIP (now SEBIN) – Venezuela's political police
ELN – National Liberation Army
ETA – Basque terrorist organization
EZLN – Zapatista Army for National Liberation
FARC – Revolutionary Armed Forces of Columbia
FDI – Foreign Direct Investment
FLACSO – Latin American Faculty for Social Sciences
FMLN – Farabundo Marti Front for National Liberation
FNRP – National Front for Popular Resistance
FONDEN – National Fund for Development
FTAA – Free Trade Agreement of the Americas
FARC-EP – Revolutionary Armed Forces of Colombia, Popular Army
FSLN – Sandinista Front for National Liberation
FSP – Sao Paulo Forum
GDP – Gross Domestic Products
MAOC-N – Maritime Analysis Operation Centre
GAO – General Accounting Office
GoB – Government of Bolivia

GoE – Government of Ecuador

GoI – Government of Iran

GoN – Government of Nicaragua

GoV, Government of Venezuela

GDP – Gross Domestic Product

IAEA – International Atomic Energy Agency

ICC – International Criminal Court

ICJ – International Court of Justice

IHL – International Humanitarian Law

IISS – International Institute of Strategic Studies

IMF – International Monetary Fund

IMPASCO – Iran Minerals Production and Supply Co.

IPR – Intellectual Property Rights

Interpol – International Police

IRA – Irish Republican Army

KPMG – International Accounting Firm

MAS – Movement Towards Socialism

MBR-200 – Bolivarian Revolutionary Movement - 200

MCB (was CCB) – Bolivarian Continental Movement

MEK – People's Mujahedeen

MERCOSUR – Southern Cone Common Market (Argentina, Uruguay, Brazil, Paraguay)

MNI – Movement for a New Left

MPM – Mothers of Plaza Mayo

MRTA – Revolutionary Movement Tupac Amaru

NED – National Endowment for Democracy

NFLP – National Front for the Liberation of Palestine

NGO – Non-governmental Organization

NYSE – New York Stock Exchange

OAS – Organization of American States

OPEC – Organization of Petroleum Exporting Countries

PCP – Peruvian Communist Party

PDVSA – Petroleum of Venezuela

PETRONIC – Petroleum of Nicaragua

PMOI – People's Mujahedeen, also MEK

PSUV – United Socialist Party of Venezuela

RCTV – Radio Caracas TeleVision

RDD – Regional Democratic Developmentalism

REPSOL – Petroleum of Spain

SICA – Central American Integration System

SUCRE – Sistema Unitaria de Compensacion Regional de Pagos Sudan

SUTEP – United Syndicate of Education Workers of Peru

TWAIL – Third World Approaches to International Law

TI – Transparency International

OFAC – United States Treasury Department's Office of Foreign Asset Control (OFAC)

UN (United Nations)

UNASUR – Union of South American Nations

UNDP HDI – United Nations Development Program Human Development Index

UNODC – United Nations Office of Drugs and Crime, UNODC

SEC – Security Securities and Exchange Commission

USAID – United States Agency for International Development

USG – United States Government

USSR – Union of Soviet Socialist Republics

VTV – Venezuelan State Television

WMD – Weapons of Mass Destruction

WTO – World Trade Organization

WWII – World War Two

Bibliography

1. "Acuerdo de San Jose," 22 de Julio, 2009. http://www.elheraldo.hn/var/elheraldo_site/storage/original/application/205307a26c541f7af1d173c22454bd5a.pdf

2. "AIR condena cierre de 34 emisoras de radio en Venezuela," El Nacional, 1 de Agosto, 2009. http://el-nacional.com/www/site/p_contenido.php?q=nodo/92617/Internacional/AIR-condena-cierre-de-34-emisoras-de-radio-en-Venezuela

3. "Bolivia admite presencia de peligroso cartel narco mexicano en el país," EFE, 15th of July, 2010. http://www.emol.com/noticias/internacional/2010/07/15/425067/bolivia-admite-presencia-de-peligroso-cartel-narco-mexicano-en-el-pais.html

4. "Bolivia aumenta ventas a Venezuela de soya y textiles," Notidiario, 22 de Febrero, 2011. http://www.notidiario.com.ve/index.php?option=com_content&view=article&id=4297:bolivia-aumenta-ventas-a-venezuela-de-soja-y-textiles&catid=45:economia&Itemid=66

5. "Bolivia aumenta ventas a Venezuela de soya y textiles," Notidiario, 22 de Febrero, 2011. http://www.notidiario.com.ve/index.php?option=com_content&view=article&id=4297:bolivia-aumenta-ventas-a-venezuela-de-soja-y-textiles&catid=45:economia&Itemid=66

6. "Bolivia elige a Iran para explotar litio," *La Razon*, 28 de Octubre, 2010. http://www.la-razon.com/version.php?ArticleId=120281&EditionId=2328

7. "Bolivia tendrá 30 Radios comunitarios y un Canal de TV," Voltairenet.org, 22 de Junio, 2006. http://www.voltairenet.org/article141096.html

8. "Bolivia: Manejo de Dinero de Evo Cumple es Secreto," *La Razon*, 26 de Agosto, 2007. http://www.offnews.info/verArticulo.php?contenidoID=9192

9. "Canal de television del gobierno comenzó a emitir," 4 de Agosto, 2008. http://legislaciones.item.org.uy/index?q=node/732

10. "Cartel quiso traficar droga a Bolivia a Africa en viajes naves," FM Bolivia, 16 de Noviembre 2010. http://www.fmbolivia.com.bo/noticia40454-cartel-quiso-traficar-droga-de-bolivia-a-frica-en-viejas-naves.html

11. "Chavez allies back ousted Zelaya," BBC News, June 29, 2009. http://news.bbc.co.uk/2/hi/8124100.stm

12. "Chavez amenaza ahora a Globovision," 30 de Mayo, 2007 EFE. http://www.cadenaser.com/articulo/internacional/Chavez/amenaza/ahora/Globovision/unico/canal/privado/critico/gestion/csrcsrpor/20070530csrcsrint_2/Tes/

13. "Chavez ha expropiado y mal administrado," La Prensa 4 de Febrero, 2011. http://www.laprensa.com.ni/2011/02/04/politica/51076

14. "Chavez propone creación de fuerza armada del ALBA," EFE, 27 de Enero, 2008. http://www.esmas.com/noticierostelevisa/internacionales/698504. html

15. "Chavez reconoce crisis por caída de petróleo," 25 de Noviembre, 2008. http://www.infobae.com/mundo/417061-101094-0-Chavez-reconoce-crisis-caida-del-petroleo

16. "Chavez, las FARC y la Coordinadora Continental Bolivariana," CNA 7 de Septiembre, 2010. http://impactocna.com/2010/09/07/chavez-las-farc-y-la-coordinadora-continental-bolivariana/

17. "Conceptualización de Proyecto y Empresa Grannacional en el Marco del ALBA – Documentos del VI Cumbre," 30 de Octubre, 2009. http://www.alianzabolivariana.org/modules.php?name=Content&pa=showpage&pid=2074

18. "Constitucion de Ecuador." http://www.asambleanacional.gov.ec/documentos/constitucion_de_bolsillo.pdf

19. "Constitucion Politica de Bolivia de 1826," http://www.dircost.unito.it/cs/docs/Bolivia%201826.htm

20. "Correa cierre canales de Television," 9 de Julio, 2008. http://www.diariocritico.com/bolivia/2008/Julio/noticias/85677/correa-cierra-canales.html

21. "Costa Rica Referendo," La Nacion, Octubre 2007. http://wvw.nacion.com/ln_ee/ESPECIALES/2007/octubre/referendo/mapa/index.html

22. "Declaracion Conjunta entre el Presidente de la Republica Bolivariana de Venezuela y el Presidente del Consejo de Estado de la Republica de Cuba para la creación del ALBA," 14 de Diciembre, 2004. http://www.alianzabolivariana.org/modules.php?name=Content&pa=showpage&pid=2060

23. "Declaracion de Adhesion de la Republica de Honduras a la Alternativa Bolivariana Para los Pueblos de Nuestra America (ALBA)," Agosto 25, 2008. http://www.alianzabolivariana.org/modules.php?name=Content&pa=showpage&pid=1969

24. "Destituido Manuel Zelaya: Cronica de la Crisis," *Contacto Magazine*, Junio (June) 2009. http://www.contactomagazine.com/articulos/zelayadestituido0609.htm

25. "Dieterich Evalua a Presidentes Socialistas," Diario Hoy, 17 de Abril, 2011. http://www.hoy.com.ec/noticias-ecuador/dieterich-evalua-a-presidentes-socialistas-470205.html

26. "Diputados aprueban leyes de defensa y seguridad nacional," La Jornada, 14 de Diciembre 2010. http://www.lajornadanet.com/diario/archivo/2010/diciembre/14/2.html

27. "Discurso de Hugo Chavez en Cumbre de las Americas," Mar del Plata, 11 de Mayo 2005. http://www.taringa.net/posts/downloads/7541770/Discur-

so-Hugo-Chavez_-ContraCumbre-Mar-Del-Plata-2005.html

28. "Dominican Leftist Leader has links to the FARC," Dominican Today, March 18, 2008. http://www.dominicantoday.com/dr/local/2008/3/18/27363/Dominican-leftist-leader-has-links-to-the-FARC-El-Dia-says

29. "Ecuador Mira al Sur y Promueve Desarrollo Endojeno," Prensa Latina 29 de Marzo, 2011. http://ecuadorinmediato.com/index.php?module=Noticias&func=news_user_view&id=146582&umt=ECUADOR%20MIRA%20AL%20SUR%20Y%20PROMUEVE%20DESARROLLO%20END%D3GENO

30. "Ecuador President's campaign to be investigated for FARC funding," Colombia Reports, 15 of April, 2011. http://colombiareports.com/colombia-news/news/15633-ecuador-presidents-campaign-to-be-investigated-for-farc-funding.html

31. "Ecuador: podrá Nubia Calderon aclarar finalmente el caso de Franklin Aisalla," Ecuador Inmediato, 18 de Agosto, 2008. http://www.ecuadorinmediato.com/index.php?module=Noticias&func=news_user_view&id=85460&umt=Ecuador:%20%BFpodr%E1%20Nubia%20Calder%F3n%20aclarar%20finalmente%20el%20caso%20de%20Franklin%20Aisalla?

32. "Eduardo Rozsa Flores and Aprad Magyarosi are the two Hungarians killed in Bolivia," Hungarian Ambiance, April 17, 2009. http://www.hungarianambiance.com/2009/04/eduardo-rozsa-flores-and-arpad.html

33. "EEUU sospecho que Venezuela impulso terrorismo en Ecuador," El Universal, 24 de Abril, 2011. http://politica.eluniversal.com/2011/04/24/eeuu-sospecho-que-venezuela-impulso-terrorismo-en-ecuador.shtml

34. "El Satelite Venezolano Simon Bolivar," 26 de Mayo, 2006. http://www.lapatriagrande.net/04_opiniones/attilio_folliero/satelite_simon_bolivar.htm

35. "Escuela de defensa del ALBA avanza," 4 de Diciembre 2010. http://www.alba-tcp.org/contenido/escuela-de-defensa-del-alba-avanza-04-de-diciembre-de-2010

36. "ETA Suspect Arturo Cubillas fails to appear in Spanish Court," El Universal, December 14, 2010. http://english.eluniversal.com/2010/12/14/en_pol_esp_eta-suspect-arturo-c_14A4853251.shtml

37. "FARC admit financing campaign of Rafael Correa," Colombia Reports, July 17, 2009. http://colombiareports.com/colombia-news/news/5050-farc-admit-financing-presidential-campaign-of-rafael-correa.html

38. "Felipe Quispe fue presidente honorario de la Coordinadora," Radio Caracol, 21 de Julio, 2008. http://www.caracol.com.co/nota.aspx?id=635893

39. "Fiber Optic Cable Linking Venezuela to Cuba, Jamaica to come Online,"

Latin American Herald Tribune. http://laht.com/article.asp?ArticleId=3709
28&CategoryId=14510

40. "FitALBA promovera a Venezuela en paquetes multi-destinos," Correo del
Orinoco, 9 de Septiembre, 2010. http://www.correodelorinoco.gob.ve/
avances/fitalba-promovera-a-venezuela-paquetes-multidestinos/

41. "FMI aplaza labor económica de Zelaya," El Heraldo 12 de Enero, 2008.
http://www.laprensa.hn/content/view/full/82502

42. "FMLN y Chavez regresaron a Zelaya," La Prensa, 8 de Diciembre 2010.
http://www.laprensa.com.ni/2010/12/08/nacionales/45854

43. "Former head of Bolivia's drugs police is sent to U.S. to face cocaine trafficking charges," Daily Mail, February 28, 2011. http://www.dailymail.co.uk/
news/article-1361384/Bolivias-drugs-police-head-Rene-Sanabria-face-co-
caine-trafficking-charge-US.html#ixzz1JbdftFcM

44. "Fourth Summit of the Americas: A New Challenge for the Hemisphere,"
Organization of American States. http://www.summit-americas.org/news-
letter/newsletter_Feb05_eng.htm

45. "Fuerzas Armadas de Bolivia Rechazan la intromisión de Chavez," Noticias 24, 12 de Septiembre, 2008. http://www.noticias24.com/actualidad/
noticia/17520/fuerzas-armadas-de-bolivia-rechazan-intromisiones-de-hugo-
chavez/

46. "Golpe de Estado de Daniel Ortega al poder Judicial," La Gaceta, 14 de
Agosto, 2010. http://www.intereconomia.com/noticias-gaceta/internacio-
nal/golpe-estado-daniel-ortega-al-poder-judicial-nicaragua

47. "Gran Colombia," Encyclopedia Britannica online. http://www.britannica.
com/EBchecked/topic/241012/Gran-Colombia

48. "Guerra de Gran Colombia – Peru," http://www.worldlingo.com/ma/en-
wiki/es/Gran_Colombia-Peru_War

49. "Ha Muerto el Camarada," Altermedia Castellano 7 de Mayo, 2003. http://
es.altermedia.info/general/ha-muerto-el-camarada_419.html

50. "Henry Rangel Silva, accused drug kingpin, Hugo Chavez's pick for General
in Chief," Huffington Post, 11 of December, 2010. http://www.huffington-
post.com/2010/11/12/henry-rangel-silva_n_782974.html

51. "Hermandad Revolucionaria." http://www.scribd.com/doc/39192834/
Hermandad-Revolucionaria-Socialismo-Siglo-21

52. "How Hugo Chavez's Petro-Dollars made it to Peru," Peru 21, June 4, 2011.
http://interamericansecuritywatch.com/how-hugo-chavez%e2%80%99s-
petro-dolars-made-it-to-peru/

53. "How much money is there in Venezuela's development fund FON-
DEN," The Devil's Excrement, March 4, 2009. http://devilsexcrement.
com/2009/03/04/how-much-money-is-there-in-venezuelas-development-

fund-fonden/

54. "Hugo Chavez crea reserve military," La Republica, 15 de Abril 2008. http://www.larepublica.com.uy/mundo/307190-hugo-chavez-crea-reserva-militar

55. "Identities Magazine." http://www.albacultural.org/__admin/imagenes//libros/Revista%20Identidades/IDENTIDADES%2019.pdf

56. "Integracion Regional: Un Proyecto Politico y Estrategico," III Informe FLACSO, P16.

57. "Inteligencia alerto sobre penetración bolivariana en el Peru desde 2006," El Comercio, 8 de Julio, 2009. http://elcomercio.pe/politica/311706/noticia-inteligencia-alerto-sobre-penetracion-bolivariana-peru-desde-2006

58. "Iran cobra deuda a Nicaragua," El Nuevo Diario, 6 de Octubre, 2009. http://www.elnuevodiario.com.ni/politica/58812

59. "Iran's Quds Force in Venezuela, Latin America: Pentagon," AFP, April 22, 2010. http://hello.news352.lu/edito-36553-iran-s-quds-force-in-venezuela-latin-america-pentagon.html

60. "Israel says Iran gets Uranium from Venezuela and Bolivia," AP, May 25, 2009. http://www.nytimes.com/2009/05/26/world/middleeast/26israel.html

61. "Israel ties two nations to Iran's Uranium," Financial Times. http://www.ft.com/cms/s/0/4848e022-9cd1-11de-ab58-00144feabdc0.html#ixzz1JKI1XZ7E

62. "Jefe de coordinadora bolivariana en Peru admite respaldo financiero de Venezuela," La Republica, 16 de Marzo, 2008. http://www.larepublica.pe/archive/all/larepublica/20080316/1/node/22454/total/01

63. "La 'guerrilla zelayista' ya entrena en Nicaragua," El Heraldo, 1 de Enero, 2009. http://www.elheraldo.hn/Ediciones/2009/08/02/Noticias/La-guerrilla-zelayista-ya-entrena-en-Nicaragua

64. "La Batalla de Boyaca," Efemerides Venezolanas. http://www.efemerides-venezolanas.com/html/boyaca.htm

65. "La carnetizacion de la ALDHU genera escándalo," Hoy, 14 de Septiembre, 2009. http://www.hoy.com.ec/noticias-ecuador/la-carnetizaci%E2%80%A6nero-escandalola-carnetizacion-de-la-aldhu-genero-escandalo-367727.html

66. "Larrea niega cita con los Ostaiza," April 22, 2010. http://www.hoy.com.ec/noticias-ecuador/etapa-decisiva-en-huracan-403924.html

67. "Las FARC aportaron a la campana de Correa," El Diario, 12 de Abril, 2011. http://www.eldiario.com.ec/noticias-manabi-ecuador/188088-las-farc-aportaron-a-campana-de-correa/

68. "Mandatos de la Cumbre de las Americas: Miami 1994." www.summit-americas.org/esp/cumbremiami.htm

69. "Manuel Zelaya," Biografias y Vidas. http://www.biografiasyvidas.com/biografia/z/zelaya_manuel.htm

70. "Maradona y Chavez encabezan una gran protesta contra Bush," El Paiz, 11 de Mayo, 2005. http://www.elpais.com/articulo/internacional/Maradona/Chavez/encabezan/gran/protesta/Bush/elpepiint/20051105elpepiint_3/Tes

71. "Ministerio de Defensa, Plan Bolivar 2000." http://www.mpd.gob.ve/prog-gob/proyb2000.htm

72. "Ministro de Finanzas Presenta Hoy Presupuesto Nacional 2010," Informe 21, 20 de Octubre, 2009. http://informe21.com/economia-finanzas/minis-tro-finanzas-presentara-martes-presupuesto-nacional-2010

73. "Ministros del ALBA: Turismo es una Actividad económica primordial," Ministerio de Turismo de Ecuador, 29 de Enero, 2010. http://www.turismo.gob.ec/index.php?option=com_content&view=article&id=1814:ministros-del-alba-turismo-es-una-actividad-econa-primordial&catid=19:noticias-ald&Itemid=151

74. "Morales impone a militares lema Patria, Socialismo o Muerte," Reuters, 12 de Marzo, 2010. http://www.eluniverso.com/2010/03/12/1/1361/morales-impone-militares-bolivianos-lema-patria-muerte.html

75. "Next Stop of Cuba's Energy Revolution: Ecuador," Cuba Standard, September 11, 2009. http://www.cubastandard.com/2010/11/09/next-stop-of-cubas-energy-revolution-ecuador

76. "Paises del ALBA adoptaran medidas para interrumpir licencias de medicamentos en manos de monopolios," Aporrea, 9 de Septiembre, 2010. http://www.aporrea.org/tecno/n165202.html

77. "Palmerola debe convertirse en un aeropuerto civil, afirmo Zelaya," Alternativa Latinoamericana, 16 de Febrero, 2011. http://alternativalatinoamericana.blogspot.com/2011/02/palmerola-debe-convertirse-en-un.html

78. "Partido comunista del Ecuador admite ser nexo entre Gutierrez y las FARC," Ecuador Inmediato, 20 de Enero, 2005. http://www.ecuadorinmedi-ato.com/Noticias/news_user_view/partido_comunista_del_ecuador_ad-mite_ser_nexo_entre_gutierrez_y_las_farc--7920

79. "Red narco en que se implica a los Ostaiza operaba en 7 provincias," El Universo, 15 de Febrero, 2009. http://www.eluniverso.com/2009/02/15/1/1355/DACC3203118B467997CD94B94476F1E8.html

80. "Se cumple audiencia en caso Huracan de la Frontera," Expreso 21 de Abril, 2010. http://ediciones.expreso.ec/ediciones/2010/04/21/nacional/judicial/se-cumple-audiencia-en-caso-huracan-de-la-frontera//

81. "Simón Bolívar, An Address of Bolivar at the Congress of Angostura" (February 15, 1819), Reprint Ed., (Washington, D.C.: Press of B. S. Adams,

1919), passim.

82. "Socialismo del Siglo XXI: La Fuerza de los Pobres," 2007 Ministerio de Comunicacion de Venezuela, If87120073201165.

83. "State Department Cable accuses Ortega of Receiving Drug Money," Insight, December 7, 2010. http://www.insightcrime.org/insight-latest-news/item/316-state-department-cable-accuses-ortega-of-receiving-drug-money

84. "The FARC Files: Venezuela, Ecuador and the Secret Archive of Raul Reyes," International Institute for Strategic Studies, May 10, 2011.

85. "Tratado para Constitucion de Empresa Gran-Nacional Energia." http://www.minci.gob.ve/doc/acuerdo_grannacional_energia_a.pdf

86. "Turkey holds suspicious Iran Venezuela shipment," AP, January 6, 2009. http://www.ynetnews.com/articles/0,7340,L-3651706,00.html

87. "Un cable bajo control," May 8, 2011, El Nacional.

88. "Un Extrano Banco Irani que Opera en Venezuela," Noticias 24, 23 de Marzo, 2008. http://economia.noticias24.com/noticia/191/un-extrano-banco-irani-que-opera-en-venezuela/

89. "Un libro de Jorge Verstrynge sobre el Islam sera editado por el ejercito Venezolano," Webislam, 18 de Agosto 2005. http://www.webislam.com/?idn=1900

90. "US General Voices Concern over Iran Venezuela ties," AFP April 5, 2011. http://www.google.com/hostednews/afp/article/ALeqM5gMdmJ9NnlROhzcDjs457Jwn0gBEg?docId=CNG.692381365d745fc505df40c97673c9ec.861

91. "US Treasury Designates Two Venezuelan Men as Hezbollah Supporters," ADL, June 24, 2008. http://www.adl.org/main_Terrorism/venezuela_hezbollah_supporters.htm

92. "Venezuela Central Bank transfers 1.5 Billion to FONDEN (Chavez slush fund)," Dow Jones, March 2, 2010. http://www.democraticunderground.com/discuss/duboard.php?az=view_all&address=405x31496

93. "Venezuela entrega 13,200 toneladas de fertilizante para productores de granos en Nicaragua," El Nacional, 14 de Septiembre 2010. http://www.el-nacional.com/www/site/p_contenido.php?q=nodo/154891/Econom%EDa/Venezuela-entrega-13.200-toneladas-de-fertilizante-para-productores-de-granos-en-Nicaragua

94. "Venezuela es el Segundo Destino de Exportaciones Nicaragüenses," El Universal 2 de Enero, 2011. http://www.eluniversal.com/2011/01/02/eco_ava_venezuela-es-el-segu_02A4920617.shtml

95. "Venezuela, Evaluating the Bolivarian Revolution," November 4, 2010, Barclays Emerging Markets Research. www.barcap.com

96. "Venezuela: El Sucre sigue siendo un experimento político," El Nacional, 27 de Julio, 2011. http://www.entornointeligente.com/articulo/1143172/

VENEZUELA-El-Sucre-sigue-siendo-un-experimento-politico

97. "Venezuela: Situacion de Libertad de Expresion e Informacion" Informe 2010, Espacio Publico. ISBN 9801218274

98. "Video de soborno a 'El Viejo' hace tambalear credibilidad en caso Rozsa," La Patria, 16 de Enero, 2011. http://www.lapatriaenlinea.com/?nota=55354

99. "Walid Makled en Tiempo Real," Tal Cual Digital 9 de Noviembre, 2010. http://www.talcualdigital.com/especiales/Viewer.aspx?id=43665

100. "Wendelin, el 'embajador' de BATASUNA en America Latina," Ideal, 28 de Septiembre, 2009. http://www.ideal.es/granada/rc/20100928/espana/walter-wendelin-embajador-batasuna-201009280902.html

101. "Wikileaks: Venezuela Sending Money to Top Bolivian Officials," Latin American Herald Tribune. http://laht.com/article.asp?ArticleId=380789&CategoryId=10717

102. "Zelaya anuncia ingreso de Honduras a PetroCaribe," Xinhua 28 de Enero, 2008. http://www.spanish.xinhuanet.com/spanish/2008-01/28/content_567861.htm

103. "Zelaya consigue entrar en Honduras," La Verdad, 22 de Septiembre, 2009. http://www.laverdad.es/murcia/20090922/mundo/zelaya-consigue-entrar-honduras-20090922.html

104. (Video), Chavez Amenaza con Intervenir a Bolivia, 9 de Mayo, 2008. http://www.marthacolmenares.com/2008/05/09/chavez-amenaza-con-intervenir-bolivia-video/

105. Al Attar, Mohsen and Miller, Rosalie (2010), "Towards an Emancipatory International Law: the Bolivarian reconstruction", Third World Quarterly, 31: 3

106. Altmann, Josette y Tatiana Beirute, "Dossier ALBA," 1ª ED., Facultad Latinoamericana de Ciencias Sociales (Secretaría General) Dossier ALBA / ed. Jossette Altmann; comp. Tatiana Beirute. – 1a. ed.—San José, C.R., 2008.

107. Altmann, Josette, "Integracion Latinoamericana: Cronica de una Crisis Anunciada," FLACSO, 15 de Septiembre, 2006.

108. Altmann, Josette, "Integracion Latinoamericana: Cronica de una Crisis Anunciada," FLACSO, 15 de Septiembre, 2006.

109. Altmann, Josette, "Integracion Latinoamericana: Cronica de una Crisis Anunciada," FLACSO, 15 de Septiembre, 2006.

110. Altmann, Josette, "La Alianza Bolivariana para los Pueblos de Nuestra America," Foreign Affairs LatinoAmerica, Volumen 10, Numero 3, Julio-Septiembre 2010.

111. American Enterprise Institute Iran Tracker. http://www.irantracker.org/foreign-relations/ecuador-iran-foreign-relations

112. American Enterprise Institute Iran Tracker. http://www.irantracker.org/foreign-relations/ecuador-iran-foreign-relations

113. Araya, Oscar Alvarez, "Valores, Humanismo y Democracia," Lara Segura Editorial, (2010) ISBN: 978-9968-930-29-1.

114. Arias, Oscar, "Culture Matters," Foreign Affairs, January-February 2011 Edition.

115. Arismendi Posada, Ignaico, "Gobernantes Colombianos, trans. Colombian Presidents"; Interprint Editors Ltd.; Italgraf; Segunda Edición: 19; Bogotá, Colombia; 1983.

116. Author interviews with confidential sources.

117. Bedoya, Felipe, "Threats to Latin American Gas Subsidies Spark Protests," Revenue Watch Institute, March 15, 2011. http://www.revenuewatch.org/news/news-article/international/threats-latin-america-gas-subsidies-spark-protests

118. Bosch, Juan, "Dictatorship with Popular Support," (1969): P116.

119. Bossi, Fernando, "10 Puntos para Entender el ALBA," Cuadernos de Emancipacion, #35, ISSN 0328-0179.

120. Bossi, Fernando, "Cuadernos de Emancipacion," N35, ISSN 0328-0179, P26.

121. Brewer-Carias, Alan, "Dismantling Democracy in Venezuela," Cambridge University Press, September 20, 2010. 9780521145572.

122. Bushnell, David, "The Liberator, Simón Bolívar." New York: Alfred A. Knopf, 1970. Print.

123. Bushnell, David, "The Santander Regime in Gran Colombia." Westport, CT: Greenwood Press. 1970 ISBN 0837129818. OCLC 258393.

124. Caicedo, Roberto Escobedo, "ALBA Drogas, S.A." Nicaragua Hoy, 19 de Diciembre, 2009. http://www.nicaraguahoy.info/dir_cgi/topics.cgi?op=print_topic;cat=Opinion;id=58080

125. Caicedo, Roberto Escobedo, "Que Persigue Ortega con la pantomima de dragar al San Juan?" Nicaragua Hoy, 6 de Noviembre, 2010. http://www.nicaraguahoy.info/dir_cgi/topics.cgi?op=print_topic;cat=Opinion;id=60136

126. Canavessi, Juan Jose, "Simon Bolivar: Sintesis Biografica de Bolivar," Reportario de Ensayistas y Filosofos. http://www.ensayistas.org/filosofos/venezuela/bolivar/semblanza.htm

127. Cardenas, Jose, "Iran's Man in Ecuador," Foreign Policy, February 15, 2011. http://shadow.foreignpolicy.com/posts/2011/02/15/irans_man_in_ecuador

128. Carrol, Roy, "20 billion barrel oil discovery puts Cuba in the big league," The Guardian October 18, 2008. http://www.guardian.co.uk/world/2008/oct/18/cuban-oil

129. Ceresole Visto por El Mismo," Analitica.com, 21 de Junio, 2000. http://www.analitica.com/va/entrevistas/1867848.asp

130. Ceresole, Norberto, "Caudillo, Ejercito y Pueblo: La Venezuela de Presidente Chavez", (1999).

131. CIA World Factbook. https://www.cia.gov/library/publications/the-world-factbook/rankorder/2188rank.html

132. Corrales, Javier and Michael Penfold, "Dragon in the Tropics," Brookings Institution Press, December 28, 2010 ASIN B004WGLDDQ

133. Correa, Rafael (Diputado), "Construyendo el ALBA: Nuestro Norte es el Sur" Ediciones del 40 Aniversario del Parlamento Latino, Mayo, 2005.

134. Cristancho, Maria Victoria, "El Incomodo Amigo de Hugo Chavez," El Tiempo, 20 de Mayo 1999. http://www.eltiempo.com/archivo/documento/MAM-872606

135. *Cuadernos de Emancipacion*, Edicion #35, ISSN 0328-0179, April 2009.

136. *Cuadernos de Emancipacion*, No. 35, ISSN 0328-0179 April 2009.

137. *Cuadernos de la Imancipacion*, #35, ISSN 0328-0179, April, 2009.

138. De la Reza, Germán A., "El Congreso de Panamá de 1826 y otros ensayos de integración en el siglo XIX. Estudio y fuentes documentales anotadas, "UAM-Eon, México, 2006. ISBN 970-31-0656-0.

139. De la Reza, German A., "La invención de la paz. De la república cristiana del duque de Sully a la sociedad de naciones de Simón Bolívar," México, Siglo XXI Editores, 2009. ISBN 978-607-03-0054-7.

140. De Soto, Hernando, "The Mystery of Capital: Why Capitalism Triumphs in the West and Fails Everywhere Else", *Basic Books*, 1st edition (July 8, 2003), ISBN 9780465016150.

141. Dieterich, Heinz, "El Socialismo del Siglo XXI," (2005).

142. Dieterich, Heinz, "Entre la barbarie y el desarrollismo," El Siglo, 27 de Octubre, 2003. http://www.elsiglodedurango.com.mx/noticia/15465.entre-la-barbarie-y-el-desarrollismo.html

143. Dieterich, Heinz, "Venezuela: Cambia el modelo o colapsara como el modelo Cubano," Kaosenlared, 28 de Septiembre, 2009. http://www.kaosenlared.net/noticia/venezuela-cambia-modelo-colapsara-como-modelo-cubano

144. Edwards, Sebastian, "Left Behind: Latin America and the False Promise of Populism," University of Chicago Press, 2010.

145. Enriquez, Haydee Ochoa, "Gestión Publica y Desarrollo Endógeno en Venezuela," Marzo 2006.

146. Escobar, Jose Benito, "Que Es el ALBA" Encuentro Regional Sobre la Flexibilidad Laboral Managua 3 y 4 de Abril de 2008, Pdte. Central Sandinista de Trabajadores.

147. Farah, Douglas, "Ecuador at Risk: Drugs, Thugs and the Citizens Revolution," International Assessment and Strategy Center, January 24, 2010.

148. Farah, Douglas, "Into The Abyss: Bolivia under Evo Morales and the MAS,"

International Assessment and Strategy Center.

149. Farah, Douglas, "Into the Abyss: Bolivia Under Evo Morales and the MAS," International Assessment and Strategy Center, (2010): P2.

150. Farah, Douglas, "Ortega steps into the breach with the FARC," July 23, 2008. http://www.douglasfarah.com/article/376/ortega-steps-into-the-breach-with-the-farc.com

151. Farah, Douglas, "What the FARC Papers Show Us about Latin American Terrorism," NEFA Foundation, April 1, 2008. www.nefafoundation.org/miscellaneous/FeaturedDocs/nefafarc0408.pdf

152. Freedom House Table on Civil Liberties and Political Rights. http://www.freedomhouse.org/template.cfm?page=15

153. Frias, Hugo Chavez "Con El ALBA, Despiertan Los Pueblos," Junio, 2008. Depósito Legal: lf87120083202647, Impreso en la República Bolivariana de Venezuela.

154. Galeano, Luis, "Albanisa es un Pulpo," El Nuevo Diario, 28 de Septiembre 2009. http://www.elnuevodiario.com.ni/nacionales/58180

155. General Accounting Office Report. "Drug Control: US Counternarcotics Cooperation with Venezuela has Declined," http://www.gao.gov/new.items/d09806.pdf

156. Geoensenanza Vol. 9-2004, ISSN 1316*6077.

157. Harnecker, Marta, "De los Consejos Comunales a Comunas" 2009, P11.

158. Harnecker, Marta, "Hacia Donde Avanzar—El Socialismo del Siglo XXI," (2010).

159. Harnecker, Marta, "Latin America & Twenty-First Century Socialism: Inventing to Avoid Mistakes," Monthly Review, July 28th, 2010.

160. Heritage Foundation Forum, "Democracy at Risk: Central America Under Siege," November 18, 2010.

161. Heritage Foundation Index of Economic Freedom. http://www.heritage.org/Index

162. High-level Panel on Threats, Challenges and Change, A more secure world: Our shared responsibility. United Nations, (2004).

163. Honduras Constitution, "Constitución De La República De Honduras, 1982"

164. Honduras: Aclaración ante campana de los embustes de el Heraldo y La Prensa sobre uso de los Fondes del ALBA," Aporrea, 23 de Agosto, 2010. http://www.aporrea.org/imprime/n163953.html

165. Inkster, Nigel, "The FARC Files Launch Remarks," May 10, 2011.

166. IV Informe del Secretario General de FLACSO, Integración Regional.

167. Izarra, Andres "El socialismo necesita una hegemonía comunicacional," Boletin Digital Universitario, 8 de Enero, 2007. http://www.boletin.uc.edu.ve/

index.php?option=com_content&task=view&id=4990&Itemid=38

168. Katz, Claudio, "La Democracia Socialista del Silgo XXI."

169. Kester, Paul, "Zero Hunger: Development or just Raindrops," February 2009. http://www.envio.org.ni/articulo/4141

170. Kozloff, Nikolas, "The Rise of Rafael Correa," Counterpunch, November 27, 2006. http://www.globalexchange.org/countries/americas/ecuador/4369.html

171. Lebowitz, Michel A., "Que es el Socialismo," *Cuadernos para la Empancipacion*, #28, ISSN 0328-0179, P4.

172. Levitt, Dr. Matthew, "Hezbollah: Financing Terror Through Criminal Enterprise," Testimony of Dr. Matthew Levitt, Senior Fellow and Director of Terrorism Studies, The Washington Institute for Near East Policy. May 25, 2005. Committee on Homeland Security and Governmental Affairs, United States.

173. Lopez, Jaime, "El entorno de ETA se infiltra en el movimiento bolivariano de Hugo Chavez," El Mundo, 8 de Mayo, 2008. http://www.elmundo.es/elmundo/2008/06/07/espana/1212867060.html

174. Luxemburg, Rosa, *Reforma o revolucion*, Obras escogidas tomo 1 Ed Pluma, Buenos Aires, (1976).

175. Lynch, John, "Simón Bolívar: A Life." New Haven and London: Yale University Press. 2006 ISBN 0-300-11062-6.

176. Maira, Antonio, "Hugo Chavez presents Gramsci to hundreds of thousands of people," Axis of Logic, June 28, 2007. http://www.axisoflogic.com/artman/publish/article_24813.shtml

177. Malamud, Carlos, "La Cumbre ALCUE de Madrid y el Estado de la Relacion Bilateral Europa-America Latina," Real Instituto Elcano, June 16, 2010.

178. Maldonado, Carlos Salinas, "El fraude electoral divide a Nicaragua," El Pais,14 de Noviembre, 2008. http://www.elpais.com/articulo/internacional/fraude/electoral/divide/Nicaragua/elpepuint/20081114elpepiint_1/Tes

179. Manifiesto General de la Primera Cumbre de Consejos de Movimientos Sociales del ALBA-TCP, Cochabamba, Bolivia, 15 al 17 de Octubre de 2009.

180. Manwaring, Max, "Latin America's New Security Reality: Irregular Asymmetric Conflict and Hugo Chavez," August 2007 ISBN 1-58487-303-5.

181. Marcano, Cristina, "Entrevista a Heinz Dieterich," Aporrea.com, 3 de Enero, 2007. http://www.kaosenlared.net/noticia.php?id_noticia=28818

182. Marcano, Cristina, "Hugo Chavez sin Uniforme," Debate Publishers, November 30, 2005, ISBN 9871117183.

183. Martinez, Emilio, "Relaciones Peligrosas," Bolivia 2010.

184. Mayorga, René Antonio, "Sociedad Civil y Estado Bajo Un Populismo Plebiscitario y Autoritario," La "Nueva Izquierda en América Latina: Derechos Humanos, Participación Política y Sociedad Civil, edited by Cynthia J. Arn-

son et alia, The Woodrow Wilson International Center for Scholars, (January 2009): P111.

185. Mejia, Thelma, "Joining ALBA, 'A Step Towards the Center Left' Says the President," August 26, 2008. http://ipsnews.net/news.asp?idnews=43681

186. Montalvo, Francisco Huerta, et al, "Informe Comisión de Transparencia y Verdad: Caso Angostura," Dec. 10, 2009.

187. Morales, Evo, "Discurso de Evo Morales en el IX Cumbre de Ministros de Defensa, 22 de Septiembre, 2010. http://www.lostiempos.com/diario/actualidad/politica/20101122/discurso-del-presidente-de-bolivia-evo-morales-ix-conferencia-de-ministros_100256_194768.html

188. Murillo, Rosario "ALBANISA, ALBA y Soberania Nacional,". http://www.presidencia.gob.ni/index.php?option=com_content&view=article&id=190:albanisa-alba-soberania-y-dignidad&catid=58:febrero-2009&Itemid=54

189. Myers, David J., "Iran and Venezuela: Capacity to Influence" CSIS. April, 2009.

190. Naim, Moises, "The Devil's Excrement," Foreign Policy Magazine, September 2009. http://www.foreignpolicy.com/articles/2009/08/17/the_devil_s_excrement

191. Noriega, Roger, "Chavez's Secret Nuclear Program," Foreign Policy, October 5, 2010. http://www.aei.org/article/102623

192. O'Grady, Mary, "Honduras Defends its Democracy," *Wall Street Journal*, June 29, 2009. http://online.wsj.com/article/SB124623220955866301.html

193. O'Grady, Mary, "The FARC's Honduran Friends," *Wall Street Journal*, August 10, 2009. http://online.wsj.com/article/SB10001424052970204251404574340570960456550.html

194. Paz, Marwan, "Chino Carias, El Ultimo Guerrillero," Al Seher Blog, 24 de Noviembre, 2006. http://alseher.blogspot.com/2006/11/chino-carias-el-ultimo-guerrillero.html

195. Pena Esclusa, Alejandro, "The Foro de Sao Paulo: A Threat to Freedom in Latin America" Alejandro Pena Esclusa, February 2009, Mary Montes, Editors, Bogota, Colombia.

196. Perez, Jose Gregorio, "Raul Reyes, El canciller de la montana." Bogota: Grupo Ediorial Norma, 2008. 277p. - (1a. ed). ISBN 978-958-45-1535-3.

197. Press Release of the Democratic United Table in Venezuela. http://www.unidadvenezuela.org/tag/perseguidos-politicos/

198. Press Release, Congressman Connie Mack. http://www.internationalrelations.house.gov/press_display.asp?id=1493

199. Report of the Secretary-General, In larger freedom: towards development, security and human rights for all. United Nations General Assembly, Fifty-ninth session (A/59/2005), 21 March 2005, P27.

200. Reporters Without Borders Press Freedom Index. http://en.rsf.org/spip. php?page=classement&id_rubrique=1034

201. Rosenau, J. "Demasiadas cosas a la vez: La Teoria de la complejidad y los asuntos mundiales." En: Nueva Sociedad, Caracas, Venezuela #148 1997.

202. Salas, Antonio, "El Palestino," *Temas de Hoy*, Agosto, 2010. ISBN: 978-84-8460-859-2.

203. Salazar, Carmen Chinas, "El neoliberalismo y el deterioro de las condiciones de vida de la clase trabajadora en America Latina." 3 de Abril, 2008. http:// revistaintereconomia.blogspot.com/2008/04/el-neoliberalismo-y-el-deteri-oro-de-las.html

204. Sanchez, Ilich Ramírez, dit Carlos (with Jean-Michel Vernochet), L'islam révolutionnaire, Monaco, Editions du Rocher, (2003).

205. State Department 2009 Human Rights Report. http://www.state.gov/g/ drl/rls/hrrpt/2009/wha/136130.htm, http://www.venezuelaawareness. com/informevaf/report2009.htm

206. Stavans, Ilan Stavans, "Hugo Chavez's Advisor: The Anti-Semitic path of Norberto Ceresole." http://zeek.forward.com/articles/116835/

207. Tapia, Nelson P., "Aprendiendo el Desarrollo Endógeno Sostenible," *Cosmovision y Ciencias* #3, Mayo 2008 ISBN: 978-99954-1-139-8.

208. Taylor, Clinton W., "Hezbollah in Latin America," The American Spectator, November 30, 2006. http://spectator.org/archives/2006/11/30/hezbollah-in-latin-america

209. Thale, Geoff, "Behind the Honduran Coup," Foreign Policy in Focus, July 1, 2009. http://www.fpif.org/articles/behind_the_honduran_coup

210. Transparency International table on perceptions of corruption. http:// www.transparency.org/policy_research/surveys_indices/cpi/2010

211. Tratado Constitutivo del SUCRE, Octubre 16, 2009.

212. Ulloa, Rodolfo, "Petrocaribe y el ALBA," *El Pregon* 30 de Septiembre, 2008. http://www.elpregon.org/opinion/100-perspectivas/351-petrocaribe-y-el-alba

213. United Nations University—Comparative Regional Integration Studies, Working Paper W/2008-4.

214. UNODC 2009 Report, "Trafficking and Instability," section 3.0.

215. UNODC 2009 Report, Section 2.3, Cocaine Use and Production.

216. UNODC, 2009 report, 1.3 "The Global Cocaine Market."

217. UNODC, 2009 report, 1.3 "The Global Cocaine Market."

218. Uriarte, Maria Josee, "Ortega viola 67 veces constitución," La Prensa, 10 de Septiembre 2010. http://www.laprensa.com.ni/2010/09/10/politica/37336

219. US Department of Energy. http://www.eia.doe.gov/cabs/venezuela/oil. html

220. US Department of Energy. http://www.eia.doe.gov/cabs/venezuela/oil. html

221. US Department of Energy. http://www.eia.doe.gov/country/country_energy_data.cfm?fips=BL

222. US Department of Energy. http://www.eia.doe.gov/country/country_energy_data.cfm?fips=EC

223. Verstrynge, Jorge, "La Guerra Periferica y el Islam Revolucionario," *El Viejo Topo*. 2003.

224. Video "Chavez Insulta a Hondurenos," Daily Motion. http://www.dailymotion.com/video/x6jsim_chavez-insulta-a-hondurenos_news

225. World Economic Forum Global Competitiveness Index. http://www.weforum.org/en/initiatives/gcp/Global%20Competitiveness%20Report/PastReports/index.htm

InterAmerican Institute for Democracy Backlist

Cayetano Llobet: *Sendas de Libertad.* (2008)

Alberto Valencia: *Historias de Guerra y Paz en el Caguán* (2008)

Alexis Ortiz: *La Política es Chévere* (2008)

Heriberto Justo Auel: *Política Estrategia Internacional Contemporánea* (2008)

Eduardo A. Duhalde: *Argentina Aflame* (2009)

Guillermo Lousteau: *Democracia y Control de Constitucionalidad* (2009)

Carlos Alberto Montaner: *Latin Americans and The West* (2009)

Douglas Farah: *The Democracy Papers N. 1 "Into the Abyss" Bolivia under Evo Morales and the MAS (2009)*

Kevin Casas, Edmundo Jarquin, Guillermo Lousteau y Álvaro Vargas Llosa: *The Democracy Papers N. 2 "La Democracia en América Latina"* (2009)

Guillermo Lousteau: *The Philosophical Foundations of American Constitutionalism* (2010)

Armando Valladares: *Contra Toda Esperanza* (2010)

Douglas Farah y Glenn Simpson: *The Democracy Papers N. 3: "Ecuador at Risk" Drugs, Thugs, Guerrilas and The Citizen's Revolution* (2010)

Juan Benemelis, Miguel Castillo, Efrén Córdova y Diego trinidad: *El Ocaso del Régimen que destruyó a Cuba* (2011)

José Ignacio Garcia Hamilton: *Cultural Legacies and the Challenge to Latin American Modernity* (2011)

Marianela Crognale, Nicolás Santos, Maria Alejandra Cardoso, Maria Teresa Garrido y Jennifer Meléndez Ochoa: *The Democracy Papers N. 4 "El Rol del Poder Judicial en el Sistema Democrático" Concurso Interamericano de Ensayo* (2011)

Eudoro Galindo Anze: *El Legado Maligno* (2012)

Carlos A. Montaner: *The Cubans* (2012)

Joel Hirst: *The ALBA*

Efrén Cordova: *El Islam y la razón* (In press)

www.ingramcontent.com/pod-product-compliance
Lightning Source LLC
Chambersburg PA
CBHW070118010626
45794CB00012B/86